SMALL BOAT LAW

1979-1980 SUPPLEMENT

HERBERT L. MARKOW
Instructor, Small Boat Law

Member of the Florida and New York Bars

NEW ENGLAND INSTITUTE
OF TECHNOLOGY
LEARNING RESOURCES CENTER

Herbert L. Markow
P.O. Box 011451   Miami, Florida 33101

Copyright© 1981 Herbert L. Markow
All Rights Reserved

Library of Congress Catalog
Card Number 77-154289

International Standard Book Number
0-934108-02-1

TABLE OF CONTENTS

Note: The "B" chapters below supplement the counterpart numbers of the chapters in the main volume of Small Boat Law ["M" page references] and its 1978 Supplement ["A" page references]. Missing chapter listings are omitted below for lack of supplementing material.

Part I - Regulation by Government

Ch. B1 Small Boat Law - A Laboratory Report

Ch. B2 Admiralty Jurisdiction

Ch. B3 Law Enforcement Authority

Ch. B4 Rescue and The Good Samaritan

Ch. B5 Florida Boating Act

Ch. B6 Florida Titles and Stolen Boats

Ch. B7 Federal Boating Act

Ch. B8 The Boating Environment

Ch. B9 Marking and Removing the Wreck

Part II - The Consumer's World

Ch. B10 Boat Sales

Ch. B11 Warranties

Ch. B12 Federal Boat Safety Standards

Ch. B13 Florida Yacht and Ship Broker's Act

Ch. B14 Florida Sales Tax

Ch. B15 Boat Charters and Liveries

Ch. B16 Marina and Boatyard Disputes

Ch. B17 Maritime Liens

Part III - Admiralty

Ch. B18 Salvage

Ch. B19 Florida Sunken Treasure

Ch. B20 Seaworthiness

Ch. B21 Personal Injuries

Ch. B22 Collision

Ch. B24 Liability of Government

Ch. B25 Insurance

APPENDIX

BI Florida Boat Registration and Safety Law

Ch. B1 SMALL BOAT LAW - A LABORATORY REPORT

THE "EXPERTS" [M1-1]

The opening of the Small Boat Law text indicated uneasiness with expertise in the areas of small boat law. Historically, the law regarded a small boat as a small ship and, understandably, applied principles of big ship admiralty. Our textual developments show a growing split in this law with the emergence of a water-based society unrelated to commercial shipping. This is as it should be, but the imputation to everyone of a high degree of knowledge of admiralty law and, for our interest, to the small boat constituency far removed from the law of shipping is disturbing, as discussed in BARGE v REAL ESTATE [B 22-1]. That proposition is criticized sharply, for it can have wide and unsuspected effect on the security of waterfront installations.

THE LABORATORY [A1-1]

Since publication of the Small Boat Law 1978 Supplement, the most significant feature appearing in the cases and materials in this two year update of the law and topics covered previously is the increasing interface between maritime and real estate law which surfaces in different chapters. Thus, BARGE v REAL ESTATE is in Ch. B22 Collision; the emerging supremacy of private lands over navigable waters is in Ch. B2 Admiralty Jurisdiction (which notes also the increasing rejection of admiralty jurisdiction over pleasure boat casualty); the new Florida boat liveaboard tax is in Ch. B5 Florida Boating Act, and in Ch. B8 The Boating Environment for consideration of the boat liveaboard's stress on its supporting shoreside community - all signs of a developing water-based society.

The tortured course of the law of search and seizure afloat is pursued in Ch. B3. While we wish this undue textual burden would abate, that is not to be, for the phenomenon of drug smuggling by small boats has spread from South Florida to all coasts. It has resulted in more stringent enforcement law and efforts including forfeiture law, Florida and Federal, which will affect those involved with the boating industry, and it penalizes the water-based society in its traditional mode.

Florida Motorboat Law amendments strengthen the State's boat title system with administrative improvements and new criminal penalties.

In Ch. B15 Boat Charters and Liveries, the growing enterprise of pleasure boat charters encounters new problems; boat livery operations require closer management to avoid liability for personal injuries to patrons.

In Ch. B18 Salvage, a double standard of awards for

salvors appears - liberal for commercial boat operators, problematical for pleasure boat operators. This concept is newly perceived, analyzed and developed.

As from the outset, the extended classroom is used as a laboratory in testing and developing the ideas presented, as appears in the text from place to place. This has been fruitful in finding new problems and directions.

THE FORMAT

As in the previous Supplement, this one updates, revises and adds new material. Similarly, "B" chapters and page references indicate the present Supplement, "A" refers to the 1978 Supplement, "M" the main volume. Bracketed [ ] references apply to "M" or "A" pages. Efforts have been made to maintain the text in topical sequence.

Ch. B2 ADMIRALTY JURISDICTION

ELEMENTS OF JURISDICTION   [M2-2, after Little v Reo Hill:]

In State v Hill, (Fla 1979) 372 So 2d 84, the Florida Marine Patrol saw Hill shrimping in the prohibited Tortugas shrimp nursery area within Florida territorial waters and charged him with violation of F.S. 370.151(2). He challenged its constitutionality because the legislature acted in excess of its lawful jurisdiction by purporting to prohibit shrimping in an area which extended in part beyond Florida's territorial limits even though he was inside those limits.

The Supreme Court held that the state had authority to proscribe shrimping within its waters regardless of whether it may prohibit shrimping outside. Since Hill was subject to the application of the statute, he had no standing to complain that it might not be enforceable constitutionally against one who might act in the proscribed area lying outside Florida's territorial jurisdiction. The fact that a statutory regulation, consistently with organic law, may apply to one class of cases but may violate the Constitution as applied to another class of cases, does not destroy the statute; instead there is a duty to enforce the regulation when it may be applied legally.

A dissent was based on Little v Reo Hill Fisheries.

Again, boundary delineation came into question in Hotoph v State, (Fla 1979) 367 So 2d 1015. Defendants were charged with violation of a statute by fishing with a net other than a cast net within one mile north or south of any inlet, here Matanzas Inlet, within the boundaries of St. Johns County.

The Supreme Court held the law to be unconstitutionally vague for failure to identify specifically the prohibited fishing areas. The average person cannot identify readily the boundaries of the protected areas. Unlike other sections of that statute, this one failed to delineate an eastern boundary (into the Atlantic Ocean). Unlike a previous section, it made no reference to "inside salt waters" and "outside salt waters" and fishermen cannot be required to guess at the location of protected fishing areas.

Intricate questions of jurisdiction are beyond our scope; yet boating issues reflect the transitory nature of boating activities and transactions which demand a passing recognition at least for orientation. An example is Templeman v Baudhuin Yacht Harbor, Inc., (CA P.R. 1979) 608 F 2d 916.

In July 1972 plaintiff bought a Chris Craft yacht from Baudhuin, a Chris Craft dealer and yard operator, after which vessel defects appeared. Plaintiffs were citizens of Illinois, defendant of Wisconsin. The yacht was built and delivered in Michigan; later it was repaired by defendant in Wisconsin, and in Florida by defendant's agents. In December 1973, while plaintiffs voyaged from San Juan to the Virgin Islands, a fire in the engine room sank the vessel. After some hours in the water, plaintiffs were rescued by the Coast Guard and private parties, and they were carried back to San Juan.

In December 1975 plaintiffs sued defendant in Illinois in Federal court based on diversity of citizenship, for strict liability, negligence, and breaches of express and implied warranties. Previously, plaintiffs had sued Chris Craft in Federal court in Puerto Rico within one year of the accident, so the Illinois court now transferred this case to Puerto Rico for trial with the Chris Craft case. But the Puerto Rico statute of limitations on the Baudhuin case required suit within one year, although this suit would have been timely in Illinois, Wisconsin, Michigan and Florida.

The Puerto Rico court dismissed the complaint because, although the accident occurred on the high seas, Puerto Rico law should apply since it was the closest state or territory, it was the place of the last act, and it was the place having the most significant relationship for that:

1. The accident occurred closest to Puerto Rico.
2. Defendant knew the boat was to be used in the Caribbean.
3. Assistance came from Puerto Rico.
4. Plaintiffs were returned to and treated there.
5. The earlier suit against Chris Craft was there.
6. The later Illinois complaint was identical.
7. Although all ten plaintiffs in the Illinois suit were Illinois residents, 7 of the 17 plaintiffs in the Puerto Rico suit were Puerto Rico residents.
8. Initial medical treatment and witnesses of the rescue were centered in Puerto Rico.

The Court of Appeals reversed. Baudhuin's connection with Puerto Rico was too minimal even to confer in personam jurisdiction on Puerto Rico courts, having only the relationship that plaintiff sailed there in a yacht that defendant had sold and repaired elsewhere. The "most significant relationship" test required a weighing against conflicting factors which might favor some other jurisdiction, but the Puerto Rico court made no comparisons. Except for the first two items above, only post-occurrence facts were weighed and, although they bore on determining the most convenient place of trial, they did not relate to where the cause of action had arisen or to the measurement of the rights and liabilities of the parties. The four significant considerations are:

- place where the injury occurred;
- place where the conduct occurred;
- place of citizenship of the parties; and
- place where the relationship of the parties is centered.

The District Court's list fits only the first of these,

and that was mere happenstance. If plaintiff had not yet left Puerto Rico waters, he was about to do so.

ADMIRALTY - THE LAW   [M2-3, add after first paragraph:]

Illustrative of intricacies in applying the saving to suitors clause is Hebert v Diamond M Co., (La App 1978) 367 So 2d 1210. While Hebert was being transferred from a crewboat to a tender barge serving an offshore platform, the crane lifting his personnel carrier malfunctioned, and he was dropped and severely injured. He sued in state court under general maritime law. The court denied his application for jury trial because there would have been none in a court of admiralty.

The appellate court reversed. In a state court, even as in federal court, if an admiralty cause is tried on the civil side, the remedy of jury trial is preserved under the saving to suitors clause. Regardless of which court or which side of the federal court (admiralty or general) in which the action may be brought, the federal substantive maritime law (law of merits as distinguished from procedural law) will apply if the claim is cognizable in admiralty in order to serve the need for uniform law on navigable waters.

What is saved under the saving to suitors clause is not a remedy at common law, but a common law remedy which is governed by the law of the court handling the case which, in turn, will apply the maritime substantive law. The remedy is the means to enforce the claim. Therefore, if a remedy is available to a maritime claimant under common law, and its prosecution does not conflict with the substantive rights of the parties under maritime law, he is entitled to the common law remedy available in the court hearing the case.

Plaintiff here is entitled to jury trial under both federal and Louisiana law. A jury trial is a fact-finding procedure to enforce substantive rights. It is purely remedial, and therefore it is available to this plaintiff, as in other Louisiana trials, under the saving to suitors clause.

MARITIME TRANSACTIONS   [M2-7, after The Wanda]

In William P. Brooks Const. Co. Inc. v Guthrie, (CA Tex 1980) 614 F 2d 509, Brooks, titleholder of a shrimp trawler, sued in admiralty to recover its possession from Guthrie who cross-claimed for rightful possession by virtue of an oral contract for its sale. Brooks replied that there was an oral charter rather than an oral contract of sale, and the charter had expired. The trial court awarded possession to Brooks.

Guthrie contended that his cross action converted the suit to one for specific performance to purchase a vessel as in The Wanda, which was outside admiralty jurisdiction.

Judgment was affirmed. Brooks brought a true possessory action to recover possession rather than to obtain original possession as legal owner who had been wrongfully deprived of possession. That is within admiralty jurisdiction which was not divested by Guthrie's contract defense.

In Gerard Construction Inc. v M/V Virginia, (DC Pa 1979) 480 F Supp 488, Gerard sold The Virginia to Mosseso and Fix for part cash and a promissory note. At Mosseso's request, Gerard had a local distributor supply fuel and oil to the vessel the next day for which Gerard was billed. To recover the sale balance for the fuel and oil furnished, Gerard filed an in rem action against the vessel and the buyers who moved to dismiss because money due on a contract of sale of a vessel is not within admiralty jurisdiction; also to vacate or reduce the amount of security.

The court dismissed the claim for the balance of the sale price. It is settled law that a contract related to a maritime service or transaction is within admiralty jurisdiction but, said the court, no bright line is to be drawn from such a statement, for the test of maritime subject matter is difficult to apply. Apparently the prevailing rule is that a contract for sale of a ship is not a maritime contract. Reviewing the cases, he noted that a contract for repair of a vessel is maritime, but one for construction or rebuilding is not, although the distinction between rebuilding and repair is difficult to draw. In a lease-purchase agreement, the maritime aspects are held to be separable, and lease aspects may be adjudicated in admiralty.

Contracts to furnish supplies or accessories to a vessel are maritime when they are for necessaries, such as fuel and oil, which give rise to a maritime lien enforceable by an in rem action. Since arrest of the property can be disruptive to the owners and maritime commerce, release by special bond is provided by statute and rule, and the right to obtain release is absolute and not subject to discretion. Defendants agreed that $1564 was owed for fuel and oil which they offered to pay. Accordingly, the vessel would be released by payment into court of that sum plus $250 to cover costs.

NAVIGABILITY IN FACT [M2-12, add:]

An important decision is Kaiser Aetna v U.S., (1979) 444 US 164, 100 S Ct 497, 62 L Ed 2d 332. Kuapa Pond was a natural 523 acre lagoon on Oahu contiguous to navigable Maunalua Bay, but separated by a barrier beach. It had been used as a proprietary fishpond under Hawaiian feudal law and passed into the Bishop Estate which leased an area in 1961, including the pond, to Kaiser Aetna for the development of Hawaii Kai subdivision. Kaiser dredged the two foot pond to a depth of six feet, built bridges and retaining walls, developed a marina to accommodate pleasure boats, and notified Corps of Engineers of plans to dredge an 8 foot deep channel connecting the pond to the bay and increase the height of the highway bridge along the barrier beach to permit boat traffic between the marina and the bay. Engineers assented without a permit.

22,000 people moved into the development around the pond including 1500 marina waterfront lot lessees who, with 86 non-marina lot lessees from Hawaii Kai and 56 nonresident boatowners, paid $72 fees for maintenance of the pond and for patrol boats that removed floating debris, enforced boating regulations, and maintained privacy and security of the pond. Kaiser controlled access to and use of the marina, the sole commercial use being the 25 passenger Marina Queen used to promote marina lot sales and, briefly, the marina shopping center.

Subsequently, Engineers required authorization for future engineering operations and demanded that Kaiser allow free access to the pond by the public because it had become navigable water of the United States. The District Court held that the pond had become such navigable water and thus was subject to regulation by Engineers (which was not in dispute), but the government lacked the authority to open the pond to the public without payment of compensation to the owner. The Court of Appeals agreed that the pond was within the regulatory authority of Congress. It reversed the holding that Kaiser did not have to allow public access to the pond - the right to public use could not be separated from the federal regulatory authority.

The Supreme Court reversed the Court of Appeals. The pond was navigable within the historical concept of Congressional regulation under the commerce clause of the Constitution, the established regulatory authority of Engineers, and the established admiralty and maritime jurisdiction of the federal courts, but the navigational servitude does not justify the taking of private property without compensation to the owner. An essential element of individual property is the legal right to exclude others from enjoying it. Government cannot invade that right without paying just compensation as required by the Fifth Amendment.

These principles were held to control the companion case of Vaughn v Vermilion Corp., (1979) 444 US 206, 100 S Ct 399, 62 L Ed 2d 365. Vermilion leased from Exxon Co. substantial acreage in Louisiana which is traversed by manmade canals 60 feet wide by 8 feet deep. The canals are subject to the tides and are navigable in fact. Constructed with private funds, the canals were in continuous control and possession of Vermilion, Exxon, and predecessors for many years. Lying between the Intracoastal Waterway and Gulf of Mexico, the canals are used for fishing and hunting, and by Exxon for oil and gas exploration and development activities. Vermilion subleases portions of the Exxon land to hunters, trappers and fishers. 400 "No Trespassing" signs are posted in various locations, Vermilion employed people to supervise activities in the canals and on land, and they prohibited entry by strangers on many occasions.

Vaughn claimed right under federal law to travel the canals and engage in commercial fishing and shrimping without Vermilion's permission, and disregarded several written notices from Vermilion. Vermilion sued in Louisiana court to enjoin Vaughn from trespassing on the land and using the canals.

As ruled by the Louisiana Court of Appeal, said the Supreme Court, no general right of use in the public arose by reason of the authority over navigation in the commerce clause of the United States Constitution.

In Cooper v U.S., (DC Mo 1980) 489 F Supp 200, in a wrongful death action arising from collision of two motorboats on Lake of the Ozarks which is sited entirely in Missouri, U.S. moved to dismiss for lack of admiralty jurisdiction. The Lake was created by Bagnell Dam impoundment of Osage River, a navigable stream, which blocks free operation of boats on the Osage. The Lake has no navigable outlet and is not used or susceptible of use by commercial navigation. Loc-Wood Boats & Motors, Inc. v Rockwell, (8th Cir. 1957) 245 F 2d 306, had held the Lake to be navigable waters of the U.S. when a sightseeing boat capsized in a sudden storm. U.S. urged now that the 8th Circuit would reverse itself and overrule the Loc-Wood decision.

The court denied the motion to dismiss. The Supreme Court in Kaiser Aetna distinguished navigable concepts: to define Congress' regulatory authority over commerce; to determine statutory authority of Corps of Engineers; or to establish jurisdiction of admiralty courts. Without dispute, the Lake is navigable for the purpose of Congress' power to regulate under the Commerce Clause of the Constitution; the vessels thereon are subject to Coast Guard regulation and inspection. There were only 8 small passenger vessels certified by the Coast Guard for use as sightseeing or excursion vessels making round trips on the Lake from their docks. Thus, while the U.S. argument is compelling on the question of admiralty jurisdiction, and the jurisdictional analysis in Adams v Montana Power and Chapman v U.S. [A2-4] would be chosen in this case, this court is bound by the direct finding of the 8th Circuit in Loc-Wood, and it is for them to reverse themselves.

[A2-4, add after Chapman:]

In Richardson v Foremost Ins. Co., (DC La 1979) 470 F Supp 699, a 16 foot bass boat with outboard power headed north on Amite River. An 18 foot pleasure boat towing a water skiier headed south. At a curve a half mile downstream of the French Settlement Bridge, the bass boat turned left into the path of the ski-towing boat. Admiralty jurisdiction was the issue in the litigation following the collision.

Even with the assumption that the river was navigable

at the place of collision, the court dismissed the case for lack of admiralty jurisdiction. Neither boat, then or previously, had been involved in any commercial maritime activity. The drivers were not paid and the operation was not part of their regular type of employment, the passengers were not engaged in any kind of traditional maritime activity, and the boats were not under hire in any traditional maritime form. Instead, the boats were purely pleasure craft, and no instrumentality such as a buoy, barge, or drilling apparatus having a relationship to admiralty or commerce was involved. Absent a commercial or traditional maritime connection which requires admiralty protection, admiralty jurisdiction should be withheld. The foregoing elements are guides to determine if admiralty jurisdiction should be applied in pleasure boat cases.

The court looked to the thinking of Preble Stolz [M2-6] and rejected aviation cases [Executive Jet, M2-4] and surfboard cases [Davis, M2-6] in reaching this decision.

Ch. B3 LAW ENFORCEMENT AUTHORITY

SAFETY INSPECTIONS   [A3-2, add:]

Administrative inspections initiate so many of the state and federal search cases afloat: documentation, safety, fishery. When state cases follow federal decisions which change, the state decisions remain in contrary stance. Often, the efforts of the courts to settle the law of search have an unsettling effect; distinctions become hairline. Classification of cases for textual presentation become blurred. Direct comparison of decisions will be preferable for exposition at times rather than to adhere to classification symmetry, and the cross-references should be helpful. Thus, after reviewing Miranda and Taylor [A3-1], consider these:

In Cacace v State, (Fla App 1980) 379 So 2d 1306, on report of a suspicious boat grounded in St. Lucie Inlet, officers met a slowly moving boat and stopped it, noticing a light brown stain on the gunwale, possibly from marijuana. It rode low in the water. Lacking registration, the operator was allowed to dock the boat to get it, after which an officer smelled marijuana. The officers boarded for a safety check and found the marijuana which defendant moved to suppress.

The court held that the evidence adduced at the suppression hearing showed that the officers lacked a founded suspicion at the time of the first stop. Therefore, any incriminating evidence later found and seized was subject to suppression.

In Roth v State, (Fla App 1979) 378 So 2d 794, Florida Marine Patrol Officers, believing there was a violation of seafood quality control laws, boarded without a warrant the shrimp boat Dudley anchored in Charlotte Harbor. They seized a large amount of marijuana and arrested Roth. The officers testified at the suppression hearing to a belief that seafood was on board unlawfully and/or there was a violation of seafood quality control. The trial judge ruled that F.S. 370.021(5) expressly authorized the search without a warrant, and probable cause was not necessary.

The appellate court reversed. The statute empowers designated law enforcement officers to board and search without a warrant if they believe the products were taken, transported, kept for sale, etc. Although probable cause is not stated expressly as a requirement, here the reason to believe is equated with probable cause as in Hill v State, 238 So 2d 608. The departmental regulation which authorized boarding and search without a warrant for enforcement of the subsection and for protection of the public health is void for exceeding its enabling statute. The case was remanded for a new hearing on suppression.

Personal motive was held to be irrelevant in U.S. v Willis, (DC La 1979) 476 F Supp 201. The Coast Guard boarded the fishing boat Seaman Blues in the Gulf 43 miles from the Louisiana coast after 5 hours of surveillance by Coast Guard aircraft. Upon a check, the documents were in order but Willis had not been signed on as skipper, and the vessel's number had been painted on an engine room bulkhead. Willis was told to raise the fish hold hatch revealing burlap bags marked "Product of Colombia" which smelled like marijuana. It was the subject of a motion to suppress.

The motion was denied. The Coast Guard had plenary authority to stop and board any American flag vessel beyond the 12 mile limit under 14 USC §89(a), Warren [A3-18]. Even if the real purpose of the boarding officer was to search for marijuana, his subjective intent cannot change what otherwise would be a valid stop and entry into an illegal one. What he thought at the time of boarding is irrelevant under Hillstrom [M3-13].

The entry into the fish hold was justified by 16 USC §971f under which an authorized enforcement officer, with or without a warrant, may board any vessel subject to U.S. jurisdiction and inspect the vessel and its catch. Also, 46 CFR §67.15-1 requires, before issuance of marine documents, that the official number and net tonnage be marked on the vessel's main beam. Thus, there were legitimate reasons to enter the fish hold to check the main beam and inspect the catch. Again, despite the personal motive of the officer in charge to look for illegal fish and smuggling activities, his personal motive to look for drugs is irrelevant in the face of the validly authorized search. The valid statute and regulations do not infringe 4th Amendment rights. Defendant had no expectation of privacy with respect to the fish hold which is not a place where one keeps personal belongings. [See discussion following Cadena, below] Crews of commercial vessels should know and expect that the hold may be subject to routine inspection by the Coast Guard or Customs when leaving or entering a U.S. port. There is no reason why the hold of a commercial vessel should be considered any more private when the vessel is on the high seas.

Part of the problem of characterizing permissible or impermissible police conduct is to distinguish between sham or bare subterfuge and colorable police action. In Mullins v State, (Fla 1979) 366 So 2d 1162, a police officer saw Mullins riding a bicycle slowly through a residential area very early in the morning, stopped him, asked his name and purpose in the area, smelled marijuana, and saw protruding from Mullins' pocket a clear plastic bag containing a brown substance. He arrested Mullins and seized the contraband. The appellate court held the search to be reasonable under the circumstances.

The Supreme Court reversed. The stop and seizure based

only on a bare suspicion of illegal activity was unlawful under authority of Coladonato [A3-15], and the evidence seized as a result of the illegal stop will be suppressed.

Two of the five Justices, concurring specially, considered that there may be instances where an officer may approach to assist, or to warn of a hazard, in which contact he may detect evidence of a crime. As a distinction, he may seize such evidence lawfully in contrast to Mullins' stop on bare suspicion.

The court found the legitimate police contact anticipated in Mullins in Carter v State, (Fla App 1979) 370 So 2d 1181. Answering a call at 5:00 AM, a Palm Beach County deputy sheriff passed Carter who was walking east on a state road 12 miles east of Belle Glade. Returning to Belle Glade after the call, he saw Carter continuing east on the road in an area of farms and ranches with few houses and no street lights. It being unusual to walk that stretch of road 30 miles from West Palm Beach at that hour, and considering that the man might be stranded with his car up the road and in need of help, the deputy got out and asked what he was doing and where he was going. Answer: To Belle Glade (which was westward, not eastward). The deputy noticed a bulge weighing down Carter's right front pocket. He tapped it with the back of his hand, felt it was metal or something hard, looked toward the pocket opening, and saw the grips of a gun. Asked what was in his pocket, Carter said, "Ah, well. I'm going to tell you the truth. I'm on the run because I just shot a man in Belle Glade." The deputy took the gun and arrested him.

His conviction, after denial of a motion to suppress, was affirmed. Unlike Mullins, the officer did not stop Carter to arrest him, but to offer assistance he might need or wish [see also U.S. v Miller, below], and as noted in Mullins, this case is an example of an instance where legitimate contact of an officer and a citizen may lead to arrest for a crime detected as a result of the contact. The search preceding the arrest was limited to a single tap and glance into the pocket to determine of Carter was armed. This is expected of an officer in his normal patrol, surveillance and investigation duties. The officer's actions were not illegal or improper. From all the circumstances, he had probable cause or reasonable ground to believe Carter might be armed and, accordingly, dangerous which permitted a reasonably limited search to neutralize the danger. The fruits of the search were admissable.

Parallel to our featured Piner case [A3-20 and below] is Casal v State, (Fla App 1979) 375 So 2d 1077. Florida Marine Patrol officers stopped defendants in the Atlantic off Monroe County simply for a check of the vessel's registration papers. There was no suspicion, founded or otherwise, of any unlawful activity; but cannabis was found aboard.

Convictions for possession were reversed, defendants were discharged. Such a stop was permissible at the time of the suppression hearing, and this had been held specifically in Miranda [A3-1]; but during the pendency of this appeal the decision of Delaware v Prouse [below] requires the conclusion that the stop was improper. "There is no basis for distinguishing between automobiles and boats in applying the Fourth Amendment's proscription of unreasonable searches and seizures. Since this is true, (emphasis supplied) and since none of the exceptions stated in the Prouse decision are applicable here, we conclude - - - that Prouse requires the conclusion that the stop was improper, and that the motion to suppress the contraband which was seized as a result of this stop should have been granted."

As discussed below, however, the Piner decision and the Prouse application in maritime searches are being whittled away.

THE SENSE OF COMMUNITY

The reader of Chapters 3 of Small Boat Law, main volume and Supplements, will be confounded by the doctrines and decisions which defy consensus. Different jurisdictions, statutes and subject matter will account for some normal variation; but the unsettled state of the law of search and seizure has been termed a quagmire. However, the serious students of Small Boat Law are entitled to something more than a shrug, and a return to basics may give some meaningful insight. When law school students would be carried away by their forensic brilliance, the late Prof. Paul D. Kaufman of New York University School of Law would halt the classroom clamor with, "Ask your uncle who never went to law school." Let us try that.

THE FREE SOCIETY MYTH [M8-3] recalls semantically the idea that when the "free" man associates with others, each pays his society dues by yielding some freedom for the communal purpose. It is axiomatic that every association has the inherent right to protect itself but, with a sense of community, this power was limited by judicial recognition that the 4th Amendment preserved to individual dignity a right to be let alone - to be protected from undue communal interference or harassment - which the courts tested by a balancing of the interests of society against those of the individual.

To the extent that such determination was not provided by legislation, judicial intervention was termed "judicial legislation" and criticized at times, but this long had been a feature of Anglo-American common law as distinguished from "code" societies (Latin law, Code Napoleon) wherein governance conformed strictly to details of codified law. The common law judge, with a sense of fairness and conscience, long ago created new law such as quasi-contract [Jones v City of Lake Charles, M16-19], estoppel (judicial refusal to hear the position of a party), and laches [M17-10] to prevent unfairness.

This brings us to the judge-created exclusionary rule,

THE EMPEROR'S CLOTHES [A3-38], THE SEARCH FOR TRUTH [A3-39], and the sense of fairness. The cases acknowledge that nothing in the 4th Amendment provides for suppression of evidence for violation of 4th Amendment rights which was borrowed from the right against self-incrimination of the 5th Amendment. It began with Boyd v U.S., (1886) 116 US 616, 6 S Ct 524, 29 L Ed 746, in which government, without a warrant, seized records in a forfeiture proceeding for non-payment of import duties on plate glass. Government's notice to produce the records was held to be unconstitutional, the court saying, "It is not the breaking of his doors, and the rummaging in his drawers, that constitutes the essence of the offense; but it is the invasion of his indefeasible right of personal security, personal liberty, and private property - -". Next came Weeks v U.S., (1914) 232 US 383, 34 S Ct 341, 58 L Ed 504, involving the warrantless seizure of policy gambling slips; and in the 1920's the exclusionary rule became embedded in the law as precedent. The test of warrantless police action was reasonableness which the court examined in balancing the interests of government against those of the individual. Mapp v Ohio and Ker v California [A3-5] imposed the federal exclusionary rule upon the states. 4th Amendment protection, said the courts, required that the usual inferences which reasonable men draw shall be made by a neutral and detached magistrate instead of an investigating officer [A3-4]. In imposing the exclusionary rule, the courts reasoned that "perhaps" the suppression of evidence would deter law enforcement officers from overreaching conduct.

That "perhaps" was unfortunate reasoning. By way of illustration, an enforcement officer at a recent educational session was asked, in casual conversation, how he fared with the exclusionary rule. He replied that he did not worry about it; he just did what he had to do and left it to the judges, prosecutors and lawyers to work it out. This confirms the commentary in Minjares, below. To add "perhapses":

- if police thought like judges, the device might have worked; or

- if judges thought like police, they might have considered that the device would not have worked; or

- if judges forfeited a police car (back to walking) or car radio (back to the call box) for each constitutional violation, the device might have worked; or

- if judges considered that not all police were impetuous, mindless bullies and, sometimes, had rational basis to follow their trained "police noses" to free judges to judge reasonableness instead of adhering mechanically to advance procurement of warrants, the device might have worked; or

- if, adhering to the celebrated requirement of due process of law, the judges had held fact-finding hearings, similar to the rule-making process imposed on administrative agencies, before the exclusionary rule was promulgated, the device might have been fine-tuned ("the seaman's vessel is his home", below, is another example of ill-conceived judicial pronouncements); or

- if, on appropriate petition, the chief executives (the president and governors) had summoned the judges to justify extraordinary powers and decisions in conformance with the constitutional concept of checks and balances (who judges the judges?) before sending messages for remedial action to the legislatures (the representatives of all the people), the law of 4th Amendment protection might have developed in a more manageable fashion.

Why these extreme speculations? Ask your uncle who never went to law school. Another legal axiom is that courts will not speculate in their proceedings; yet when the courts perhapsed the deterrent effect of the exclusionary rule they institutionalized a doctrine that has produced public and judicial outcry ever since, as in Coolidge [A3-5].

It continues in California v Minjares, (1979) 443 U.S. 916, 100 S Ct 9, 61 L Ed 2d 892. Two men with handguns robbed a Safeway Store in Fremont about 8:30 PM in the presence of several witnesses, one of whom followed, saw them get in a car, trailed the car several miles until he could identify it as a 1968 or 1969 Fairlane and record the license number, and reported this information at the police station. At 9:00 PM an officer, who had the broadcast information, spotted a suspect vehicle, called for a backup, and made a stop. The driver, the sole occupant, fit the description of one suspect and he was arrested, but a search of him and of the car gave no clue to the whereabouts of the other robber. The officers couldn't find the car trunk key, so the car was towed to the city yard, the lock was picked, a red tote bag in the trunk was opened. It held clothing similar to that described by robbery witnesses, three guns, and a roll of pennies in a wrapper of Safeway's bank.

At the suppression hearing the officer who made the stop testified he did not get a warrant while making the decision to search the car and trunk because time was a factor of hours in their search for the second suspect. The trial court refused to suppress the evidence in the tote bag, and defendant was convicted of armed robbery, but California's Supreme Court reversed because, although the warrantless search of the car was based on probable cause and was permissible after the tow to the police station, the search of the container in the trunk was invalid without a warrant.

The State petitioned the U.S. Supreme Court to stay the order of the California Supreme Court. That petition was denied, and the foregoing was reported in the biting dissent of Justice Rehnquist joined by Chief Justice Burger.

He acknowledged the conscientious police work that fell short with good-faith error in judgment of the officers who did not realize the search of the trunk at the city yard under the exigent search exception was constitutionally permissible, but not the tote bag in the trunk which they did not know existed before they opened the trunk. He reviewed the history of the court-created exclusionary rule and concluded that police should have rules easily understood for carrying out their work, that rights infringed by wrongful official conduct should have redress for that damage; but these need not be done in the same forum. He cited Oaks: Studying the Exclusionary Rule in Search and Seizure, 37 U Chi L Rev 665 (1970) as the most comprehensive study on the exclusionary rule which states it to be an open question whether the exclusionary rule deters police.

In making a comparison with Canada which has no rule excluding illegally obtained evidence, Oaks observes (pp.705-706):

"Another possible factor in the control of Canadian police, difficult to isolate but of great potential importance, is their tendency to obey the rules, irrespective of sanctions. Toronto police officials, prosecutors and a judge all insisted that their police are greatly concerned about obeying the rules and very sensitive to and quick to be influenced by judicial criticism of their conduct. It is doubtful that comparable United States officials would similarly describe the attitudes of their police."

This is not to say that tainted evidence never should be excluded. Our system boasts it is a government of laws, not men. That system includes judges whose function it is to exercise judgment. It should be for them in their traditional mode, in fairness as they perceive it, to nullify sham police conduct as in Moorhead v State, (Fla App 1980) 378 So 2d 123. At 6:30 PM, Moorhead walked toward a recreation center in Reddington Beach carrying his personal pool cue. The center, located above the city fire station, was due to open at 7:00 PM. When stopped by a police officer for identification, he produced his driver's license and blood donor card. As requested by the officer, he went to the police station to fill out a field interrogation card. There, the officer admired the cue and asked to examine it. He consented and handed it to the officer who shook it. It rattled and, thinking some sort of weapon might be inside, he unscrewed the cue and saw a piece of paper with something inside. It was phenobarbital.

At the suppression hearing the officer testified that, while there had been a purse-snatching in a neighboring community the previous day, he had no suspicion that Moorhead had committed that or any other crime at the time of the stop and that it was not unusual to see young people near the recreation hall at that time of evening. The judge refused to suppress because Moorhead had consented to the search.

The appellate court reversed. No consent was requested or given to search the pool cue. The police conduct was tainted and could not support a criminal charge. The cue was handed over for admiration, not search; without consent, there was no voluntary basis for the illegal police activity.

Finally, in <u>State v Greene</u>, (Or 1979) 285 Or 337, 591 P 2d 1362, Justice <u>Linde</u>, noted that the present approach of the courts in administering the law of search and seizure, in effect, is to send out the police with the latest U.S. Supreme Court advance sheets (paperback supplements) in their pockets. This, for students of Small Boat Law, we are unable to do.

<u>THE COAST GUARD</u>   [M3-3, add:]

Since initial publication of this text, drug smuggling from south of the borders has become a giant industry. The large number of search and seizure cases that intruded into the 1978 Supplement showed the surge of this activity which continues to climb. It disadvantages boating in several ways.

As noted in <u>THE SUNTAN PATROL</u> [M3-12], the 7th Coast Guard District, through which most of this waterborne contraband passes, serves a vast area. Operations against it - "square grouper" - have deprived the legitimate maritime community, including boating, of normal Coast Guard services by the drain on personnel, equipment, funds, and time. In an address in Miami by Rear Admiral Benedict L. Stabile, Commander of the 7th, he presented an insight into the magnitude of the enforcement problem that barely had been covered in the press. To cover the sealift from Mariel, Cuba, the Coast Guard had to bring in personnel and equipment from as far distant as Alaska and borrow elements from the Navy and Marine Corps. Patrol patterns fanned out from the Straits of Florida with this sea and air armada so effectively that it blocked seaborne drug traffic; but this was a temporary operation. Yet, the Mariel sealift and the influx of Haitian refugees were but a part of the pressures building in the entire Caribbean basin in which there is severe economic depression caused in part by the worldwide fuel stringency - more so there than here. At the same time, billions of dollars are moving into that area from the United States, but into the wrong hands in the drug trade, which serves to aggravate the economic imbalance in the area and increase the social turbulence.

Returning from this digression into international affairs, how does this affect normal pleasure boating? In addition to the lessened expectation of Coast Guard services as above, the boater is coming under stronger suspicion and law enforcement of the criminal kind. The classroom demand to know the extent of enforcement authority mentioned in <u>FEDERAL AGENCIES</u> [M3-3] occurred in early 1975 by students more deeply <u>involved</u> than weekend boating who felt they were being harassed unduly by law enforcement officers. Things are much worse five years later, and there is less pleasure in pleasure boating as it moves into an aquatic jungle. The boating commercial enterprises, too, are affected as we are about to see.

Coast Guard enforcement of smuggling laws was hampered by legal loopholes in territorial jurisdiction, flag jurisdiction, or proof of criminal intent in their interceptions at sea. Essentially, their cases were based on conspiracy to import. Accordingly, on September 15, 1980, P.L. 96-350 (21 USC §955a), Importation of Controlled Substances - Enforcement, went into effect. It provides that:

Sec. 1(a) It is unlawful for any person on board a vessel subject to the jurisdiction of the United States on the high seas to knowingly or intentionally manufacture or distribute, or to possess with intent to manufacture or distribute, a controlled substance.

(b) It is unlawful for a citizen of the United States on board any vessel to knowingly or intentionally manufacture or distribute, or to possess with intent to manufacture or distribute, a controlled substance.

(c) It is unlawful for any person on board any vessel in customs waters of the United States to knowingly or intentionally manufacture or distribute, or to possess with intent to manufacture or distribute, a controlled substance.

(d) It is unlawful for any person to possess, manufacture, or distribute a controlled substance

(1) intending that it be unlawfully imported into the United States; or

(2) knowing that it will be unlawfully imported into the United States.

(e) (Certain lawful exceptions.)

(f) Violators will be tried in federal court at the point of entry into the United States, or the District of Columbia.

Sec. 2 defines customs waters, high seas, and vessels of the United States including those numbered under the Federal Boat Safety Act of 1971.

Sec. 3 includes attempts and conspiracies to violate.

Sec. 4 subjects to seizure and forfeiture any property used or intended for use to commit, or to facilitate commission of, an offense. [See FLORIDA CONTRABAND, below]

But again, how does this affect normal pleasure boating? Recall in WHY SEARCH AND SEIZURE [A3-3] the observation that pleasure boats are used widely in smuggling operations and that smugglers merge indistinguishably into the spectrum of the water-based society. Thus, all boats with any capability to transport contraband increasingly will be subject to suspicion, surveillance, and what the boatman may deem to be harassment. A scan of Enforcement Authority cases will show the variety of watercraft that have become involved. To the degradation of the finer traditions of pleasure boating, the pattern leads from the mother ship.

PROFILE OF A MOTHER SHIP

In U.S. v May May, (DC Tex 1979) 470 F Supp 384, the court's extensive findings of fact reveal the elements of Coast Guard enforcement techniques in the suppression of smuggling of drugs. Reasonable cause thus appears in sharper focus for search of non-U.S. flag vessels, and to the degree that the court considered prior cases, the decision represents an exposition of this law.

Cdr. Ikens, Chief of Intelligence and Law Enforcement, 7th Coast Guard District-Miami, testified on the techniques and modes of drug smugglers from Colombia, Guajira Peninsula at its northen tip being the primary shipping point for marijuana headed for the United States. The mother ship technique employs usually a 70 to 90 foot non-U.S. flag vessel to hover off the U.S. coast with a large quantity of marijuana which usually is off-loaded into smaller vessels from the U.S. at rendezvous outside U.S. territorial waters. Mother ships generally are older vessels originally designed for fishing or short run merchant trading. They carry unusually large crews to handle the large bulky cargoes. Rendezvous vary from 20 to 200 miles offshore and the long voyages, usually from Colombia, require extra fuel often carried in extra drums on deck. They fly false flags, typically of Panama, Venezuela or Honduras. Upon seizure, the crews often tell a standard story of the master's recent departure in a small boat in mid-ocean. Since 1973 most mother ship seizures were off the Atlantic and Gulf coasts of Florida, but enforcement efforts caused a shift of smuggling to the New England coast.

A Coast Guard patrol routinely will try to determine the nationality of an encountered ship by its name, home port, and nationality. If it is not identified properly, the patrol will check with the country of the flag flown to determine the vessel's registration in fact. If the flag flown is proper and there is no suspicion of illegal activity, the ship is passed on; otherwise, through a chain of authority, permission is requested of the foreign flag nation to take action as its agent. If the flag flown is incorrect, the patrol will investigate by boarding to check documentation. A vessel on the high seas shows nationality by the flag it flies and the documents issued by the flag nation. The vessel's permanent number is marked on its main beam and the number usually is registered by the flag country. The number is on the vessel's documents. If no documents are available, other sources such as Lloyds of London can be contacted for the information. Boarding personnel, by policy, first should check the pilothouse and captain's cabin, usually above deck, for the documents. If a suspect vessel is flying a proper flag, the flag country usually grants permission for Coast Guard boarding and investigation, Colombia being the only nation which has denied permission to board.

Coast Guard patrols are provided with a list of suspect vessels, but names of smuggling vessels are changed routinely and frequently. Therefore, patrols regard with suspicion improper markings, name or home port not permanently attached, failure to fly a flag, failure to identify itself, condition of the vessel, and unusual activities aboard.

In August 1978 an unknown informer told an officer of Coast Guard Cutter Durable that a mother ship with 30-50 tons of marijuana would rendezvous with two shrimpers from Freeport and one from Corpus Christi. The information could not be amplified or verified. Durable is a well-armed warship. On patrol August 15th its helicopter spotted a vessel, 10 miles northeast of Durable, on a northwesterly course. It was 100 to 120 feet long with a blue hull and white superstructure. It showed no flag or hailing port. Superfly II was painted on white boards in some temporary manner. Blue paint on the stern seemed fresher than the sides which indicated possible deletion of the hailing port. It carried both whip and long wire antennas. 9 men were visible aboard. Durable approached from the stern where its commander, Crosby, saw with high-powered binoculars the lack of a flag and hailing port, the name Superfly II on a white board, M/V Johnette Walker painted on a white life ring on the port side, extra fuel drums on deck, and a hull shape of a type commonly built in the United States. At first sighting, Crosby saw nobody on deck, but he knew from the helicopter report of at least 9 that Superfly was over-manned.

He got no response to radio and flag signals or to a battery operated megaphone. As Durable lowered a 26 foot boat, Superfly raised a new Panamanian flag with fold marks as if taken out of a protective plastic bag. In response to questions from the small boat in English and Spanish, the crew's spokesman, William May May, said the crew was Panamanian bound from Honduras to Tampico, Mexico. It was now many miles northeast of Tampico and headed northwest. Crosby radioed for a check with Pamana, his suspicions being aroused by the hand-lettered non-permanent name board, lack of home port on the stern, presence of oil drums on deck, and excessive crew. It fit the classic mother ship pattern in his experience. When the small boat returned to Durable, Superfly circled to the right in 20° increments and altered its heading from 310° to 300° true. Crosby had experienced this maneuver as a test of surveillance which strengthened his suspicions.

But August 15th was a Panamanian holiday, and Crosby got no response from that country that day. At 3:00 AM Superfly changed course abruptly forcing Durable to change course and increase speed to avoid collision. Now it was 105 miles from the Texas coast whereas it had been 220 miles off when first sighted, so it had gone 115 miles toward the U.S. and further from its stated destination. At 9:00 AM it stopped and hailed Durable. They were lost and needed assistance; they were headed for Tampico but did not know about any charts aboard and did not know how much fuel they had. Also, at 6:00 AM on the 15th, prior to the initial encounter, the master had left the ship on a raft with a small motor, and he said before leaving that a heading of 310° true would get them to Tampico. Both vessels then simply drifted all day until 7:34 PM when Crosby, who had received word that Superfly was not a legitimate registered vessel of Panama, now received word of "no objection to boarding". Crosby ordered Ens. Farrel to board to examine documents; if none, to locate the beam number. This took place 135 miles offshore. As he boarded he smelled marijuana. The crew disclaimed knowledge of any documents, and he decided to find the main beam number because that would take only a few minutes whereas a search of the ship for documents could take hours. On entering the hold he found it filled with 32 tons of marijuana upon which the ship was seized and the crew arrested. Crosby was ordered to sail Superfly toward the U.S. with a custody crew to draw out contacts with the mother ship. Several vessels approached, then turned away, and an airplane circled it, all with the probability that lack of a recognition signal defeated the ruse.

A number of charts were found aboard. One bore an x mark southeast of Matagorda Bay, Texas along a pencil line running easterly from Port Aransas. Another mark was on a depth number between latitude 27° 30' and 27° 20'. Another chart had the upper left hand corner torn off. A number of pencil markings that looked like course lines converged toward the missing part. North-south lines off the Yucatan Peninsula marked with times indicated that these were used as lines of position. A pilot chart bore a number of small pencil marks, one mark being a circled x. All points and lines transposed from the charts appeared to converge on the same general area off the Texas coast. But clearly, it would have been impossible for Superfly to reach Tampico on its heading.

Defendants had moved to dismiss for lack of jurisdiction, and to suppress the evidence. The motion to dismiss was denied. Whether the events took place in territorial or international waters, defendants in a criminal trial may not challenge successfully the jurisdiction of the court on the ground that their presence was obtained unlawfully. It was not necessary for government to allege or prove an overt act if it can demonstrate conspiracy to import and/or to distribute, thereby having an impact within the U.S. The evidence amply supported the conclusion that the illegal cargo was headed for this country alone.

The motion to suppress also was denied. Superfly was a stateless vessel - one without a nationality - as shown by the efforts to conceal its identity and its lack of registration in Panama even though flying the Panamanian flag with the claim by the crew that it was a Panamanian vessel. As held in Cadena [see below], 14 USC §89(a) grants power to the Coast Guard to board, search and seize foreign vessels on the high seas when there is probable cause to detect and prevent a violation of U.S. laws. The evidence in this case justified such action. Superfly, as a stateless vessel flying a false flag, was not entitled to the protection accorded a ship registered in a foreign nation which is a signatory to the Convention on the High Seas. As noted in Cadena, suppression of evidence acquired by an improper seizure, if such there was, is not required if a violation of international law may be redressed by other remedies. The facts known aboard Durable were sufficient to support reasonable suspicion of criminal activity to warrant the conclusion that probable cause existed for a boarding and search. Nobody aboard could challenge the constitutionality of the seizure inasmuch as none had a legitimate expectation of privacy in the holds of the ship. Probable cause combined with exigent circumstances of the ship's capability of movement justified the warrantless search. Even so, the evidence discovered in plain view was not the subject of a search.

A series of important and widely cited cases will show the situations and challenges that led to the new enforcement legislation [B3-9] and illuminate other issues; but first, let us return to the Piner case [A3-22]. In U.S. v Piner, (CA Cal 1979) 608 F 2d 358, the 9th Circuit Court of Appeals affirmed, with a dissent, the District Court's suppression of marijuana seized aboard Delphene in the random and routine safety inspection by the Coast Guard without suspicious circumstances. The court noted the Coast Guard practice of inspecting pleasure boats only when underway because safety equipment such as life jackets and fire extinguishers may be stored at home when the boat is not in use, relatively safe from theft, contrary to dockside inspection of commercial vessels which are subject to rigorous safety regulations with which compliance is required at all times. Such random boardings were upheld by the 5th Circuit in Warren [A3-18], as also for Customs authority [A3-29]. The lower court had held that the random stop and search of Delphene violated the 4th Amendment, and the present appeal centers on the validity of warrantless administrative search because of the need for and the nature of the administrative search.

Meanwhile, the Supreme Court decided Delaware v Prouse on March 27, 1979, 440 US 648, 99 S Ct 1391, 59 L Ed 2d 660. That case dealt with reasonableness of a random stop of an automobile by state police to check the driver's license and registration. It balanced the intrusion against the promotion of legitimate governmental interests to insure safety of the roadways. The court rejected random stops because checkpoint stops were less frightening and less intrusive to the lawful traveler as an alternative mechanism to achieve highway safety.

Accordingly, the Court of Appeals concluded that the random stop of Delphene after dark solely for safety and registration inspection was not justified by governmental need to enforce compliance. Even though 330,534 pleasure craft were registered in the San Francisco Bay area in 1977 of which

3,245 were boarded by the Coast Guard, 40% of which were found not to be in compliance with safety regulations, and check points at sea were not practicable, the court saw no reason why the Coast Guard's governmental purpose could not be accomplished sufficiently during daylight hours.

The dissenting opinion said that Prouse, which deals with automobiles only, does not establish a rule against all random stops. Thus, that decision excepted random inspections by game wardens. The Prouse court noted that the automobile spot check did not appear sufficiently productive to qualify as reasonable law enforcement practice. Unlike that experience, Coast Guard practice is highly effective. The roadblock alternative is not available at sea where conditions are incompatable with a safe orderly queue for the systematic check of vessels. The alternative of limiting Coast Guard stops to daylight hours ignores the fact that nightime safety violations may be more dangerous to boaters and those who may be called upon to rescue them. Nightime stops may be more intrusive with the specter of uniformed officers rousing people from sleep, but someone ought to be awake when a boat is underway.

Two hundred years of history make it plain that there is no legitimate expectation of privacy in this instance. Based on the historical acceptance of Coast Guard document and cargo inspections and the special rules applicable to certain administrative searches, random safety checks of vessels are not unreasonable within the meaning of the 4th Amendment. The 5th Circuit upheld the constitutionality of documentation and safety checks without probable cause or particular suspicion. Statutory authority for the purpose at any time is granted by 14 USC §89(a) which originated in the first Congress which, as traced by Carmichael [A3-36], has continued to modern times. This is pursuasive authority for the reasonableness of the boardings which is not overcome by the reasoning of the majority opinion.

Moreover, the Coast Guard document and safety checks fall within the exception for administrative searches to fulfill an important governmental objective of insuring safety of pleasure boats while in use. This would be frustrated by the requirement of a particular suspicion when the safety devices are not visible to a passing vessel. This, too, has been the subject of historical federal regulation.

Therefore, this safety check is not a substantial invasion of privacy. Although search of certain portions of a vessel, such as crew quarters on an oceangoing tanker or a locked compartment on the bridge, may constitute substantial invasion of privacy, here the evidence was in plain view when the officer boarded Delphene. Stepping onto the exposed deck is not an invasion of an area in which defendants had a legitimate expectation of privacy.

The order of suppression, he said, should be reversed.

Note that the Court of Appeals turned away from the trial court's reliance on inspection of buildings and boats at dockside in favor of inspection at sea, as narrowed to day or night, to serve a significant governmental purpose of assuring safety at sea; also that the dissenting judge questioned privacy protection for non-personal areas of a vessel which, increasingly, arises in the cases.

Although appeared to be headed for the Supreme Court, it has been said that government chose not to appeal it because better cases were pending for that purposes. Meanwhile, it appears to have little support in the other Circuits which favor Warren [A3-18].

In U.S. v Harper, (CA NC 1980) 617 F 2d 35, Coast Guard Cutter Alert, pursuant to intergovernmental agency cooperation, patrolled Caribbean sea lanes for general enforcement purposes with special emphasis on drug interdiction when it boarded the North Carolina shrimper Lady Ellen in Mona Passage between the Dominican Republic and Puerto Rico. The policy was to board all U.S. vessels under 250 feet without particularized suspicion. The master admitted it carried 25 tons of marijuana. With his cooperation, it was allowed to proceed under surveillance upon entry into U.S. waters. A navigator boarded at Morehead City to pilot the boat to its remote landing site where various government agents closed in by land, sea and air on the enterprise participants.

Affirming the convictions, the 4th Circuit alined with the 5th and undercut Piner:

- The stop and boarding was lawful without particularized suspicion because it was done as a sysyematic "border" operation.

- 4th Amendment protection against unreasonable searches was not involved because stops and searches at established border check points are reasonable per se. Statutory authority governs the conduct of the officials.

- The Coast Guard action under 14 USC §80(a) did not violate the 4th Amendment. It was statutory, plenary, traditional and historical.

- Unlike a stop at the will and whim of officers in the field as condemned is Prouse, this was done under established policy to intercept all American flag vessels equipped and of a size sufficient for large scale smuggling operations which could not be detected easily in isolated coastal waters. Check points were in well-known sea lanes for such clandestine operations. Routine boardings could have been made at port without particularized suspicion, and they were not unreasonable on the high seas. Check point control in a well-traveled sea lane is like a roadside truck weigh-station and inspection point expressly approved in Prouse as reasonable non-discretionary intrusions on private interests beyond the warrant and probable cause requirements of the 4th Amendment.

- Such operations were a minimal and reasonably necessary intrusion on private interests under the circumstances. Administrative and regulatory searches of commercial enterprises, and vessels generally, intrude on interests and expectations of privacy very different from those involving the integrity of persons and residences not subject to ongoing regulation.

- American flag commercial shipping, since the beginning of the republic, was subject to boarding and inspection with no reasonable expectation of privacy in the industry. International law of the sea requires each nation to maintain the navigability and safety of its own commercial fleet as a condition of non-interference from other nations. Regulatory inspection derives from this.

- Requirement of a particularized suspicion in the systematic inspection plan would encourage flaunting of navigation, safety and administration laws of the United States at the expense of its sovereign international obligation to police its flag vessels. Departure of U.S. territorial waters with probability of return, historical regulation of vessels on the high seas with lessened expectation of privacy, and practical difficulty of policing U.S. vessels on the high seas if some standard of prior suspicion is required make a special case for high seas search in much the same sense as a border search.

- Halting all motorists by road blocks in the vicinity of Lady Ellen's landing to catch crime participants known to be fleeing the scene was a necessary means of law enforcement under the circumstances to justify the minimal intrusion on privacy rights of the passing motorists. This was not the random stop at will and whim condemned in Prouse.

In U.S. v Cadena, (CA Fla 1978) 585 F 2d 1252, DEA agents had a tip that Albernaz sought a vessel to meet a freighter on the high seas to receive and deliver a marijuana shipment to Florida, so they plotted with Albernaz and others to supply a vessel, Catchalot II. Catchalot found the Labrador 200 miles off Florida and gave a pre-arranged code signal. Cadena, Labrador's master, said he had 1000 bales of marijuana to deliver and he requested $1000 cash payment. He had his crew unload 150 bales during daylight hours after protesting he had never done anything like this before in daylight.

Summoned by Catchalot, Coast Guard's Dauntless arrived that evening and hailed Labrador in Spanish and English. Cadena radioed "Shark, Shark", the prearranged warning to Catchalot, and sailed away. Labrador stopped only after Dauntless fired several machine gun bursts and a cannon volley across the bow.

The boarding party found 54 tons of marijuana in sacks in the holds. They found a 1975 Canadian registration certificate and a 1976 Colombian certificate indicating that the ship had been inspected for rats. It was sailing without lights, it had shown no flag by day, and it was flying none when it hove-to. During the chase the crew had been seen discarding papers and small packages into the ocean.

They were convicted of conspiracy to import and to distribute within the U.S. They appealed legality of search and seizure for lack of authority over a foreign vessel in international waters; violation of the Convention on the High Seas (450 U.N.T.S. 82, 13 U.S.T. 2312, T.I.A.S. No. 5200) if there was such authority; 4th Amendment violation for lack of a search warrant; and unreasonable search under the 4th Amendment for lack of authority for search and violation of the Treaty.

Convictions for importation were affirmed, those for distribution reversed, and the case was remanded for further proceedings. 14 USC §89(a) empowers the Coast Guard to search and seize any vessel on the high seas that is subject to the jurisdiction or operation of any law of the U.S., Warren [A3-17], "Winds Will" [M3-12], and Hillstrom [M3-13]. It is not limited to domestic vessels or domestic waters, but it contemplates that vessels on the high seas, under some circumstances, will be subject to the statute. Jurisdictional and territorial limits are not co-terminous in determining its scope, for jurisdiction extends to persons whose acts have an effect within the sovereign territory (conspiracy to import) even though the acts themselves occur outside it. Thus, even though the 200 mile offshore scene was beyond the limits of a customs enforcement area or other territorial jurisdictional statutes, the Coast Guard authority to search was extended by the purpose of the section to detect and prevent violation of U.S. laws - the conspiracy.

International law is codified in the Convention on the High Seas which purports to bind signatory nations of which neither Canada nor Colombia is a ratifying party. It was not intended to confer rights on non-member nations or their citizens. Even if the Coast Guard search violated international principles, the 4th Amendment rule for exclusion of evidence would not apply because none of the signatory nations has such an exclusionary rule, and there is no basis to give such expanded relief to these defendants.

Turning from international law, when foreign vessels or aliens are subjected to criminal prosecution under domestic law, they are entitled to equal protection of all our laws including the 4th Amendment's prohibition of warrantless searches which, in general, are unlawful if made without probable cause. An exception to this prohibition, however, is one made pursuant to 14 USC §89(a) with respect to domestic vessels for legitimate safety and documentary search purposes for the national interest in the conduct and operation of its citizens' vessels.

Here there was probable cause to search without a warrant because of exigent circumstances even though government had advance notice of the conspiracy to import. Dauntless was lying in ambush for a considerable time during which a warrant could have been obtained. It was impossible to know where the two vessels would meet - they themselves did not know - and there was no way to await their union without being seen. Moreover, when Labrador refused to stop after signal and attempted to flee, that created exigent circumstances, if none existed previously, in justification of warrantless search.

No privacy issue was present under the 4th Amendment for there was no search of crew's quarters apart from the general area of the ship. If there were violations of international law, 4th Amendment principles would not apply because unreasonable search and seizure must be determined under a showing that the interests to be served were 4th Amendment violations, not violations of international law.

On a petition for rehearing, denied in 588 F 2d 100 (1979), the court amplified the prior ruling. The attempted flight created exigent circumstances which, with probable cause, justified warrantless search. The Coast Guard does not have complete authority to search on the high seas except for the type situations authorized by the en banc opinion in Warren [A3-18]. A warrant should be obtained where there is prior probable cause, and officers should not rely on exigent circumstances created by attempted apprehension. Despite the similarities in mobility of automobiles and vessels, motor vehicles are not designed to be used as residences, but a ship is a sailor's home (emphasis supplied). Little expectation of privacy in the former is expected in the latter. However, the boundless seas traversible in any direction make it difficult, for purposes of application for a warrant, to state where and when a vessel is to be searched.

The Supreme Court has not created an exception to 4th Amendment warrant requirements for automobiles, and this court will not now create one for vessels.

The court's observation that a ship is a sailor's home is a misleading expression. A ship is not a sailor's home; his living quaters may be his home. A ship usually has a cargo area, dining area, engine area, an executive or administrative area, and other specialized areas where the seaman works, not where he lives. His living area usually is comparatively miniscule and of little interest to searchers unless, perhaps, smuggled diamonds or high potency drugs are in question.

By these considerations the small pleasure vessel poses a different problem because the entire enclosed space usually constitutes living quarters. A liveaboard vessel truly is a permanent home; the livery boat is at the other extreme; for such as these, the elements require a closer examination to determine the actual expectation of privacy. However, the 5th Circuit was quick to modify the "sailor's home" language in subsequent decisions.

In U.S. v Postal, (CA Fla. 1979) 589 F 2d 862, Coast

Guard's Cape York sighted the 51 foot Morgan sailboat La Rosa sailing southwesterly 8.5 miles southeast of Matecumbe Key. It showed no flag and had no name or home port on the stern. Cape York inquired the origin and destination of the voyage and nationality of the vessel. Postal said they were en route from the Bahamas to Belize, of Grand Cayman registry, and the crew was Australian. Two held up a flag later determined to be of Grand Cayman Islands. Cape York notified Coast Guard Miami; then Lt. Beardsworth, commanding, decided to board to verify documentation papers, and he ordered La Rosa to stand by for boarding which Postal refused to do. Miami ordered boarding. Beardsworth saw Postal holding a pistol which turned out to be a Very flare pistol. When Beardsworth explained that the boarding was for violation of international agreements for lack of name and home port on the stern, Postal agreed to receive one boarding officer; but then La Rosa maneuvered erratically to hamper boarding while papers were being jettisoned, which Cape York retrieved. They were pieces of charts and log entries showing La Rosa's presence a month before near Aruba and points in South America.

Now CPO Lewis boarded about 10.5 miles from the coast. Postal agreed to show documents but refused to show identification, asked Lewis if he could be bought, persisted, and added that he had been in the Coast Guard but found a better way to make a living. Lewis questioned that they were Australians. He saw that the hatches, open before boarding, now were closed with Chitty sitting on the forward hatch. One of the defendants, in the interval, asked if they were not yet outside the 12 mile limit. The documents showed Grand Cayman registry and Lewis was recalled to Cape York where he told Beardsworth he believed "they were dirty". Miami ordered Cape York to maintain overt surveillance. La Rosa changed course from parallel to the coast to 35° away from the coast, and varied erratically between.

Miami ordered a second boarding for customs search some three hours later when La Rosa was 16.3 miles out. An armed party found defendants "stoned". Lewis read them their Miranda rights. During defendants' banter, Forsythe opened the forward hatch and disclaimed any allegation that he was Australian. Postal added, "does that mean you want to see the pot?" Lewis saw bales of marijuana down the hatch, one opened, and Postal admitted having 8000 pounds of it. Now Lewis asked Forsythe if he was "really going to Belize"; answer, "No".

Lewis searched La Rosa and took photographs. He noted there was little food aboard and the meat was putrified; fuel was almost gone. A few hours after the arrest Chitty commented to his guard that they made a mistake throwing the papers overboard and not waiting offshore until a pickup. An entry in La Rosa's log the day before Cape York's sighting read: "32 hours and 95 miles to go" (which would have put La Rosa at American Shoal near Key West).

Defendants appealed convictions of conspiracy to import and to possess with intent to distribute. They challenged jurisdiction over persons arrested aboard a foreign vessel seized beyond the 12 mile limit in violation of treaty protection.

The Court of Appeals affirmed and detailed an examination of international law. Grand Cayman came under the protection of The Convention on the High Seas by virtue of ratification by the United Kingdom. The first boarding was justified by right of approach under international maritime law because the facts, circumstances and conduct raised a reasonable suspicion that this was an American vessel making a last ditch effort to avoid apprehension. The second boarding outside the 12 mile limit was not justified under the doctrine of hot pursuit because the signal to stop, which controls, was given just prior to the boarding. Having established that the vessel was of foreign registry, there was no reasonable suspicion of the other two treaty exceptions for halting foreign vessels: La Rosa's engagement in pirating or slaving. However, the applicable provisions of The Convention were not self-executing; that is to say, implementing Congressional legislation would have been required to limit jurisdiction of the courts. The United States did not intend to limit that jurisdiction. Nothing in the circumstances surrounding adoption of The Convention shows an imposition on domestic law of a limitation on jurisdiction on the courts in criminal actions. Thus, the violation of the treaty by Cape York was not a defense to jurisdiction of the court.

The Coast Guard has authority under 14 USC §89(a) to act against a foreign vessel outside the 12 mile limit when there is probable cause to believe defendants were conspiring to smuggle contraband, Cadena. Lack of authority of the arresting officer for a customs boarding outside the 12 mile limit does not affect jurisdiction of the court and it not of sufficient constitutional weight to invoke the rule of exclusion of evidence. Coast Guard boarding power under 14 USC §89(a) exceeds that of Customs even though a customs boarding was Cape York's purpose, for that section was intended to give the Coast Guard the broadest authority available under law, as was held in Warren [A3-18].

Chitty directed the outfitting of La Rosa in Ft. Lauderdale in late January 1976. He paid $21,000 cash on the $153,000 purchase price. It was delivered in Bimini July 3rd when Postal and Chitty flew there. It left Bimini on the 4th for South America, arrived back off the Bahamas September 13th, and continued toward Miami and the Florida Keys until the seizure on the 15th. The magnitude and deliberateness of the enterprise supports the finding of a conspiracy at the time of La Rosa's purchase. The United States has jurisdiction to prohibit extraterritorial acts intended to have effect in the United States.

The first boarding in the 12 mile limit was proper for

routine documentary checks of foreign or domestic vessels without probable cause or suspicion. The information derived coupled with the conduct of defendants gave probable cause to believe La Rosa Carried contraband to justify the second boarding and seizure. The search was consented to by Forsythe who opened the hatch to reveal the marijuana. All government actions were proper and the evidence supported the convictions.

A tracking beeper arose in U.S. v Conroy, (CA Fla 1979) 589 F 2d 1258. Budal, a DEA informer, had conversations in New England with Schubert and Conroy to smuggle marijuana from Jamaica. He joined Schubert and Dahl in Ft. Lauderdale when Schubert obtained a 53 foot Gulfstar sailboat. They were joined by Jacobs, and they lived on Nahoa together until they sailed for Jamaica September 3, 1976. Conroy remained in New England for cargo delivery.

DEA had supplied Budal with two electronic beepers, one to be activated when the vessel was loaded. He hid one in the engine room, the other in the air vent. The contraband was loaded about 40 miles from Jamaica.

Coast Guard's Dauntless, on patrol in the Windward Passage between Cuba and Haiti, was on guard for Nahoa and was alerted when an overflying plane received the signal from one of Budal's beepers. Dauntless spotted Nahoa on radar 9 miles southwest of Haiti and signaled by radio, flags and flashing lights to heave-to; but Nahoa headed straight into Haitian waters. The Haitian Chief of Staff gave oral approval, later confirmed, to enter Haitian waters to search Nahoa, so Dauntless continued in pursuit. When Nahoa continued to ignore signals, Dauntless flagged "stop or we'll shoot", and Nahoa hove-to. Lt Council, commanding, drew up in a small boat, smelled marijuana, boarded, and requested ship's papers. Schubert Prevented him from entering the vessel's cabin. Council ordered a search and found 7000 pounds of marijuana.

Defendants contended, on appeal of their conviction of either conspiracy or both conspiracy and attempt to import, that the installation of the beepers was an illegal search, that boarding in Haitian waters exceeded Coast Guard statutory authority, and that the search was unreasonable and warrantless.

The court affirmed. Under the court's prior holding in U.S. v Holmes, 521 F 2d 859 (1975), a beeper installed on an automobile is a search under the 4th Amendment because it defeats the expectation of privacy of the car's occupants, and a warrant must be obtained for it unless there is sufficient basis for failure to get one to render the action reasonable because the information yielded by beepers normally would not be accessible to the reasonably curious person. However, Budal was not a trespasser. Although not the owner, he had a right to be aboard the vessel. There was probable cause to believe Nahoa would be used to transport contraband. The signal transmission was not an invasion of privacy of others because Budal had no obligation to conceal his whereabouts. Defendants had no legal protection of their erroneous belief that the secrets they divulged would be safeguarded by their confidant. If the informant may reveal the information at a leter time, he may transmit it contemporaneously to third parties.

The 4th Amendment shelters U.S. citizens worldwide from unreasonable searches by the U.S. and the mere consent by a foreign government to a seizure that would be unconstitutional in the U.S. even though the search might have been valid under local law. 14 USC §89 covers a stop on the high seas. It does not authorize search of an American vessel in foreign waters but it does not restrict it, and an examination of its legislative background does not show Congressional intent of the term "high seas" to be restrictive; thus the authority for search is implicit.

International law is part of the domestic law. The law of nations classifies Coast Guard vessels as warships. Haiti and the U.S. were parties to The Convention on the Territorial Sea and Contiguous Zone by which they acknowledged that a warship of one may enter the territorial waters of the other without first giving notice and receiving authorization, and Dauntless had implicit authority to enter Haitian waters. Even so, permission was obtained. If there had been improper seizure in foreign waters, redress is not due to the owner or crew of the subject vessel, but to the foreign government whose territoriality has been infringed by the action. Thus, these defendants have no basis for complaint on that ground.

The statutory authority to make a search does not obviate the need for 4th Amendment compliance; but Dauntless had authority to stop and board, and Nahoa's flight of itself created exigent circumstances which, with probable cause to believe it was engaged in smuggling, justified the warrantless search of the vessel.

An intricate combined enforcement operation appeared in U.S. v Weinrich. (CA Fla. 1978) 586 F 2d 481. Special Agent Layman, Florida Department of Criminal Law Enforcement, had a confidential tip November 10, 1976 that Ryder was involved in importing and distributing narcotics. On January 18, 1977 Layman received further information from a second confidential source. Upon these and information from his independent investigation, he obtained a court order February 18, 1977 to tap Ryder's phone, the information from which supported a second wiretap order for Mitchell's phone which, similarly, led to a total of eight sequential taps. These disclosed an operation discussing "125,000 pounds of gold", "Bogota", "pot", "offloading sites", and a house on the Intracoastal Waterway in Nokomis.

Pinellas County Deputy Sheriff Sgt. Grass reported to FDCLE June 13th that an informant told him a load of marijuana would arrive from South America in 20 days to be offloaded at a Nokomis house matching the one under surveillance. Four days later a 34 foot cabin cruiser Big Daddy moored behind the house until the afternoon of June 21st when it headed for open sea. At 6:30 PM it rendezvoused for an hour with 31 foot Bertram Cat's Paw and a 60 foot converted shrimp trawler Deux Dauphins. Then the two smaller boats headed in tandem toward the Florida coast while Deux Dauphins headed toward international waters. Aerial and marine surveillance of the three boats continued.

At 1:30 AM, as the two boats entered Boca Grande Pass, Big Daddy flashed a spot-light, apparently to locate a buoy. It lit a surveilling Florida Marine Patrol boat, and the FDCLE agent in charge ordered boarding of Big Daddy and Cat's Paw. 6000 pounds of marijuana were found on them, plus hashish on Cat's Paw. A document pertaining to Deux Dauphins was found on Big Daddy. A Customs officer in the team immediately radioed Coast Guard's Point Thatcher which had been trailing Deux Dauphins into the Gulf, and illumination from surveilling aircraft showed the crew to be rinsing the deck with water. Customs officers boarded, smelled lemon-scented disinfectant and marijuana, and a field test confirmed marijuana residue under the carpet on the rear deck.

Those involved were convicted of various offenses of distributing, importing, and possessing. Their appeal charged that the initial Ryder wiretap was illegaland all subsequently developed evidence should have been suppressed as fruit of the poisoned tree; also, the warrantless searches of the vessels lacked either probable cause or exigent circumstances to excuse failure to obtain warrants. And the Coast Guard lacked authority to stop Deux Dauphins, allegedly a Canadian vessel, in international waters.

The convictions were affirmed. The wiretaps were upheld. There was ample probable cause to search Cat's Paw and Big Daddy after intercepting Weinrich's telephonic references to "pot", "125,000 pounds of gold", "Bogota", and "offloading sites"; the independent information of offloading Colombian marijuana to the Nokomis house traced previously to Weinrich; and the one hour rendezvous at sea by the three vessels.

The automobile exception to requirements for a warrant where there are the exigent circumstances of Coolidge [A3-3] applies to sea-going vessels at night when all the vagaries of vehicular travel on land are compounded by random courses and devious actions made possible by open water and darkness. Thus, although surveillance was maintained for seven hours, immediate boarding was ordered when the surveillance was discovered because the suspects might have been armed, they could have resisted boarding, they might have attempted escape, and they might have destroyed evidence. During surveillance the officers were not required to search or arrest at the exact moment probable cause arose. They had the option to wait while developing further evidence rather than interrupt their operations to seek out a magistrate to obtain a warrant. This choice did not vitiate the existence and validity of exigent circumstances as an exception to the requirement for a search warrant.

TRADITIONAL AID

Note [B3-9] the motivation for traditional assistance in U.S. v Miller, (CA Me 1978) 589 F 2d 1117. At 5:45 AM a marina employee at Arrowsic, Maine noticed the yacht Cold Duck to be fouled in a marina mooring 250 yards offshore. It was strange to the area and no effort had been made to rent the mooring, so an employee rowed out in mid-afternoon to investigate. Nobody was aboard, the rubber dinghy was in the cockpit, and part of a meal was on the stove. A phone call to the home port revealed the boat recently had been sold to Jackie Miller. The Coast Guard was notified of a suspected drowning and a group of marine agencies gathered, the sheriff assuming responsibility for employing divers. The Coast Guard learned from the former owner that Miller had paid $19,500 in small bills but asked for a receipt showing a $15,000 price. Aboard were a bill of sale and registry to Jackie D. Miller, PO Box 42, Woolwich, Me.

While clearing the fouled lines the next morning, deputies noticed several thousand dollars worth of new electronic equipment which had been installed in a sloppy manner, marijuana butts in an ashtray, and a folded navigation chart lying on the floor. After opening it on the table, there appeared a penciled course line from the marina toward Mill Isle, a secluded peninsula in Arrowsic. The boat came under suspicion of drug involvement.

Now Miller drove up in a black Chevrolet Blazer and asked Muise, a marina employee, about leasing a mooring for Cold Duck. He saw law enforcement officers aboard, he asked Muise about them, and he was told they brought the boat to the dock to free the mooring. Miller departed, Muise reported the conversation to the officers, and three went in search for him. Deputy White passed Miller on the highway with mutual recognition, and he caught Miller after a high speed chase. Miller produced his license and registration and admitted he owned Cold Duck. At the marina he said the ownership papers of the boat were on Cold Duck which he boarded voluntarily with the officers, one of whom informed Miller of suspicion of drug smuggling, noting two roaches in the ashtray. Several officers in the parking lot were admiring the Blazer when they saw marijuana debris on the floor through the doorway left open by Miller, and they so informed the officer on the boat. Miller denied involvement with drug smuggling but the officer seized the vessel.

They returned to the Blazer which had been locked by the officers. Miller denied knowing who owned it, but he unlocked it with his keys. He denied knowledge or ownership of the four suitcases taken from it which were searched without his objection. The fourth had a combination lock which Miller opened, and they found a 2 ounce cube of hashish. Miller was arrested and the drug and Blazer seized. A search of Miller produced a sales receipt for an industrial vacuum cleaner sold May 13th - that day - to a John Davis which Miller later admitted to be his false name. He was placed in a holding cell in Bath.

Meanwhile, officers went to the Woolwich address which corresponded to the PO Box. They found an empty house which neighbors said he had vacated several weeks before. Considering the marked course on the chart, the officers decided to visit Mill Isle to inquire about unusual activity which may have been observed at the deep water dock. A telescope protruded from a trash barrel on the dock upon which was scattered marijuana debris. Fresh tire tracks showed the distinctive tread pattern of the Blazer. Their knocks at the chalet were unanswered. On a short cut to the main house they saw a tarpaulin-covered large object by the side of the road. Trash bag twists were scattered about and tire marks matched those at the dock. They found a 40 pound bale of marijuana under the tarp and seized it. They went to Bath to interrogate Miller who refused to cooperate. They returned to the chalet with a search warrant where they found 60 bales of marijuana, warehouse rollers and stands, and a new industrial vacuum cleaner matching the one bought by Miller.

Subsequent investigation revealed that Miller leased the Mill Isle property for $26,000 on behalf of Carlisle Estate Venture Ltd. and paid $15,000 for an option to purchase it for $260,000. Two weeks before the arrest he had purchased a 48 foot ocean going vessel, Harvard, for $17,400, the bill of sale for which was found in the main house at Mill Isle. But Miller was 25 years old, an unemployed high school graduate with no ascertainable capital resources. On his conviction, he challenged the validity of each official action.

In a detailed and lengthy review, the Court of Appeals affirmed. Cold Duck was abandoned at the marina mooring fouled in its lines for 12 hours 250 yards from shore with its dinghy aboard, which triggered the responsibility of state officials for safety of property as a community caretaking function. The circumstances justified a reasonable fear of drowning, and exigent circumstances justified an intrusion upon the limited expectation of privacy surrounding the vessel to determine its ownership and the safety of its mariners. The boarding the next morning to clear the fouled lines and to secure the vessel to the dock was part of this function. The subsequent search yielded the chart leading to Mill Isle and the marijuana, but before this, the sheriff's deputies and the Coast Guard had called DEA because they noted the marijuana cigarettes and the poorly installed equipment. The 4th Amendment does not countenance warrantless exploratory rummaging on every unattended vessel that smells of smuggling; but the search was constitutional without a warrant because the search by the officers was motivated by the non-criminal purpose of investigating a drowning, and it was limited to that purpose. In seeking the owner, if they had limited their inquiry to the Woolwich PO Box, they would have had only a lead to an empty house while divers searched the waters around Cold Duck. The exigent circumstances of the Maine tides made it likely that a body would disappear in a short delay. The chart found in plain view was relevant to a possible drowning. By happenstance, it proved later to be incriminating.

As to the contention that even if Deputy White had probable cause to arrest for speeding, the detention and arrest at that time was but a pretext for a drug arrest without probable cause, the individual facts known to White, apart from speeding, taken as a rapidly developing whole - the recent purchase of a large yacht for cash in small denominations by one requesting two receipts for different prices which supported an inference that the buyer did not want to be traced and was deceptive about available cash; the recent sloppy installation of expensive long range navigational equipment which supported an inference of a hastily planned or executed ocean voyage; the charted course to secluded Mill Isle having a deep water harbor suitable for smuggling near an area under investigation as a smuggler's port; presence on the boat of marijuana in support of an inference of drug traffic; the abandonment of the yacht at night at an unauthorized mooring for over 24 hours; the apparent guilty flight from the marina by the yacht's owner on learning of the presence of the officers; the second flight past the marina entrance upon sighting White - were sufficient to warrant a reasonable prudent man's belief that Miller was involved in furnishing drugs. More than a courier profile, the flight signified guilt.

As to the marijuana debris in the truck, Miller had a limited expectation of privacy which he eliminated by leaving the door open for any passerby to see the evidence in plain view. The opening of the combination lock of the suitcase by Miller after he denied its ownership was a consent in fact. The expressed intention by the officers to seek a search warrant did not negate the voluntary nature of unlocking the suitcase, for no physical abuse or lengthy detention was present as a coercive element. Bowing to events, even if one is not happy about them, is not the same thing as being coerced.

The key to the Mill Isle building, found in the search of the truck, became obvious evidence when the Mill Isle cache was discovered before the truck inventory was completed. But now the discovery of the vacuum cleaner, the tire tracks, and the marijuana debris on the floor of the Blazer associated them with Mill Isle. Moreover, the false statement of address coupled with Miller's living at Mill Isle, and the scene of the crime, made the house key obvious evidence.

When the officers went to Mill Isle, which was not posted

or barred, they went to inquire about Cold Duck, not to search. Their entry without a warrant was permissible, and the bale of marijuana in plain view was properly seized without there having been a search.

In U.S. v Ricardo, (CA Tex 1980) 619 F 2d 1124, Coast Guard Cutter Point Hope was sent to a point 125 miles southeast of Galveston to find a fishing boat of unknown nationality reported by a passing freighter, later by a Coast Guard spotter plane, to be drifting northerly without power but with the assistance of a makeshift sail. Approaching a vessel of matching description, the cutter noted tobacco-like sweepings 100 yards astern of the boat. It had no flag or markings and showed only at the side of the deckhouse "Sincere Progress I".

Two Americans aboard, Neuman and Durrange, said they had been on a sailboat built in Florida by Neuman which sank off the coast in a trial run, and they were rescued by Sincere Progress. They did not remember the sailboat name or registration number. During this conversation, objects were being thrown overboard. The cutter recovered them: marked nautical charts showing origination of the voyage in Colombia, through the Caribbean Sea and Yucatan Channel, into the Gulf to a probable destination 60 miles off Matagorda, Texas. The 5 Colombians aboard could not speak English, but when the vessel's papers could not be produced, Neuman explained that the papers and logs had been washed overboard in a storm. No registry information could be found on the engine room main beam. "Atlantic Marine, 1969" was on the manufacturer's nameplate in the wheelhouse. The hold, upon examination, held marijuana.

At Galveston, defendant Conrado told the Immigration investigator, during citizenship and alien interview, that the crew had been hired by two unknown Cubans who gave them the course coordinates to follow to a rendezvous off Texas to transfer the marijuana, and he produced a chart showing similar coordinates of those on charts thrown overboard. The American and Colombian defendants appealed convictions of conspiracy to import and to possess with intent to distribute. They challenged extraterritorial jurisdiction, authority and justification to board and search, and legality of seizure.

The convictions were affirmed. Jurisdiction attached on the showing of the intended territorial effects of the actions taken to import the marijuana even though no actions were taken within the U.S. The evidence showed that the effect of the actions would be in the U.S. The stop was not a pretext for an unauthorized search. Under 14 USC §89(a), the Coast Guard has authority to board, without any particularized suspicion, any vessel of the American flag beyond the 12 mile limit and conduct documentation and safety inspections with additional authority to search, seize evidence, and make arrests upon reasonable belief of violation of U.S. laws. This authority over American vessels, as declared in Warren [A3-18], extended to foreign vessels under international law when a stop of a foreign vessel may be made if there is reasonable suspicion to believe that criminal activity may be afloat as declared in Cadena [B3-16]. Under international right of approach, the cutter was authorized to board Progress on suspicion of U.S. nationality. Here its failure to fly a flag, exhibit nationality, the presence of American interpreters, proximity to and bearing toward the U.S. coast, generated ample suspicion that Progress may have been of American registry - this in accordance with Postal [B3-18]. Point Hope's mission to intercept a seemingly disabled vessel, the failure of attempted contact under right of approach, the tobacco-like sweepings trailing the stern, the jettisoned charts, furnished reasonable suspicion and justification for boarding.

Dicovery of the marijuana in the hold during investigation of the vessel was proper, for defendants had no expectation of privacy in the hold of a shrimp boat. Once there appeared to be a violation of U.S. law, the Coast Guard was authorized to conduct searches, seize evidence, and make arrests on any vessel, American or foreign, on the high seas.

CUSTOMS BORDER SEARCHES [A3-31, add after Freeman:]

In U.S. v Whitaker, (CA Fla 1979) 592 F 2d 826, a Customs patrol officer off Miami saw a 42 foot yacht two or three miles offshore heading north toward land. Nearing Biscayne Channel, it was noticed to be riding low in the water and making a big bow wake. It showed no name or home port, but it carried a registration number on a sign posted inside a window which was normal for a new boat but not for a 15 year old boat. Windows were closed and curtains were drawn. Following the yacht into Biscayne Channel, the patrol observed it handled sluggishly which indicated a heavy load. Computer check of the boat number yielded four possible "hits", and the officers decided to board. There was a strong odor believed to be marijuana, and they saw residue on the deck; on opening the cabin door they found 9000 pounds.

Defendants appealed convictions for importation and possession with intent to distribute because of lack of probable cause to stop and search, and a border search did not apply because there was no probablity that the vessel came from foreign waters.

The convictions, following Freeman, were affirmed. Unlike the facts in Freeman where the stop was made in customs waters, this one was made in inland waters. "We hold that, at least as to vessels initially sighted within customs waters, the fourth amendment does not prohibit document stops in the absence of suspicion, reasonable suspicion, or probable cause." The officers could have stopped Whitaker at first sighting without suspicions but they checked further with the computer. Their actions were reasonable and constitutional in exercising their authority under 19 USC §1581(a) for a simple document check of a vessel sighted in customs waters. Having the right to board and to be in a position for a plain view of the residue on deck, they had probable cause to believe there was smuggling. Exigent circumstances justified the search without a warrant.

In U.S. Kleinschmidt, (CA Fla 1979) 596 F 2d 133, from an observation tower, a Customs officer sighted the vessel Business Stinks at 11:30 PM, and he notified Customs patrol officers that it had an apparent capability for foreign cruising, but it had not been seen to leave port that evening. On approach, Officer Settle noticed it was wallowing as if under heavy load, but the water line mark appeared normal which suggested it had a false water line. The cabin was dark, the front windshield was covered with canvas, and two men were on the bridge.

A suspect list given to Settles two weeks earlier by his supervisor, obtained from the Ft. Lauderdale Police Department, included Business Stinks which, thereupon, was stopped by the patrol. The men refused to identify themselves or produce registration papers. Settles went to the bridge to check for registration. Officer Collins went to the cabin, smelled marijuana, and found a large number of bales; Settles smelled it too on his way to the bridge.

Refusal to suppress the evidence was affirmed. Although the Customs officials did not have reason to believe the boat had a sufficient connection with the border to justify a border search, they have the power under 19 USC §1581(a) to stop and board in customs waters for a routine document check even without a modicum of suspicion. Freeman, Whitaker. The events combined to provide reasonable suspicion of wrongdoing sufficient to justify, even if this had been necessary, an investigative stop and boarding.

Once aboard, probable cause and exigent circumstances were necessary for further search. Cadena, Weinrich, Freeman. The smell of marijuana provided probable cause; exigency was created by the inherent mobility of the vessel, possibility of escape, limited visibility at the time, and the fact that the two men may not have been alone or they may have had secret arms aboard to endanger the officers if they did not secure the vessel immediately.

In U.S. v Whitmire, (CA Fla 1979) 595 F 2d 1303, two Customs patrol officers saw a 25 foot Nova come in through Bakers Haulover in Dade County at 40-45 mph in choppy waters. At 8:00 AM December 23rd, the day was overcast, cold and windy. The boat left a heavy wake and its bow spray was higher than the top of the boat which, in their experience, indicated a heavy load. It had two occupants with no visible fishing gear and the officers decided to investigate, but their slower boat could do no better than to follow. The Nova turned north into the inland waterway, sped past a Customs inspection station and through two "no wake" areas, and the patrol caught up only after the Nova was docked on a canal behind Whitmire's house. They saw salt crust on the boat as from an extended ocean voyage. Whitmire and Williams wore brand new orange sweatshirts with "Bimini" across the chest. They were walking toward Whitmire's back door when the officers called to them for identification and registration papers. Whitmire helped them to dock, then produced his identification and an unsigned boat registration made out to Excellent Car Company. Williams had no identification. Suspecting a stolen boat and contraband, one officer boarded the Nova to investigate and met an overpowering odor of 1000 pounds of marijuana. Whitmire's wallet, after arrest, produced an American Express receipt showing a large fuel purchase in Bimini the day before.

Defendants' appeal of conviction challenged the warrantless search on which the court considered: border search or functional equivalents; limited investigatory stop on reasonable suspicion of law violation; and the force of 19 USC §1581(a) in the light of its unique character and history.

The convictions were affirmed. A border crossing does not arise because the boat was sighted inside the coastline, perhaps after an early morning cruise, inside or outside the coast, without some probability of having just entered the country. Initially, there was no reason to believe the boat crossed the border.

The observations produced articulable facts and inferences amounting to reasonable suspicion that contraband, carried overseas, was aboard. This supported a limited investigatory intrusion, but not a search of the vessel or further detention because probable cause did not accrue until the boarding for search and the smelling of marijuana. Had the patrol overtaken the Nova, it could have been boarded underway and the marijuana smelled thus.

The court then reviewed at some length the nature and history of 19 USC §1581(a) in its relationship to the 4th Amendment. The search was within the authority of the statute, it was constitutional, and the fruits were admissible in evidence. The officers saw defendants flout traffic rules, there was reasonable suspicion of boat theft and customs violation. Although the boat possibly had been solely in domestic travel at the time of sighting, it was reasonable in the light of the suspicions generated to detain and inspect even without border crossing facts. The smell which justified the search was discovered immediately upon boarding.

In U.S. v Castro, (CA Fla 1979) 596 F 2d 674, at 8:00 AM Customs officers at Panama City had word from a Florida Marine Patrol officer that an unknown shrimp boat captain saw a shrimp boat, Tanila, 5 miles from St. George Island which ran parallel to the coast near Apalachicola, being a known area of contraband smuggling. The captain had seen high speed boats going to and from Tanila, a 65 foot shrimper, white with blue trim, home port Key West. The Customs officers estimated it to be in international waters, although it could have been in intracoastal or other national waters.

At 1:30 PM Tanila, matching the earlier description, passed under a bridge on the Intracoastal Waterway near Choctawhatchee Bay heading eastward toward open water 20 miles away. The Coast Guard Documentation Officer in Washington, D.C. reported no Tanila was documented, so the Customs officers boarded to determine if it came from foreign waters. No documents were produced. Marijuana debris, verified by field test, was scattered on the open deck; the crew was arrested and the vessel was seized. Defendants challenged constitutionality of the search.

The court held that recent connection with the border is not a prerequisite for an investigatory stop based on suspicion. Whitmire. There were sufficient articulable facts to support an inference that the vessel was involved in smuggling contraband. Boarding to determine the vessel's identity and documentation was a reasonable response to that suspicion. Once aboard, the marijuana in plain view gave probable cause for an intensive search of the vessel.

In U.S. v Serrano, (CA Fla 1979) 607 F 2d 1145, Customs officers on routine patrol in Tampa Bay saw a 65 foot shrimper running in the shipping channel toward Tampa without running lights. The officers, following by use of night vision devices, saw the shrimper leave the channel for shallow waters as it neared Apollo Beach, a residential area with a public launching facility and marina. It stopped, went completely dark, and flashed lights with an approaching smaller vessel. 45 minutes later the shrimper, without lights, returned to the shipping channel, turned on navigation lights, and headed toward the Gulf where several smaller boats were seen in its immediate vicinity. The officers boarded the shrimper, took the documents, inquired who was the master and what was the fish cargo, but they smelled marijuana. Search revealed 1312 bales.

Conviction was affirmed. The officers' observations and the rational inferences engendered reasonably warranted suspicion that the shrimper was engaged in smuggling. Customs search and seizure authority under 19 USC §1581(a) must meet the 4th Amendment general standard of reasonableness. Freeman. Inland waters cases indicated that those bodies adjacent to the sea are not customs waters but they did not decide whether random Customs boarding and document checks would be permissible in these waters. Customs boardings were approved in inland waters on reasonable suspicion of a Customs violation. In Whitmire, where the boat was sighted in the Intracoastal Waterway but was boarded after docking and landing of the occupants, the court upheld the boarding upon reasonable suspicion and an unsatisfactory document check ashore. But the search in Williams [A3-22] of a probably unseaworthy craft moored in a marina 4 miles from the Gulf without knowledge of articulable facts and reasonable inferences to reach Customs' area of concern, or of a violation of law aboard, was unconstitutional. Castro to the contrary, where the boat headed from the Intracoastal Waterway to open water 20 miles away, the boarding before reaching the coastline was constitutional on the basis of articulable facts to support the inference of involvement in smuggling.

Customs officers may make an investigatory stop of a vessel in inland waters adjacent to the open Gulf under 19 USC §1581(a) on facts justifying reasonable suspicion of illegal activity. The evidence need not support suspicion of a border crossing, but only of the presence of contraband. This boarding was constitutional.

RE-EXAMINATION

In U.S. v Williams, (CA Ala 1980) 617 F 2d 1063, in January 1978 the 270 foot Panamanian cargo vessel PHGH loaded sulphur in Venezuela. Karavias, the owner, came aboard, and the captain told the crew they would be paid after the ship picked up a cargo off Colombia and delivered it in the Gulf of Mexico. Karavias debarked at Aruba leaving behind special radio equipment to be operated by two Dominicans who came aboard. Off Colombia, small vessels came by with cargo, and all were ordered below except the captain, the two Dominicans and two officers. Williams boarded at that time, apparently armed, and blocked the crew from coming topside.

A DEA plane spotted that rendezvous and reported it to the El Paso Intelligence Center. Coast Guard's Acushnet saw PHGH on January 30th about 100 miles east of Yucatan. PHGH hoisted a distress signal on Acushnet's approach and radioed a reply that it was en route from Aruba to Mobile with sulphur and it had a generator problem which required no Coast Guard assistance. It flew no flag, but "Panama" appeared on the stern. Acushnet kept visual surveillance, and on February 1st at 5:00 AM crew members waved clothes, toilet paper, flashlights, and gave hand signals for six hours. By 4:30 PM the ship stopped dead and a crewman jumped and swam to Acushnet to say there was "dirty business aboard". The next day the State Department relayed word that Panama authorized a stop, boarding, and search, and to seize and arrest on discovery of contraband. The boarding party found no registration number in the engine room, so they went to the cargo hold where 22,000 pounds of marijuana in paper bags were atop the sulphur cargo; the sulphur was destined for Peru.

Convicted of conspiracy to import, Williams appealed on the legality of the stop and search. The Court of Appeals affirmed in 589 F 2d 210, but now the case was reviewed by the court en banc to harmonize precedents in the 5th Circuit and to change 4th Amendment standards for offshore search and seizure.

The en banc court affirmed the panel court as to jurisdiction but differed on 4th Amendment aspects. Government had met the standard of having reasonable suspicion of criminal activity afloat in order to make a stop - the vessel hovering off Colombia with support vessels nearby, the beckoning by crew members for six hours before one swam to the cutter, the merchant vessel remaining dead in the water which is unusual in a business in which time is money, rejection of offers of assistance. The panel had ruled that Williams had no expectation of privacy in the hold of a merchant vessel. That would be true of a crew member, but the record does not show he was one. He could have had a proprietary interest in the vessel, the marijuana, or both to support a privacy interest. However, the facts provided reasonable suspicion the vessel carried contraband, and the search could not have violated 4th Amendment rights. But more, there could be no expectation of privacy of anything in the hold in plain view, or smell, in the course of an identification check.

The panel should not have applied automatically Brignoni-Ponce [M3-23], and other land-based stop and search cases, to seizures on the high seas, nor try to define in the abstract the minimal constitutional requirements for a seizure. Some 5th Circuit cases had held that the 4th Amendment did not prohibit Coast Guard documentation and safety checks without suspicion as in Warren [A3-18], Odom [M3-13], 43 Foot Sailing Vessel [M3-12]. Also, Customs could board American or foreign flag vessels in customs waters without a modicum of suspicion for a routine document check as in Whitaker [B3-28], Freeman [A3-29]. But Kleinschmidt [B3-29] implied that the question on a high seas stop remained open. Some cases approved high seas warrantless searches without considering exigent circumstances or suggesting need of a warrant. Postal [B3-18], Warren, Odom. None considered justification in the absence of probable cause. Reasonable suspicion standards supported the idea that 4th Amendment search warrant requirements on land applied at sea. The case ambiguity and inconsistency hampered counter-smuggling enforcement at sea. Although several cases had spoken of a warrant requirement, what federal court could issue such a warrant? How could a law enforcement officer obtain one for a search far from shore? What would be the degree of specificity for definition of the search area?

The method of testing validity of a search is to determine if there was a statute authorizing warrantless search; if so, did the search violate the Constitution nonetheless?

Here, 14 USC §89(a) authorized Coast Guard boarding of a vessel subject to U.S. jurisdiction on the high seas in the absence of suspicion of criminal activity. The power extends to foreign vessels engaged in violating U.S. smuggling laws. However, the Coast Guard must have reasonable grounds for suspecting a violation of U.S. laws to permit a seizure of the vessel. This conforms with "right of approach" under international law. Acushnet's suspicions were aroused sufficiently by the actions of PHGH for a lawful boarding and search. Collaterally, Panama gave consent to the search and seizure.

But 14 USC §89(a) searches must be reasonable under the 4th Amendment. Historically, this power pre-dated the Constitution and they were enacted simultaneously. It was reasonable and necessary for collection of duties and prevention of smuggling. The constitutionality of a particular search and seizure must be considered in the light of its enabling authority. In balancing governmental and private interests, the seizure of a vessel is a very limited and foreseeable intrusion. Thus, seafarers in international waters know that their vessels will be subject to seizure in 19 USC §1581 Customs checks in U.S. customs waters without any suspicion. 14 USC §89(a) is at least as reasonable as the Customs statutory and international right of approach. The Coast Guard seizure of PHGH satisfied the requirement of reasonable suspicion under the facts in comparison to the Customs statute and international right of approach which have no such requirement.

Customs statutes for searches without any suspicion satisfy the 4th Amendment's requirement for balancing the interests of government against those of privacy. Equally reasonable is Coast Guard authority for limited administrative search in a safety or documentation check of an American flag vessel without any suspicion, or for a foreign vessel reasonably suspected of having the same nationality as the inspector which would require no suspicion that the inspection will result in discovery of contraband or evidence of wrongdoing.

The Coast Guard had grounds for reasonable suspicion that they would find contraband in the hold of PHGH, and the warrantless search satisfied the requirements of the 4th Amendment. Williams' conviction was affirmed.

[But let us note that of the judges participating in this en banc opinion, 12 voted for the majority opinion as summarized here; the 11 others voted in 3 concurring opinions.]

CORPORATE BOAT PRIVACY

In U.S. v Vicknair, (CA Fla 1980) 610 F 2d 372, a neighbor notified Coral Gables Police November 22, 1977 that the house and grounds of a residence were not well kept and the house seemed uninhabited, but at odd hours of the day and night people entered and left by boats at the rear canal. Police observed the boat Sky Top II, owned by FBV Corp., docked behind the house titled in the name of Alvero Carrera. Investigation showed that Sky Top II and Felix B. Vicknair, president of FBV Corp., were suspected by federal authorities of involvement in marijuana smuggling. 24 hour police surveillance revealed nothing until the 25th when they decided to visit with a Customs officer. Knocks were unanswered, so they boarded and searched Sky Top. Apparently a pleasure craft, the interior was messy, carpets were rolled up, and normal accouterments of luxury were lacking. They entered the screened patio of the house, knocked on the rear door, and had no answer. They could not see through the drapes and shutters, but while returning to their car they detected an odor like marijuana from an air conditioning vent at the side of the house.

On December 13th they received information that the boat had left. They staked out the house, made a 5 hour coastal search by helicopter, but small craft warnings were announced, so they concluded that the boat had gone to sea. A police task force was assembled. The boat returned after midnight December 14th. Police saw a human chain unloading bales so they moved in, arrested the persons on the property, and seized 30,000 pounds of marijuana, which the trial judge suppressed.

Cabrera was a straw man but Felix B. Vicknair owned the house. From him, the 10 defendants had an invitation or permission of one of his invitees to enter the house or reside in it, or use the vessel or stay on it. The judge concluded that the November search of the house and boat were illegal, that each defendant had an expectation of privacy in the areas searched, and that evidence obtained in December was tainted by the November police activities.

The Court of Appeals reversed. The November search of the house premises and boat were unlawful; but for challenge to admissability of evidence obtained unconstitutionally, each defendant must show violation of his expectation of privacy by the challenged conduct. They did not have automatic standing to object because the fruitless search in November and the seizure two weeks later were separate events in fact and law.

The boat was the property of the corporation, not of any defendant. There was no corporate action that would give any defendant a reasonable expectation of personal privacy while using corporate property even though invited by the corporate president and even if the defendants were stockholders of the corporation. Expectations of privacy by law must arise outside the 4th Amendment in principles of real or personal property law or policies recognized and permitted by society. When corporate property is seized or searched, an individual cannot assert the corporation's 4th Amendment rights without showing he had an independent privacy interest in the goods seized or the area searched.

Defendants who had keys to the vessel and sometimes slept on it claim a privacy interest similar to those who have a key to a friend's apartment or store possessions with a right to exclude others. Factually, Felix B. Vicknair gave his three sons permission to use the vessel, none of whom lived on it, plus come-as-you-wish access shared by six other defendants, plus the wife, daughter, and son of defendant Kersting who stayed on the vessel sometimes, but none used it as a home or permanent living quarters. Considering the latitude

of use by so many second and third hand from the corporate
president, lack of separate space, quarters or lockers, and indiscriminate coming and going of so many, there was no expectation of privacy for anyone aboard, and none was personally ag-
grieved by the illegal search of Sky Top. The effect of illegal
entry on the residence grounds was more substantial. However,
no evidence was obtained and the only lead was the odor of
marijuana from the air conditioning vent which may have produced self-assured smiles but contributed nothing to the continuance of the investigation in the light of the police appraisal
already made. No illegal information contributed to the investigative effort. The smell was not so 4th Amendment-noxious as
to require suppression of everything that followed, and there
was no evidence that the December seizures resulted from the
grounds-walk in November. The seized evidence resulted from
sources and means independent of defendants' 4th Amendment
rights and was admitted properly against them.

<u>DOG SEARCH</u>   [M3-23, add:]

Reflecting increasing use of dogs, a court reviewed
extensively the cases and authorities on dog search, not repeated here, in <u>State v Walshen</u>, (Wash App 1979) 23 Wash App
813, 598 P 2d 421.

Detective Ray and his "canine cannabis connoisseur"
Chinook patrolled the Greyhound Bus express package area in
Phoenix during regular assignment for mass transportation
areas. Chinook alerted to a book-sized parcel, Ray opened it
(the bus was scheduled to leave Phoenix in 1-1/2 hours), and
found 1-1/2 pounds of marijuana. It was addressed to defendant at Yakima, so Ray phoned Yakima police. The phone call and
a teletype of Chinook's reliability record - 40 cases with 42
arrests - supported issuance of a search warrant in Yakima upon
which defendant was arrested the next day as he carried the
package from the bus terminal.

His conviction was affirmed on the basis that the response of the dog's unerring nose was reliable information by
itself to furnish sufficient probable cause for issuance of
the search warrant. A legitimate expectation of privacy means
more than a subjective expectation of not being discovered.
A sender or receiver of a parcel by common carrier has only a
limited expectation of privacy as distinguished from first
class mail transmission, and common carriers have the right to
protect themselves and not be unwitting carriers of contraband. Defendant did not have a reasonable expectation of privacy in the parcel area, a semi-public place, nor in the odor
emanating into the air space surrounding the package. Ray and
Chinook were in that semi-public place, not as trespassers,
and Chinook's sniffing was not an illegal search under the
"plain smell" doctrine. The dog alone gave probable cause for
the warrant to issue. Said the court in a footnoted dictum:

"While the issue is not before us, we entertain grave doubts whether the above rationale would permit a similar search in a public waiting room or of carry-on luggage, parcels or other personal effects on or near the person. Obviously, such a search would invade a person's legitimate expectation of privacy."

The distinction in that dictum soon will confront the courts as cases approach dog-hairline variations. The anticipated dog confrontation did not quite take place when it was Goodley, rather than the dog, who alerted in State v Goodley, (Fla App 1980) 381 So 2d 1180. Goodley's visible reactions to the sight of narcotics dog Le Dur accompanying 3 narcotics officers near the ticket counter at Miami International Airport aroused suspicions of the officers. Goodley checked in a suitcase tagged "Mr. Martin Joyce". Two officers took Le Dur to the baggage area where an airline supervisor permitted Le Dur's examination. Goodley's suitcase with 4 or 5 others was moved about a foot from the luggage cart onto the floor, and the dog reacted immediately to Goodley's bag only. It was set aside, Goodley was brought to the baggage area, a search warrant was procured from a judge, and a search of the bag yielded a half-pound of cocaine which the trial judge suppressed for lack of probable cause to seize the bag, and unreasonable seizure to remove it for testing.

The appellate court reversed. The officers and dog did not intrude on Goodley's legitimate expectation of privacy. A traveler who checks his luggage has no knowledge or real concern as to its precise location in the airline's custody at any given time, and the one-foot movement from cart to floor was not a seizure, much less a search. By checking the bag, Goodley exposed its exterior to the public and those the airline permitted to approach it, and he had no constitutional complaint that the dog's nostrils intruded into the aromatic airspace surrounding it.

[A3-34, add after Commonwealth v Hernley:]
Standing on a chair to see without binoculars was prohibited in State v Adams, (Fla App 1979) 378 So 2d 72. Miami police officers had a tip that defendants possessed marijuana at a rooming house where they resided. At the apartment, the officers could not see through the window which was above eye level, so one stood on a chair on the porch and saw the defendants sitting in the room which contained marijuana. The arrest area was secured as there was no back door to the apartment. When the door was opened to their knock, they saw the marijuana in the room, so they made the arrest and seized the contraband. There was no attempt to get a search warrant.

The order to suppress the evidence was upheld. Defendants had a reasonable expectation of privacy that the officers would not climb furniture to look in the window. No exigent circumstances were shown to excuse the need for a prior search warrant. The view of the marijuana through the window was not "plain view"; thus its view through the doorway was tainted so that the contraband seized was not in plain view. <u>Morsman v State</u> [A3-13].

NIGHTSCOPE   [A3-35, add after <u>BINOCULAR SEARCH</u>:]

In a joint law enforcement stake-out and raid at night in <u>State v Denton</u>, (La 1980) 387 So 2d 578, an officer had a clear field of vision of marijuana transfer at a fish house from 100 feet away. With unaided eye he saw silhouettes of people, using head lamps and flashlights, carrying burlap bales and moving in a pattern from the direction of the fish wharf through the fish house to a loading dock and into parked trucks. He heard the characteristic sounds of offloading bales of marijuana based on previous investigations. During 6 or 8 minutes of watching he used a nightscope part of the time, and it intensified what he was looking at so he could see individuals much clearer than by naked eye.

The court rejected the contention that use of the nightscope violated the 4th Amendment: "- - we see no significant difference between binoculars that magnify and a 'night scope' that clarifies the observations made by the naked eye."
But one of the justices who concurred in the decision because the officers saw enough by naked eye to furnish probable cause for arrest excepted to use of the instrument:
"As I understand this device, it not only magnifies what the viewer could see with the naked eye, but also makes possible the observation of activities which the viewer could not see because of darkness. There is little difference, therefore, between a night scope and electronic bugging devices or telephone-wire tapping instruments. By electronic means, the investigator is able to gather evidence which could not be obtained without the use of ingenious scientific devices."

FLORIDA CONTRABAND   [M3-25, add:]

Florida changed its contraband law in 1980. "Uniform" and "Transportation" were stricken from the title, now "Florida Contraband and Forfeiture Act".
943.41(2) was expanded to include in the definition of contraband article:
(a) Any controlled substance as defined in Ch. 893 or any substance, device, paraphernalia, <u>or currency or other means of exchange</u>, which has been, is being, or is intended to be used in violation of any provision of Ch. 893.
(e) <u>Any personal property including, but not limited to, any item, object, tool, substance, device, weapon, machine, vehicle of any kind, money securities, or currency, which has</u>

been or is actually employed as an instrumentality in the commission of, or in aiding or abetting the commission of, any felony.
    943.42 adds that it is unlawful:
        (4) To conceal or possess any contraband article.
    943.43, dealing with forfeiture of a vessel, motor vehicle, aircraft, or other personal property, or contraband article, provides:
        (1) that such property shall be seized, and all rights, interest and title thereto shall vest immediately in the state, subject to perfection in the state in accordance with procedures of this act, excluding other forms of court proceedings. If the offense be a felony, the contraband shall be subject to forfeiture. It shall be presumed that the carrying vehicle was intended to be used to violate the law;
        (2) excepts from forfeiture the property of an owner who establishes that he neither knew nor should have known, after reasonable inquiry, that the property was being used or likely to be used in criminal activity;
        (3) excepts, similarly, the interest of a bona fide lienholder, that the use was without his express or implied consent, and that the lien was perfected pursuant to law before the seizure. A lien so established shall be preserved for payment from the proceeds of sale of the property.
    943.44 deals with the forfeiture proceedings.
    (Emphasis supplied)

    Note that these changes withdraw Florida from the federal uniform law which was addressed to illegal furtherance of a drug operation as interpreted in Griffis [A3-40], and seek to reach money as questioned in Baker [A3-42]; that 943.41(2)(e) extends contraband forfeiture to any personal property implicated in commission of a felony offense; that the amendments now can reach stolen boats as raised in Ch. B6; and that the burden of establishing innocence is on the owner or lienholder after reasonable inquiry.

    The previous rule appeared in One 1973 Cadillac v State, (Fla App 1979) 372 So 2d 103, in which Jack Agnew, Jr. was arrested on various charges of possession of contraband when he was in possession of the car at the time of seizure. At the forfeiture hearing Jack Agnew, Sr. explained that the car was owned by Hughes Marketing Systems, Inc. of which he was president, he and his wife being sole stockholders. The company engaged in a wholesale jewelry and coin business. His son's only connection was as an employed sales person who used the car in the course of the business, but Sr. had no idea Jr. used the car for any illegal purpose, and Sr. had nothing to do with the crimes for which Jr. was arrested. The court ordered forfeiture under the Florida Uniform Contraband Transportation Act.
    The appellate court reversed. By 49 USC §§ 781-782

upon which the Florida Act was patterned, the subject vehicle may be forfeited regardless of the innocence of the owner as long as the person involved in the illegal activity was in charge of the vehicle legally, and even an innocent lienholder has no redress. The Federal Act does not exempt innocent parties, but F.S. 943.44 does. The testimony of Sr. was sufficient to show Hughes Marketing was the innocent owner. When the State failed to show that the car had been used to transport contraband with the corporation's express or implied knowledge, the court should have released the vehicle.

In *Agnew v State*, (Fla App 1979) 376 So 2d 376, the Hendry County Sheriff's office had a call from a local resident on a Sunday evening stating that a DC-3 airplane landed at the Airglades Airport, several vans were backed up to it, and he believed dope was on it. Cpl Sloan arrived 15 minutes later and saw the plane parked near a hangar leased by Gostomski for his airplane repair business. Sloan saw nobody in the area, drove to within 30 feet of the plane, opened his car door, crouched with weapon drawn, and ordered anybody out of the plane. Nobody responded. He circled behind his car, saw no movement near the plane, but noticed that the cargo door was open 3 or 4 inches and he could see inside. Capt. Higdon arrived, and they could see brown burlap bags inside. There were no markings and there was no particular odor. Sloan believed the sacks contained contraband but he could not be certain. Sloan told Higdon he thought they had a jackpot, but he didn't think anybody was inside.

Then somebody ran up and told the officers a white Eldorado Cadillac left the airport only moments before containing four white males and perhaps a female. Sloan radioed this information to local units for a lookout. Sgt. Hendry arrived and he and Sloan, by ladder, climbed through the plane's door. They found 10 stacked bags, presumably marijuana, and decided it was such when they examined an open bag.

Deputy Thomas, approaching the airport, saw a white Cadillac leaving. He radioed Sloan who told him to stop and detain it. When Sloan and Higdon arrived, they saw a CB walkie-talkie and aerial maps on the floor of the car. In the trunk they found a Bearcat scanner, another walkie-talkie, and several antennas. They arrested the occupants.

They returned to the airport to process the plane. Gostomski lived in a mobile home adjacent to the hangar and they asked him for lights so they could complete the investigation. When the hangar lights were turned on, Sloan saw a similar bale on the floor of the hangar. The single access road to the airport had been blocked by Higdon's son shortly after the officers arrived at the scene.

The trial judge denied a motion to suppress because the defendants had abandoned the plane prior to the search which they challenged. Agnew, McKenzie and Temens were sentenced to five years imprisonment, Gostomski to two. The court's findings did not address the evidence seized from the Cadillac, and the bale in the hangar had not been included in the motion to suppress.

On appeal, defendants contended that the evidence did not support an abandonment to allow a warrantless search; and if the search of the plane and seizure of the contraband was illegal, then the subsequent stop of the Cadillac and arrest of its occupants was tainted by illegal search of the plane. The State argued that the absence of people in the immediate area of the plane in a flyable condition and not tied down indicated abandonment; further, that the citizen's tip on unloading dope was corroborated by Sloan who found the plane as described, saw that it contained burlap sacks similar to those he saw confiscated in the area previously; and that the search was on a Sunday evening at a time when there were no personnel on duty at the sheriff's office to type any affidavit and the nearest judge was 25 miles away, all of which constituted exigent circumstances to justify a warrantless search.

The court reversed as to Agnew, McKenzie and Temens and remanded the case to the trial court to determine if there was any basis other than abandonment to deny their motion to suppress, but Gostomski's conviction was affirmed because the bale in his hangar was in plain view and was admissable against him.

Leaving a plane in a flyable condition in an area where repairs often are made does not mean that one relinquishes his interest in the property and no longer has a reasonable expectation of privacy in it. Only after the search did the officers determine nobody was aboard. The right to search a vehicle does not depend on the mere fact that it is unattended.

Next, in One Douglas DC-3 Aircraft v State, (Fla App 1979) 376 So 2d 46, under F.S. 943.43 the trial court forfeited the airplane in Agnew v State, finding that its seizure and the cannabis aboard was justified on any or all of the grounds of abandonment, plain view, probable cause, and exigent circumstances, and its seizure for forfeiture based on reasonable belief that it had been used to facilitate transportation of contraband.

The appellate court affirmed. Agnew was reversed and remanded as to three defendants to determine if there was a basis to deny a motion to suppress; but here the trial court concluded that, in addition to the theory of abandonment, there were other reasons to justify seizure of the aircraft. There was ample evidence to support that finding.

Febles, in 1975 Pontiac Grand Prix (Alvarez v State), (Fla App 1979) 374 So 2d 1119, had borrowed Alvarez' car several times, but on this occasion he got it from Alvarez' mother-in-law without Alvarez' knowledge or consent, and was arrested while using it to transport marijuana. The trial judge ordered it forfeited under F.S. 943.41-44 based on a finding of consent to use.

The appellate court reversed. §943.44 clearly provides that its provisions shall not apply to innocent parties. Pursuant to One 1973 Cadillac (above), it is incumbent on the State to show that the owner had knowledge, either express or implied, of the illegal use of the car. There was no such showing. Therefore, Alvarez was an innocent owner and there was no basis for forfeiture of his car.

Burden of proof, as explained in the law of bailments [M16-2], appears in Cadillac for the showing of innocence in which Agnew Sr.'s testimony was held to be sufficient. In Agnew and Douglas DC-3 the abandonment ruling controlled, but in Alvarez the court imposed burden of proof on the State to show the owner had express or implied knowledge of illegal use. §943.43(2) now will place the burden heavily on the property claimant by requiring the owner - lienholder under (3) - to establish that he neither knew nor should have known, after reasonable inquiry. This is the standard of care imposed by the United States in Calero-Toledo [M15-8] and by Alabama in U-Haul of Alabama [M15-10]

FEDERAL CONTRABAND

The federal law changed also. Recall the $41,500 and Pesos aboard the shrimper Stormy Seas bound from Apalachicola for Colombia to invest in South America real estate in U.S. v Warren [A3-17]. In a subsequent Warren decision, 612 F 2d 887, the court held that the government had to release the money because there had been no prior warning requiring a report of more than $5,000 being taken out of the U.S.

But like the new Florida Contraband Act, P.L. 96-350 (21 USC §955a) Importation of Controlled Substances, effective September 15, 1980 [B3-9], in Section 4, subjects to seizure and forfeiture any property used or intended for use to commit, or to facilitate commission of an offense. The related forfeiture statute, 21 USC §881, states the property subject to forfeiture to the U.S., and no property rights shall exist in such; briefly:

    (1) The violating controlled substances,
    (2) Raw materials and equipment,
    (3) Containers,
    (4) All conveyances, including aircraft, vehicles, or vessels,
    (5) All books and record, etc.,
and added November 10, 1978:
    (6) All moneys, negotiable instruments, securities, or other things of value involved, except to the interest of an owner, by reason of any act or omission established by that owner to have been committed or omitted without the knowledge

or consent of that owner.

The federal courts, however, have tried to temper the harshness of forfeiture. One examined the elements closely in U.S. v One 1976 Lincoln Mark IV, (DC Pa 1979) 462 F Supp 1383. In September 1977 Kallaway resided with his brother in law, Pesci, and their wives, at Lincoln Park, Michigan while awaiting completion of his new house. Kallaway, a Ford employee, bought the Lincoln July 6, 1977 with the intention of reselling it. He insured it under a fleet policy of Pesci's trucking company, Franco Freight, and so one of the named insureds was Pesci.

While the wives, sisters, were staying at the family's vacation cottage on September 19th, Pesci borrowed the Lincoln as he had done on several occasions. Kallaway later testified he loaned the car because Pesci's van was in the repair shop, but the government contended it was a weekend exchange for use of the van.

DEA arrested Pesci and Benevides in the early morning of the 20th in the parking lot of Holiday Inn at Corapolis, Pa. after transfer of 13 ounces of heroin for $16,900 to an undercover agent, Carroll Gibson, acting as a street dealer. Gibson had met Benevides in Detroit and had spoken with him several times by phone. About the 16th, upon information from Montero which yielded 3 ounces of heroin for $4500, Gibson expected Benevides to bring two pounds of heroin to Pittsburgh.

On the 19th Benevides called "Boots" Gipson, a government informant, to advise he was in Pittsburgh to arrange a meeting with Carroll Gibson. Gipson met Benevides in the lobby of the Inn and they went to Pesci's room where he produced 13 ounces of heroin from under the mattress. Benevides left to go to Gipson's apartment but stopped at the parking lot to get a change of clothes from the Lincoln.

Later that night they negotiated a sale at the Inn bar, and Gibson negotiated for a larger future sale through Pesci. Transfer took place in Gibson's car in the parking lot in the presence of Gibson, Gipson, Pesci and Benevides, the actual exchange of drugs and money being between Benevides and Gibson. After other agents closed in for the arrest, Pesci gave Gibson the Lincoln keys.

The U.S. filed for forfeiture of the Lincoln which had been used by Pesci and Benevides to travel from Detroit to Pittsburgh to negotiate and carry out the heroin transfer. There was no evidence that Kallaway had knowledge on the 19th that his car would be used in a scheme to distribute narcotics, or that it was being taken to Pittsburgh, or that he had any implication in the events surrounding the arrest. He testified he would not have loaned the car to Pesci if he knew of the planned trip to Pittsburgh, and that he had no knowledge Pesci was involved with drugs, although he did know Pesci had served time for a securities violation in 1973.

The court denied the forfeiture. Upon the showing of

probable cause to believe that the car was used to transport narcotics or facilitate the sale, it was properly seized, and claimant had to prove that the forfeiture was not within 21 USC §881 and 49 USC §§ 781-782 even though there was no direct proof the drugs ever had been in the car. Apart from the inference of transportation, facilitation alone would be sufficient since the forfeiture proceeding is against the vehicle under the fiction that it is guilty of facilitating a crime. Upon probable cause for seizure, forfeiture is automatic unless the claimant can absolve the vehicle of culpability or establish that forfeiture is not properly within the forfeiture statute. Innocence of crime, by itself, is not a defense to a forfeiture proceeding. Authority to remit a forfeiture is vested in the executive branch of government and not the judiciary, and the unlimited discretion vested in the Attorney General does not bear upon the constitutionality of forfeiture in individual cases. Remission is a matter of grace, not right, and federal courts have no power to intervene. As held in Calero-Toledo v Pearson [M15-8], to fit within the constitutional claim exception to the forfeiture statute, the owner must prove not only that he was unaware of and uninvolved in the wrongful activity, but also that he had done all that reasonably could be expected to prevent the proscribed use of the property.

Kallaway acted as a reasonably prudent person under all the circumstances to do all that could be expected of him to prevent illegal use of the property. Here a forfeiture would be improper under the standard established by the Supreme Court. The purpose of forfeiture is to impose a penalty only upon those who are significantly involved in a criminal enterprise to remove the operating tools of crime from criminals. The practical result here would be only to deprive an innocent party of his car. The court noted that the language of the Supreme Court in Calero-Toledo - doing all that reasonably could be expected to prevent the proscribed use of the property - is difficult to apply.

"Doing all" connotes an affirmative duty, whereas innocence of crime and ignorance of potential wrongdoing are passive conditions. If one knows of criminal involvement, one might be charged with a greater degree of care than if no such knowledge is established. By the dictates of logic, common sense, and a new trend in the district courts, the forfeiture of Kallaway's car is not constitutionally within the application of the forfeiture statutes. What one reasonably could be expected to do to prevent criminal use of the property is a standard that must be tailored to individual circumstances. Kallaway did all that could reasonably be expected of him to prevent illegal use of the car.

An innocent subsequent purchaser of a car had relief in U.S. v One 1976 Chevrolet Corvette, (DC Pa 1979) 477 F Supp 32. At a gas station in Philadelphia on September 14, 1977, Carmen

Garcia sold heroin to a person who was cooperating with DEA. She operated the defendant vehicle registered to Adelbert Torres. Diane Morales bought it from Torres for $4000 on September 28th or 29th, receiving a temporary registration certificate on October 1st and a title certificate October 31st. She kept the car in a garage rented from Garcia "located in the 400 block of Airdrie Street" at which it was seized by the U.S. November 22nd.

On or about October 4th, DEA agents saw Garcia operate the car, and that day "inside a garage in the 400 block of Airdrie Street", she delivered heroin to a person cooperating with DEA. Morales claimed the vehicle in the forfeiture proceeding. The court found that there was no evidence linking her with the transportation, possession or sale of contraband after September 14th, nor evidence to show that her purchase of the car was a sham transaction to avoid the operation of the forfeiture statute, nor evidence that she was aware of Garcia's heroin sale on the 14th, and that she did not give Garcia permission to use the car after its sale.

The court denied forfeiture and granted possession to Morales. The forfeiture being an action in rem against the car, the innocence, non-involvement and lack of negligence of the owner is not a defense to forfeiture; but this is one of the narrowly circumscribed instances in which forfeiture against the innocent owner would be an unconstitutional deprivation of property. Unlike the claimant In Calero-Toledo [M15-8] who "Voluntarily entrusted the lessees with possession of the yacht" and who made no allegation of proof that "the company did all that it reasonably could do to avoid having its property put to an unlawful use", Morales did not own or control the car at the time of its unlawful use. She made a bona fide purchase after the illegal use without knowledge of illegal use. She did all that reasonably could be expected to prevent the illegal use of the car. A forfeiture in this instance would be unduly oppressive.

In Alabama, similarly, the court extended relief to a lender in Chrysler Credit Corp. v State, (Ala App 1980) 379 So 2d 624. On July 28, 1978 Loggins bought a Dodge van from Crimson Dodge in Tuscaloosa. The dealer phoned his credit history to Morris, Chrysler's customer service supervisor, who followed corporate procedure in checking credit. Chrysler made an independent investigation and checked with the credit bureau in Loggins' residence area and received his age, residence, parents' names, occupation, and record of other purchases on credit. This revealed he was a suitable credit risk and gave no reason for suspicion that the car would be used illegally or that he had a record or reputation for law violations. Chrysler bought the security contract on the van from the dealer. On January 1, 1979 his brother-in-law, Robison, was arrested for transporting beer illegally in Fayette County, and the van was condemned to the State, which Chrysler appealed.

The decision was reversed. When the State shows prima facie violation of the liquor transportation statute, the seizure, condemnation and forfeiture of the vehicle is permitted, and the claimant must prove lack of knowledge of illegal use and that, by reasonable diligence, it could not have obtained knowledge of such intended use. Evidence of a buyer's bad general reputation for liquor dealing tends to give notice of probable future use of the vehicle for illegal transportation. The bad reputation must be general reputation to be notice or knowledge imputed to claimant so as to be culpable negligence in allowing the purchaser to obtain the vehicle, and it must exist at his place of residence, business or occupation at the time the vehicle was sold.

Chrysler's credit bureau information and limited credit check gave no reason to suspect a use for illegal purposes. There was no evidence of general bad reputation of Loggins at his place of business or residence for dealing in illegal whiskey, and Chrysler had no reason to inquire about possible charges against him for violating prohibition laws. The sheriff of the county of the arrest testified he spoke to officers of Loggins' home county who said Loggins had a reputation among them for dealing in illicit whiskey based on whiskey violation records. That is not the required general bad reputation in the community to put claimant on notice for further inquiry about possible illegal use of the financed vehicle. Thus, Chrysler was not shown to be culpably negligent in financing the vehicle for Loggins.

Ch. B4   RESCUE AND THE GOOD SAMARITAN

GOOD SAMARITAN STANDARDS   [M4-2, add:]

The inter-dependence of boating people afloat and their frequent need for message transmission highlights our interest in Mixon v Dobbs Houses Inc., (Ga App 1979) 149 Ga App 481, 254 SE 2d 864. Mixon's job was to load food and clean planes which Dobbs catered for Delta Airlines. He had no access to a telephone, so in mid-April he told his shift manager, Braley, that his wife was pregnant and he might have to take her to the hospital at any time. Braley agreed to relay the message. This was repeated in May when Mixon told Braley he expected a call any day. On June 7th Mrs. Mixon phoned and told Taylor, a timekeeper, she had an emergency message for Mixon. Taylor acknowledged and notified Braley. 30 minutes later Mrs. Mixon phoned again because Mixon was only 10 minutes distant by car. Taylor relayed the message to Sample, a supervisor. Mrs. Mixon called a third time, crying and desperate, and was told her husband had been given the message and was on the way home.

Braley had gotten the message but failed to deliver it even though he knew that Mixon was in the kitchen area and could be met easily, or Mixon could have been paged over the intercom. When Mixon's shift ended, Taylor asked if he got the message. By time he got home his wife had given birth alone, unassisted and unmedicated, with total fear and excruciating pain.

Mrs. Mixon sued for negligence of Dobbs employees in failing to deliver the emergency message. The court held, overruling a summary judgment for defendant, that the gratuitous undertaking by Taylor and Braley to deliver Mrs. Mixon's messages to her husband can rise to a duty to perform under the requisite standard of care. Clearly, she relied on the promises to relay her emergency messages. One who undertakes to warn of danger and thereby induces reliance must perform his good Samaritan task in a careful manner. Thus, there was a jury question as to negligence in transmitting the message.

Ch. B5 FLORIDA BOATING ACT

Florida has made significant legislative changes in the past two years [Appendix BI] dealing with tax on liveaboard vessels and the strengthening of the Florida boat title system. The title features will be considered in the next chapter.

The liveaboard tax is addressed to "floating houses", but conventional boats are drawn into the concept by inclusion of "legal residence". Highlights are:

371.021(1) excludes "liveaboard" from definition of "boat" for boat license fee purposes if it is assessed as tangible personal property.

371.021(18) identifies liveaboard with the floating house concept by a more detailed definition.

371.63, declaring a registered boat to be a motor vehicle, excludes a liveaboard assessed as tangible personal property.

371.64 conformably exempts from the boat license fee a liveaboard assessed as tangible personal property.

371.65(6) again exempts the liveaboard from the boat registration fee. The owner must exhibit proof of assessment as tangible personal property. Collateral tax laws provide in 192.032(6) that a liveaboard which meets the provisions of 371.021(18) at any time in the prior year shall be assessed as tangible personal property on January 1st in the county of situs when meeting those provisions; but after January 1st and before April 1st of any year, it shall be taxable for that year if the appraiser has reason to believe it will be removed from the state before January 1st of the next succeeding year. For split situs during any year, it will be taxed in the county where located when meeting the said provisions for the greatest period of time. 193.052(8) provides for the appraiser to issue to the owner an acknowledgment, on a prescribed form, of ad valorem tangible personal property assessment on the liveaboard. The owner must present the form to the county tax collector or Department of Natural Resources, pursuant to 371.65(6) license fee exemption, when applying for a certificate of registration.

Plainly, it is government's intention to tax living facilities in the community that are in the water instead of on the land as discussed in THE BEST OF BOTH WORLDS in Ch. B8. A 63 foot seagoing yacht moored for storage purposes will pay an annual license fee of $51.00. The same yacht or a floating house will have to pay a substantially higher ad valorem tax as a liveaboard, so avoidance of the legal residence classification and its higher tax will become controversial. Owners contend they are paying their way through rentals of space and this constitutes double taxation. Ultimately, the answer lies in how much money goes to pay for which communal services, for the stress of family living on a community is much greater than for property storage.

  371.66 adds a fillip. It subjects liveaboards to all applicable safety regulations and requirements. We shall defer to another day consideration of the effect of 371.57, anchor and line, fire extinguishers, life preservers, ventilation of compartments, electrical wiring, and Coast Guard safety standards to confront house builders who are not boat builders.

  Note that 371.65 exempts a liveaboard from paying a registration license fee, but not the registration. 371.051(1)(b)(5), discussed in the next chapter, requires the registration certificate to state the hull identification number and boat number. The Coast Guard is having problems with boat manufacturers who are remiss in proper display of hull identification numbers; add, probably, "house builders". For placement of boat numbers, there may be problems of determining the port and starboard sides of the forward part of a "house". Does situs of the "front door" govern? This reaches the absurd until we recall that the powerless 60 Foot Houseboat [M17-3], a waterborne place to live, was held to be a boat, and that identification of a runaway barge was involved materially in liability imposed in Loveland v East West Towing as discussed in BARGE V REAL ESTATE in Ch. B22, below. These considerations, also, we shall defer to another day.

  Yet, these are signs of development of the water-based society.

PROHIBITED ACTIVITY [M5-11, add after §371.50:]

  Presumptively, the elements of reckless or negligent operations of vessels are well understood by marine law enforcement officers who are confronted by and called upon to assess such conduct in their daily affairs. Not true, and they said so in conjunction with a recent seminar: What are the differences in slight, ordinary, gross, wilful, wanton, culpable, and criminal negligence, and reckless operation? These questions posed by a variety of state and local officers demonstrated widespread confusion among them (and logically, therefore, among boatmen-enforcees). This recalls the position of the U.S. Supreme Court on obscenity - hard to define; but they know it when they see it. In like vein, we have one hardly-enlightening exposition: Negligence depends on the circumstances of the parties at the time and place of occurrence in each particular case. Yet, that is the way it is. [See Negligence Elements, M21-1].

  Unlike state and local marine law enforcement units, newly-formed comparatively, the Coast Guard has a well established training program in which Coast Guard Boating Safety Training Manual (CG-464) notes that the Federal Boat Safety Act of 1971 [MII] changed reckless or negligent operation to negligent and grossly negligent. It offers these definitions:

  Negligent operation is the failure to exercise that

degree of care necessary under the circumstances to prevent the endangering of life, limb or property of any person. Negligent operation may be caused by the operator's ignorance, inattention, indifference, or general carelessness.

Grossly negligent operation implies extreme forms of negligence - an absence of all care. The operator of a boat knows that a certain act can create an unreasonable risk of harm even though he does not necessarily intend to cause harm.

Examples of negligent operation in the Manual are:
- Excessive speed under storm conditions or fog, or under restricted conditions.
- Operating erratically under the influence of intoxicants or drugs.
- Towing skiers where a fallen skier may be hit by another vessel or where there are obstructions.
- Operating in swimming areas where bathers are present; if a posted area, this may be gross negligence.
- Operating near dams which are known to be hazardous; posting increases the degree of negligence.
- Cutting through a regatta or marine parade to the hazard of participants or spectators to interfere with safe conduct or cause an unreasonable nuisance.
- Bow, gunwale, or transom riding.

Compare the language of §12(d) of the Federal Act [MII-5], Florida Act Sections 371.50 [MI-14], 371.51 [MI-14], 371.522 [MI-16], 371.53 and 371.54 [MI-18] which correspond to the examples in the Manual. Review the cases in Chapters 21, Personal Injuries to note that they deal with these varieties of boating conduct.

Parenthetically, former Section 13(a) (46 USC §526L) of the Federal Motorboat Act of 1940 stated: No person shall operate any motorboat or any vessel in a reckless or negligent manner so as to endanger the life, limb, or property of any person. Between the 1940 and 1971 Acts, the Coast Guard promulgated the model State Act which Florida and most other States enacted during the 1960's. Probably, therefore, the limited use of "negligent" and "grossly negligent" operation was not considered for conformance in the Florida Act which continues use of "reckless operation" and "willful and wanton disregard for the safety" in §371.50.

Another notable item is that §13 of the 1971 Act [MII-5] provides separately for termination of unsafe use [see M7-3]. A Coast Guard circular states that overloading beyond manufacturers recommendations or evidenced by instability or insufficient freeboard is negligent operation. Termination authority in the Florida Act is in §371.67 [MI-30].

Reckless operation approaches intentional misconduct in that the operator is or can be found to be aware that his conduct creates a risk that a forbidden harm probably will result, but he is consciously indifferent to that risk; it differs from willful and intentional misconduct in that the operator does not deliberately intend that the harm should result, or seek to cause it. State v Dodge, (NH 1960) 103 NH 131, 166 A 2d 467.

Wilful, by dictionary definition, confirms the above use: Done by design; intentional.

Wanton is defined similarly as reckless; heedless; with utter disregard of right or consequences.

Culpable negligence, in F.S. §784.05, addresses one who exposes another person to personal injury (a second degree misdemeanor); one who inflicts actual personal injury on another (a first degree misdemeanor). In State v Greene, (Fla 1977) 348 So 2d 3, Greene was charged under the statute with culpable negligence or reckless disregard for the safety of another by discharging a pistol and injuring a person. On a constitutional challenge of the statute for vagueness, the court held that culpable negligence is the omission of an act which a reasonably prudent person would do, or the commission of an act which such a person would not do. Reckless indifference or grossly careless disregard of the safety of others is necessary to prove culpable negligence.

Criminal negligence is encompassed in a variety of acts, such as above, prohibited by criminal statutes, all criminal statutes being codified.

Slight, ordinary and gross negligence, as they relate to each other, are beyond this discussion, for the involve civil tort liability. Slight negligence is the lack of great care; ordinary negligence is the lack of ordinary care; gross negligence is the lack of slight care. These are discussed in TYPES OF BAILMENT [M16-1].

FLEEING BOATS

Rather than in Chapters 3 which deal principally with search and seizure and warrants, probably it is most appropriate to introduce a new law criminalizing flight at this juncture even though it is not part of the F.S. Ch. 371. F.S. 861.045 Boats; fleeing or attempting to elude a law enforcement officer (effective October 1, 1980) provides:

It is unlawful for the operator of any boat plying the waters of the state, having knowledge that he has been directed to stop such vessel by a duly authorized law enforcement officer, willfully to refuse or fail to stop in compliance with such direction or, having stopped in knowing compliance with such a directive, willfully to flee in an attempt to elude such officer, and any person violating this section is guilty of a misdemeanor of the first degree, punishable as provided in ss 775.082, ss 775.083, or ss 775.084.

There are similarities to the cases in RESCUE AND PURSUIT OF PROPERTY [A17-2], but those were under special statutes. The Florida statute is general, and "duly authorized law enforcement officer", perhaps, will apply to civil property cases.

EQUIPMENT REGULATIONS [M5-15, add after 2nd line:]

In State v Nettleton, (La 1979) 367 So 2d 755, on investigation of nighttime harassment of local fishing, the Nettleton brothers were charged with a number of violations of Louisiana's motorboat law, but they were convicted only of operation without running lights. Their appeal argued that 46 USC §1459 [MII-4, §10] and the regulations thereunder preempt expressly to the federal government the law of boating safety on navigable waters as to which the Louisiana statute purported to legislate.

The court upheld the Louisiana statute. The purpose of the federal preemption is to promote boat safety through uniformity of regulations, including those applicable to navigation lights. The Federal Act went on to provide expressly that the states may establish boat safety regulations which are identical to federal regulations. The fact that federal regulations allow the option to display lights in accordance with the Federal Motorboat Act of 1940, or in accordance with 1972 Colregs which Louisiana did not provide, does not operate to preempt and deny enforcement of state regulations which do not offer the optional use of two different sets of lights.

WHAT IS A BOATING ACCIDENT? [M5-17, add:]

That was the question of a marine law enforcement officer. He was troubled by the question of reportability in a Boating Accident Report of such as a boat falling off a trailer on land at a launching ramp. By happenstance, there appeared that day in the published law reports the case of Boudloche v Conoco Oil Co., (CA La 1980) 615 F 2d 687.

Boudloche, a tractor-trailer driver, was sent by his employer to load and transport four small boats on the back of his rig. He backed it down the shelled incline to two feet from the water and loaded the boats by a winch on the rig with help from other employees. Three were loaded, but when the last was removed from the water, before being secured to the rig, it fell and crushed Boudloche who was standing on shore. His suit alleged admiralty jurisdiction under the Admiralty Extension Act (46 USC §740).

The case was dismissed for lack of jurisdiction. Maritime torts are limited to those on the navigable waters of the United States, and they must bear a significant relationship to a maritime activity. The Act extends admiralty jurisdiction to personal injury done on land by a vessel on navigable waters. This boat, out of the water, struck plaintiff on the shore, and the boat came to rest on land. There was no admiralty jurisdiction.

Ch. B6 FLORIDA TITLES AND STOLEN BOATS

As mentioned in Ch. B5, new legislation strengthens the Florida boat title system, as contained in Appendix BI. These highlights are:

371.051(1)(b)(5) adds the hull identification number to the certificate of registration.

371.053 sets forth crimes relating to registration decals.

371.75 requires the application for a certificate of title to state the boat hull identification number.

371.76(5) provides that the certificate of title shall have a labeled place to show the seller's price. After such a place is provided in the form, a title transfer shall not be notarized without its disclosure, nor shall an agent of the state accept a title for transfer without such price disclosure.

371.763 imposes a felony penalty for transfer of title to a vessel by one knowing or having reason to believe it is stolen, or holding or dealing with false documents relating to indicia of title.

371.77(1) brings the hull identification number situs into conformity with Coast Guard requirements [M6-9]. It must be affixed in such a way that tampering would be obvious or evident.

(2) requires display of a hull identification number for vessels completed before November 1, 1972.

(3) prohibits tampering with a hull identification number or hull serial number.

(4) prohibits, as a felony, the dealing in or possession of a vessel or parts thereof on which the identification number has been tampered with so as to conceal or misrepresent the identity of the vessel. It is noteworthy that boat theft legislation suggested at M6-11 to define "forged" boats as contraband, by these new provisions, has upgraded stolen boats to a parity in legislative concern with stolen automobiles and can affect such property as contraband with its forfeiture implications. And Florida's contraband law has been made more stringent, as discussed in Ch. B3.

(5) provides probable cause for a marine or other authorized law enforcement officer to inspect a vessel to ascertain its true identity when a hull identification number is not clearly displayed.

371.791(1) requires the seller of a new boat to furnish to the purchaser a manufacturer's certificate of origin.

(2) imposes a third degree felony penalty for issuance of a false certificate of origin.

THE REPOSSESSED BOAT   [M6-4, add after Northside Motors:]

Like Florida, Mississippi upheld contractual repossession by self-help for lack of state involvement in McComb Equipment Co., Inc. v Cooper, (Miss 1979) 370 So 2d 1367. On May 5, 1976 Cooper traded his log truck with McComb for a $11,375 difference payable in 48 monthly installments. The security agreement provided that Cooper, on default, would deliver the vehicle to McComb on demand, or McComb could enter the premises where the vehicle might be and take possession of it without legal process, and with or without previous notice of demand for performance. Thereafter, McComb, if permitted by law, could retain the truck as its property or sell it under Mississippi law, whereupon Cooper agreed to pay any difference on demand.

Cooper made one payment, defaulted because the truck was unsatisfactory, and left it at McComb's parking lot. On June 1, 1977 notice of sale was posted at the courthouse. After sale, McComb got a $9728 deficiency judgment. Cooper's appeal challenged the constitutionality of §9.503 of the UCC for allowing repossession by self-help which, allegedly, was tantamount to taking property without due process of law.

The court held that this was not so. 14th Amendment restraint is against deprivation of property without due process, but action by the state is lacking in this statute.

THE FLORIDA BOAT LIEN   [M6-4, add after first paragraph:]

Failure to perfect a lien cost a lender its security in Gulfstar, Inc. v Advance Mortgage Corp., (Fla App 1979) 376 So 2d 243. Gulfstar, a yacht manufacturer, sold Yankee Doll and Windsong to Underwood, a boat dealer, who sold them to Underwood Marine Corp. (UMC) which financed the purchase through Advance. UMC primarily was a real estate holding company, but not a boat dealer.

Gulfstar had sold Yankee Doll to Underwood for full payment in April 1974, submitting the Manufacturer's Statement of Origin (MSO) and Master Carpenter's Certificate (MCC). [See M6-1 and forms at end of the chapter] Underwood told Gulfstar that the MSO and MCC were lost and requested replacements. Gulfstar submitted duplicates which, however, were not so marked. Five weeks later Advance wrote to Gulfstar that it had a lien on Yankee Doll by reason of its purchase of the installment contract between Underwood and UMC, and it asked to be advised by Gulfstar of any requests for additional certificates. There were no additional requests, and Gulfstar did not advise of the previous duplicates issued.

In December 1974 Gulfstar sold Windsong to Underwood, received full payment, and issued the original MSO and MCC. Persons unknown forged duplicate documents on Gulfstar stationery and Coast Guard forms. Underwood or UMC used the duplicates or forged papers to arrange financing with Advance to sell both yachts to bona fide purchasers.

Advance bought the financing papers from Underwood, not Gulfstar, so there was no privity between Gulfstar and Advance.

The MSO and MCC, though not title certificates, were necessary for Florida titling or Coast Guard registration. Although Advance told Gulfstar it had a lien, it did not. It collaborated with Underwood and UMC to avoid titling the boats so that the mortgagors would not have to pay title tax and UMC could sell the boats later as new even though they had been used. Advance had agreed to this procedure, so it did not file a lien [see M6-4] or a preferred ship mortgage [see M17-18] which would have protected its security interest. Also, Advance was able to finance the sales to Underwood or UMC at a higher rate of interest than that which would have been usurious against an individual under Florida's usury laws. UMC defaulted in payment to Advance which sued Gulfstar for negligence and won $102,000 damages.

The appellate court reversed and dismissed the case. The complaint did not allege any privity between Gulfstar and Advance. The documents on Yankee Doll had been sent to Underwood before any notification from Advance, and Gulfstar owed no duty to Advance. Underwood's acts in selling the vessel and pledging it as collateral constituted a criminal act which was an intervening cause of any loss to Advance which broke any chain of foreseeability occasioned by Gulfstar's issuance of duplicate documents.

Without conceding that Gulfstar breached a duty to Advance, Advance's loss by financing between Underwood and UMC was occasioned by the intervening criminal acts of pledging and selling the same collateral on Windsong, as in the Yankee Doll matter, and the further criminal act of presenting forged documents by Underwood and UMC to Advance. Advance could have perfected liens against the boats. It did not have liens when it notified Gulfstar that it had them. Advance knew that Charles Underwood controlled Underwood and UMC and that UMC was not a boat dealer per F.S. §371.021(12). The vessels should have been titled in accordance with F.S. §§ 371.041 and 371.76(1) when the purported sales were made between Underwood and UMC. Advance's losses were caused when it failed to perfect its liens and elected affirmatively not to comply with the statutes enacted to protect such a compensated finance company.

[M6-5, add after 1st paragraph:]
On the other hand, a mortgagee that failed to record a boat lien survived an attack by a bankruptcy trustee because the court found the trustee was not harmed in In re Collins, (U.S. Bcy Ct 1980) 5 B R 56. On May 9, 1978 Collins bought a bass boat and gave a note and security agreement to the bank. Two months later he sold it to Branch by oral agreement whereby Branch agreed to assume and pay the debt to the bank, and the bank apparently had agreed to this. The bank held a certificate of title on the boat, and a new certificate never was issued to transfer title from Collins to Branch. When Collins

filed bankruptcy October 24, 1979 he listed the bank as a secured creditor and listed the boat as property with no value. The trustee in bankruptcy sought determination of the status of the boat title. He contended that, Florida being a title certificate state, no title could pass until a new certificate was issued pursuant to F.S. Ch. 371.

The court ruled against the trustee: the boat was not a part of the bankrupt estate and he had no rights in the boat. Failure to record the sale made it vulnerable intervening rights of creditors or subsequent purchasers. §371.81 provides that no prior lien is valid against creditors or subsequent purchasers unless notice of the lien is recorded. This protects creditors or subsequent purchasers against prior liens, but not prior conveyances. Here, creditors were not prejudiced by failure to record and get a new certificate, and the trustee had no better rights.

THE INTERSTATE LIEN   [M6-6, add:]

As in state court in General Electric v Hollywood Bank, the mortgagee lost its lien in bankruptcy court in Matter of Unger, (U.S. Bcy Ct Fla 1980) 4 B R 224. Unger bought a 24 foot boat in Indianapolis on August 4, 1977 and financed it with a bank which recorded a security interest August 10th with the court clerk of the county. Unger moved to Florida and continued payments to the bank for 6 months. The bank knew of the change of residence. He filed bankruptcy October 1978, and the trustee claimed title to the boat as against the bank.

The court held that after the 4 month grace period of the UCC in F.S. 679.9-103(3), the bank's security interest expired, and under §70(c) of the Bankruptcy Act, the trustee with the rights of a lien creditor had a superior claim to the boat, the bank then having only an unperfected security interest.

The Indiana recording statute distinguished between motor vehicles and motorboats, and it did not require notation of a security interest on the title certificate to perfect the lien. But Florida, a certificate of title state, requires notation of the security interest on the title certificate. Under F.S. 371.81 the bank had a duty to see to the application for a title certificate in Florida by the debtor or by the bank itself. The 4 month grace period is long enough for remedial action failing which the lien lapsed.

PRIVATE SALE   [A6-5, add after 4th paragraph:]

Summary sale to enforce a possessory lien required strict compliance with statutory procedures in Richwagen v Lilienthal, (Fla App 1980) 386 So 2d 247. Richwagen bought a 27 foot boat from Wilson in 1974 for $4500. Wilson gave a receipt and signed the registration and title certificate for the transfer, but Richwagen never obtained a new title. He made an oral agreement to leave it at Lakeside Marina at $25 per month so he could work on it from time to time. The yard filled out a card showing name, address, telephone, and $25 payments to be made. Payments were irregular, and Richwagen said later he did not have to make them because of damage from the yard's negligence, which the yard denied.

In May 1977 the yard asked Tallahassee how to dispose of various boats. The reply listed this boat as titled in the name of Wilson; and explained F.S. 85.031 which allowed sale without judicial proceedings when personal property is entrusted to a mechanic or laborer for alteration or repair, and more than 3 months elapsed without payment, with prescribed procedures for publication and sale. The yard sent a letter to Wilson which was returned unclaimed, and in June it published notice of sale in the community. The yard sold the boat to Lilienthal by private sale. Richwagen was uninformed until October 1977 when he learned the boat was gone, and he sued to recover it by replevin, which was denied. On appeal he contended the yard was not a warehouse man; but if it was, no warehouseman's lien existed to warrant the sale, and Lilienthal was not a bone fide purchaser under the UCC.

The court, reversing, held that the yard, under F.S. 677.102(1)(h), was a warehouseman as one engaged in the business of storing goods for hire; but the file card was not a warehouse receipt as defined in F.S. 671.201(45) as a receipt issued by a person engaged in business of storing goods for hire. It need not be in a particular form, but F.S. 677.7-209 provides that a warehouseman has a lien on the goods covered by a warehouse receipt; yet none was issued to Richwagen. F.S. 677.7-210 provides for enforcement of the warehouseman's lien by public or private sale upon procedures to be followed, and a purchaser in good faith then will take the goods free of rights of persons against whom the lien was valid despite non-compliance by the warehouseman with the requirements of the section. When the yard's warehouseman status failed for lack of an underlying warehouseman's receipt, the yard might have relied on F.S. 713.58(1) creating a lien in favor of one performing labor or services for another on the personal property of the latter. Such a lien may be enforced by a sale pursuant to F.S. 85.031 which, however, permits only a public sale and does not specify that a bona fide purchaser will prevail over the lienee where there is non-compliance with sale procedure. Thus, Lilienthal was not entitled to possession of the boat.

BOAT REPAIRER v MORTGAGEE   [A6-6, add]

Balancing of interests in the statutory procedures for enforcement of a possessory lien was held to be constitutional in the battle for position in State v Miller, (Fla 1979) 373 So 2d 677. Graven delivered her automobile to Miller for body work at his auto repair business. After a dispute over the correct cost of repair, Miller asserted his possessory lien for labor and services on personal property under F.S. 713.58. Graven sought release of the car by posting bond 713.62, but he refused to surrender it because he maintained that the bond was insufficient to cover the value of his services, so he was arrested under 713.76(3). The county court dismissed the charge against him because 713.76 deprived him of his property without due process of law.

    The Supreme Court reversed the dismissal and remanded for further proceedings. Certain procedural safeguards must precede a significant deprivation of a person's property interests. The safeguards seek to avoid mistaken or wrongful deprivation between the initial taking and the completion of the main suit. §713.76 is constitutional because it does not effect a significant deprivation of property interests. 713.58, which gives a possessory lien for 3 months after which the property may be sold without judicial proceedings to cover the debt, is extremely limited. It is a form of leverage looking solely toward full payment. The lienholder under 713.76 has a position at least as favorable as under 713.58. He loses possession in exchange for a liquid fund on deposit in court sufficient to cover the final bill, and he need not wait 3 months to proceed against it. The writing of his final bill decides initially the existence of the debt, the amount in dispute and value of his lien, and the attendant amount that must be bonded. This strikes a constitutional balance between the interest of the owner in the use and possession of her property, and the interests of the laborer in the existence of a secure collateral measured by the value of his services.

Ch. B7 FEDERAL BOATING ACT

PURPOSE [M7-2, add:]

The Federal Boat Safety Act of 1971 does not include a basis for private suits. In <u>Montgomery v Harrold</u>, (DC Mich 1979) 473 F Supp 61, on October 18, 1976, Harrold loaned Montgomery his pleasure craft which remained moored to a dock in the Detroit River at all times material. Accompanied by a female companion while aboard, allegedly he was overcome by lethal fumes and died, apparently of asphyxiation. His estate sued Harrold in admiralty.

The case was dismissed. Jurisdictional basis alleged in the complaint was the Federal Boat Safety Act of 1958. It had been repealed in favor of the Federal Boat Safety Act of 1971 which was designed by regulatory scheme to provide criminal and civil penalties for unsafe boat operation, but not remedies in the form of civil actions by private citizens, although specific provisions may provide a relevant standard by which to gauge a boat owner's duty of care.

The Jones Act mentioned in the complaint is designed to permit recovery by seamen from their employers for work-related injuries. It has no application in this case. Similarly, the doctrine of seaworthiness applies to seamen, not to guests.

Finally, a jurisdictional claim was alleged under general maritime law, but that does not confer jurisdiction automatically. A maritime tort would confer jurisdiction, but the boat was not loaned for use as a boat qua boat but merely as a place of recreation. The lethal fumes alleged are not unique to boats, and the same type casualty could have occurred on land. The death was not unique to the sea, nor was the sea its source, such as a drowning. No navigation or trade was involved, and the fact that death occurred on the water was purely fortuitous. No maritime cause of action was alleged.

OPERATOR LICENSING [M7-4, add:]

The pressures for regulation of boating will vary with its prevalence and locale. The latter part of 1980 saw actions portending the spread of pleasure boat operator licensing in Florida, and beyond. Florida is a giant among the boating states, and Dade County probably is its leading center. A direct portent is the announcement by the Executive Director of Florida's Department of Natural Resources that Florida will have operator licensing.

Indirectly, pressures are building through the Coastal Zone Management Act of 1972 (P.L. 92-583) and its 1976 amendments (P.L. 94-370) for the protection and development of the coastal zone. The states were found to have given marine matters a low priority. The Office of Coastal Zone Management under NOAA supervises plans of the coastal states. Florida's Department of Environmental Regulation, therefore, issued its Coastal Management Program Hearing Draft of August 1980 which touches upon every conceivable issue involved - the answers are to come later after public hearings and deliberations. Conformably, as with other affected counties, Dade County's Planning and Environmental Resources Departments promulgated a Proposed Biscayne Bay Management Plan which, for resolving Bay user conflicts among other things, calls for more stringent marine law enforcement and operator certification. It is a fair speculation that this feature of the broader program is being scrutinized in other coastal areas of heavy and dangerous boating traffic around the country.

But more, the Coast Guard's Fall 1980 issue of SAFE BOATING, the Boating Safety Newsletter, reports in "Water Management Survey" that the Coast Guard has contracted for a study of state and local water management techniques in six to nine sites for the purpose of identifying and evaluating water management schemes and producing a manual covering them. There is a symmetry in these plans, but the Coast Guard disclaims an intent to "impose restrictions or controls on the boating public in an effort to reduce boating accidents and congestion. Each state and locality has specific water related problems and interests to which no catchall solution can be applied. The Coast Guard does, however, have an obligation to the state and local governments to provide guidance in the management of their recreational waters." The Coast Guard having favored education over compulsory operator licensing [M7-4], the translation of this lofty language is that they will hand over the weaponry and let local government impose the compulsion.

These programs and studies contemplate such items as areas of speed and wake control, user separations (skiers and fishermen), traffic flow patterns, markers, and the like. They will superimpose a new layer of boating regulation. If a large segment of boaters, from ignorance or indifference or both, has failed to conform with the needs of boating conduct, there is no prospect for altruistic compliance with a more intricate scheme, and the coming of compulsory qualification is plain to be seen.

Opponents of operator licensing have argued that a practical testing system is impossible; but aviation has used simulation trainers for many years, and the Coast Guard is demonstrating similar devices at boat shows. Now, modern technology of electronic game manufacturers makes plausible a testing system for the management of this feature of the water-based society.

Ch. B8 THE BOATING ENVIRONMENT

THE FLOATING HOMESTEAD [M8-9, add:]

THE BEST OF BOTH WORLDS

Presaging an expanding mode of living, in 1947 a houseboat was moored at the seawall of a vacant lot in Miami Beach on Biscayne Bay. This was not the current two-story shingled house on a raft, but an elegant small ship from bright white hull, to the large mahogany framed windows enclosing the salon, to the ocean-liner type stack. The owner also owned the lot which carried water and electricity ties. His car was kept on the lot. He was served by a captain and staff aboard the vessel which wintered at the mooring except for cruises of choice.

Who can fault that mode? However, if the living accommodations and amenities for those aboard were on the lot instead of being in the water, the lot would have been assessed and taxed as improved property.

The Floating Homestead [M8-8] was considered for constitutional change in Florida, without success. Such abodes have had and will have their legal status problems. Recently, a sheriff seized a liveaboard boat as part of mortgaged property under a business foreclosure. The owner lost not only his place to live - instantly - but his clothing, personal effects and papers were beyond reach, which would not have happened in a house foreclosure. The judge, who happened to have a boating background, could give the owner no homestead exemption relief, but he directed the sheriff to yield to the owner the personal property items which were not appurtenances of the mortgaged vessel.

For taxation, however, liveaboards received major attention in Florida as detailed in amendments to F.S. Ch. 371 in Appendix BI and discussed in Ch. B5. For additional governance, the Florida legislature amended F.S. Ch. 125 which covers powers and duties of County Commissioners. §125.0106 provides:

(1) Any county, by local ordinance, may adopt restrictions relating to the construction of "floating residential units" in state waters.

(2) For the purposes of this section, the term "floating residential unit" means a structure primarily designed or constructed as a living unit, built upon a floating base, which is not designed primarily as a vessel, is not self-propelled although it may be towed about from place to place, and is primarily intended to be anchored or otherwise moored in a fixed location.

(3) The provisions of this act shall not apply to any floating residential unit in existence or under construction prior to the effective date of this act (October 1, 1980).

Pressures are building. In Dennis v City of Key West, (Fla App 1980) 381 So 2d 312, Dennis lived on her houseboat off Key West since 1951. With others, it was moored to pilings driven into the sea bottom and tied to a bulkhead built in the tidal waters to protect the beach from erosive wave action. City Electric Co. supplied electricity, Florida Aqueduct Authority supplied water.

In 1970 the territorial and jurisdictional limits of the City were enlarged to extend 300 feet into tidal waters for prevention of crime, abatement of nuisances, regulation of zoning, and enforcement of sanitation, after which ordinances were passed making it a violation to moor any watercraft without a permit, and making it unlawful to sleep or live aboard watercraft moored in the jurisdiction unless equipped with compliant marine sanitation devices. The ordinances provided that no vehicle or vessel could be kept on public or private property while used as a residence except in a licensed trailer park or other area designated by the City, and it was unlawful for a utility to furnish water, electricity, or other services to a vehicle or vessel used in violation.

Excepted was a vessel, having an approved marine sanitation device, which was tied to private property and did not constitute a navigational hazard, or a vessel connected to an approved sewer system. Designated live aboard areas were Key West Yacht Club, and City docks at Garrison Bight.

In proceedings against Dennis under the ordinances, the court held that the ordinance making it illegal to live aboard any vessel unless it was docked at Key West Yacht Club or Garrison Bight had no discernible relationship with the general health, welfare or safety. Accordingly, those provisions were unreasonable and were quashed.

In California, in Derfus v Far West Villa Del Mar, Ltd., (DC Cal 1979) 471 F Supp 1082, plaintiff, a live-aboard tenant, was served with a 30 day notice to vacate his berth. When he did not, the landlord filed an unlawful detainer action. Plaintiff lost and went though several appeals in state court until he sought an injunction in federal court.

The injunction was denied, the case dismissed. The right to dock a boat at a particular berth or marina cannot be equated with the right to decent low-cost housing and it does not rise to the level entitled to constitutional protection which would override traditional landlord-tenant relationships. The Los Angeles County live-aboard boat tenancy ordinance (§11,704) was enacted 13 months after the unlawful detainer action was started, and it is inapplicable; but even if it were, it does not give rise to any constitutional rights or any rights granted by federal statute. Defendant did not act in a capricious or arbitrary manner or violate plaintiff's constitutional rights protecting him against retaliatory eviction, restriction of free speech, or unconstitutional discrimination. The mere failure to provide plaintiff with a statement of good cause does not support federal action in the absence of a statute or regulation requiring it to accompany the notice.

THE LIVEABOARD PROFILE

As noted in RESCUE FOR THE ENDANGERED [M8-6], the liveaboard can become anybody's target, but what is the profile of the liveaboard - the person, not the vessel? Do we need one? We know that liveaboard communities are long-established in the orient. Reportedly, floating homes are everywhere in Holland, but there were riots in Amsterdam recently because the people had no place to live - not even on the water.

In the United States, "Wastes From Watercraft", Sen. Doc. 48 (1967) [M8-9], reported on the numbers of liveaboards on Lake Union at Seattle, on the Columbia and Lewis Rivers at Vancouver, on the Willamette and Columbia Rivers and Howard Prairie Reservoir at Portland, on Lake Pend Oreille in Idaho, on Dewey Reservoir in Kentucky. The Proposed Biscayne Bay Management Plan [B7-2] reports there are 800-900 houseboats and liveaboards on Biscayne Bay and its tributaries at any given time. We have noted the colorful confrontation in SAUSALITO STANDOFF [M8-5]. Some communities have banned or have considered banning liveaboards. National boating magazines feature departments on living aboard which consist mainly of food recipes or devices for amenities aboard. National television programs increasingly portray the glamor of living aboard. Whatever the partisan view, living aboard appears to be well-entrenched and spreading across the United States. Consider also that the popularity of motor homes grew rapidly until quenched by the shocks of successive fuel restrictions; and that enthusiasm for modular living can attach to boat liveaboards as the result of some form of mass media presentation - a television documentary, a magazine article. Yet, there appears to be no liveaboard background study to prepare for such a turn.

A study, more than of engineering, should probe the people and communities. Consider this: A real estate developer sought a permit from pollution control authorities to open a finger canal so that property owners could run their boats to open water from their private docks. Preservation of water quality was in question. Hearings spanned a year. Engineers testified on details of construction and configuration of the canal; chemical tests were made of water samples at various locations and depths; a pond was built to receive storm water run-off; a hydrologist studied the annual tide, current, meteorological and other data, prepared a mathematical model (Computerized analysis), and testified that 90% of the water in the canal, if opened, would be exchanged in an 18 day period. But would the fish live or die in those 18 days? Nobody knew. Several government marine biologists who were present throughout were asked for an opinion, but they could not answer because sufficient information had not been gathered.

Similarly, for liveaboard communities, knowledge of size, configuration, and numbers of vessels would be important for space occupancy, density, and storm safety at a given location; water pollution factors would be central. But would a projected liveaboard community and its land-support community live or die in particular circumstances? Would sufficient information be available for a determination? For concept rather than detail:

- On a personal basis, what kind of people are these? Stability, occupation, quality of citizenship, education, age brackets, family size and composition - social factors that profile a community should be examined.

- On a marine community basis, what are their requirements and effects? Demands on police and fire security, utilities, amenities from the shoreside community - how and to what extent will they stress a marina?

- On a shoreside community basis, are they an asset or liability? Effects on surrounding real estate values, business community, taxation balance or imbalance - how will they enhance or stress the greater community?

By now, the cases and comments offered in THE BOATING ENVIRONMENT, more than a nuts-and-bolts presentation of legal and social skirmishes, should mirror the larger problems in the development of this part of the water-based society. The sea grant colleges, now established around the country, study the fish and their environment. It appears appropriate that they include a study to determine to what extent and upon what terms the liveaboard phenomenon should be managed for which they have the advantage of access to related academic disciplines. What is not permissible, however, is for us, "like those who sponsored The Titanic", to believe what we want to believe [M1-2].

THE IMPACT OF REAL ESTATE LAW   [A8-2, add at bottom:]

Restrictive covenants on waterfront use were enforced in Dauphin Island Property Owners Assn. Inc. v Kuppersmith, (Ala 1979) 371 So 2d 31. Restrictive covenants and building restrictions were imposed on a real estate subdivision in 1953 with respect to erection of buildings, and the prior approval by the architectural committee of plaintiff which, however, would be waived if it failed to act within 90 days. Means of notice of approval were specified, and failure to enforce a restriction at the time of violation were not to be deemed a waiver of later enforcement. The Indian Bay Addition restrictions limited further a pier or wharf to two feet above the adjacent sea wall, and no roof, shelter, or other permanent structure, except hand rails, benches and tie pilings, might be built on it. Two tie-off pilings at each wharf were permitted if they were not more than 35 feet distant from the sea wall into the water. A majority of other owners in a particular block might authorize variances after approval by the architectural committee and two-thirds vote of plaintiff's directors.

Defendant got a building permit from plaintiff to erect a house on Lot 43. In 1971 he got another permit for the garage which extended partially into Lot 42, and he also obtained a variance to build a boat stall cover. On March 12, 1977 defendant orally requested of Young, plaintiff's secretary, a permit to build a boat lift, and Young presented the request to the board of directors that afternoon. It was denied. Young's letter of March 16th, mailed to Mobile because defendant did not live on Dauphin Island, advised of the fact, but defendant began to build a boat lift in April after he received Corps of Engineers approval. He said he got the letter after construction began, but he admitted he began to build without plaintiff's permission, and he suspended construction after contact from plaintiff's lawyer.

The structure consisted of 8 large creosoted pilings in the water and 6 on land which were 10 or 11 feet above the sea wall. Beams tied the pilings together and supported a boat lift hoist. Defendant proposed to top this with a one foot roof which would have been 11 or more feet above the Bay water.

Plaintiff sued to compel removal of the boat lift and won in the Supreme Court which said "building" does not mean only a habitable structure, and the architectural control suggests contemplation of a variety of structures. Various categories of buildings were listed in a fee scale. A pier has been held to be a building; thus, the boat lift structure was a "building" which required a permit. The evidence showed that the structure, however interpreted and argued, was higher than the limiting two feet above the adjacent sea wall.

Even though plaintiff did not enforce the two tie piling limitation, plaintiff was not estopped by that acquiescence from enforcing other restrictions on height of roof or building permit. Boat tie pilings and a boat lift building obviously are dissimilar in appearance and character. Also, plaintiff was not estopped by proof of existence of another boat lift building in Indian Bay Addition for which a variance had been granted in conformance with specified procedures. Deliberate adherence to the variance procedures cannot be deemed an estoppel or waiver.

The boat house lost for its own deficiencies in <u>Jansen v Fair Harbor Marina, Inc.</u>, (Ala App 1979) 373 So 2d 325. The parties owned adjoining properties on Fly Creek in Fairhope. Plaintiff's property bordered on a drainage easement located between the two parcels, and he built a boathouse which encroached 4 feet on the easement. Defendant, owner and operator of a marina, bulkheaded along the creek and engaged in earth moving operations. Plaintiff claimed $12,000 damages for trespass and negligence when his land and docking facility became silted because defendant trespassed on his property and altered the original elevation so that runoff and sand washed on his property. He claimed that the bulkhead was constructed negligently so that his dock filled with sand to the damage of his property and his boat.

The trial court awarded damages for the trespass but found that plaintiff negligently constructed the boathouse so as to prevent installation of proper drainage facilities by defendant and the city. On appeal, plaintiff contended that defendant's grading activities caused the land to be covered with 30 inches of sand, and defendant caused the dock to fill with sand which caused his boat to become stuck and sink.

The appellate court affirmed. There was evidence that runoff and consequent buildup of sand on plaintiff's property was caused by his negligent construction of the boathouse on the drainage easement, and that docking facilities along the creek silt-in naturally every two or three years. There was evidence to support the decree of the lower court. Plaintiff's contributory negligence caused his damage and it bars his recovery as a matter of law.

A "stiltsville" home lies, perhaps, between a liveaboard and a dock, and faced its stress in U.S. v Ferrer, (CA PR 1980) 613 F 2d 1188. Ferrer appealed a conviction of unlawfully erecting a building on navigable waters without obtaining a permit from Corps of Engineers. He had begun rebuilding a house on stilts with ramp which had been burned by vandals. For this, he had obtained a permit from Puerto Rico's Department of Natural Resources and he had applied to Engineers, but he had no answer. 33 USC §403 prohibits erection, without Engineer's permit, of certain structures and buildings. Engineers and DNR held public meetings in June and July 1977 with local residents to explain the authority of each agency and the permit requirements of each with emphasis that no new illegal construction would be allowed. Ferrer was present and he filed the required application form with Engineers on July 13, 1977. In September he began construction of the house and catwalk.

Affirming the conviction, the court held that there was no inconsistency between the local and federal permits merely because both were required. Concurrent jurisdiction is acceptable under §403 and implies a need for compliance with both federal and local requirements, absent an inconsistency between them. There was no inconsistency, and procurement of a valid Puerto Rico permit was not a basis for dismissal of the charges.

Marine facilities draw our interest increasingly. In Gulf Fishing and Boating Club, Inc. v Bender, (Ala App 1979) 370 So 2d 1026, plaintiff, a non-profit social club, owned property on Dog River, and in 1960 it leased for 30 years a part that adjoined its club facilities to Bender, operator of River Yacht Basin, Inc. Bender was to build and operate a full service marina, maintain it in clean condition and good repair, and pay to plaintiff 3% of gross monthly receipts as rent. In 1960 plaintiff had 250 active members and had plans to build a new clubhouse; but membership declined to 50, only a few having boats, and the new clubhouse never was built. In 1970 plaintiff leased its club facilities to the Elks Club.

Bender cut back on services offered to the declining membership so that the principal business at the time of suit was the renting of boat stalls. Defendant used trash and debris for landfill; some of the debris was scattered over defendant's premises; some of the marina facilities deteriorated to an unsafe and unsightly condition; and during 1973 Mobile Bertram, Inc. stalled four boats there, and these were sold for $119,000. Plaintiff sued to terminate the lease and recover delinquent rent payments. The trial court awarded rent due, but plaintiff appealed the court's refusal to terminate.

The appellate court affirmed. The lease recited that a moving consideration was to provide adjacent boating facilities for boat storage, repair, construction, and care, "a principal feature of the club objectives being the conduct of a boating club" for which lessee agreed to operate and conduct a first class boat repair service and boat-stall rental service, and all such operations would be of top quality and be kept in first class condition and repair, free of dilapidated and unsafe wharves, stalls, buildings and the like. The trial court construed the contract as being ambiguous which required a determination of intent which it found to be to maintain a full service marina to serve the membership; but significant demand for it declined with declining membership, and the contract did not require defendant to continue an unprofitable business. Those findings will not be disturbed.

While unprofitability of a contract is insufficient excuse for non-performance, this was only one factor. The parties did not intend that defendant maintain full facilities if plaintiff abandoned active operations. This is a reasonable construction because it does not deprive plaintiff of the right to the rent. The lease required defendant to maintain a "reasonably adequate" facility. This is unclear, so ambiguity will be construed favorably for defendant. The business was a reasonably adequate facility under the facts and circumstances. For this determination, the trial court in its discretion allowed testimony as to the condition of similar marinas. Trash scattered about the premises was a normal condition for marinas in the area; and the trial court ordered defendant to repair those structures that were dilapidated, but defendant's operations were not unsafe.

Plaintiff is not entitled to 3% on Bertram's boat sales. Bertram advertised that the boats were kept at the site, they were demonstrated there, and defendant's employees worked on them, but Bertram had no office, telephone, or salesmen there. The sales were not covered by the contract which expressly required, for plaintiff's entitlement to a percentage, that the boats must be "sold by a business conducted on the leased premises". This, again, was an ambiguity for interpretation by the trial court. If plaintiff had desired such coverage it could have drawn the agreement in clear language.

In Ralo, Inc. v Jack Graham, Inc., (Fla App 1978) 362 So 2d 310, the State deeded certain submerged lands to the City of Sarasota with a proviso that the lands be used solely for municipal purposes. The City lease of the premises to Marina Mar, Inc. called for use for a municipal park and recreational purposes only. Later amendment provided for construction, maintenance and operation of docking and marina facilities for boats and other watercraft, and the facilities were to be offered and leased to the general public for such use. Marina Mar assigned the lease to Graham which served notice on Ralo, a sightseeing tour operator at the site since 1970, to vacate the dock and slip. Ralo had paid a monthly fee but it had no written lease. There was no default, but Graham planned to use the space to operate a boat featuring dinner cruises.

The trial court held there was a tenant-subtenant relationship between the parties, that Ralo was a tenant at will, and that Ralo had to vacate pursuant to the notice.

The appellate court reversed. In this case Graham was not in the position of a landlord because its use of the property was conditioned by the restrictions upon use which derived from the State. Ralo appears as part of the general public, and it was incumbent upon Graham to offer space to Ralo on the same terms and conditions as it would offer comparable facilities to other parties for the same purposes.

WHERE ELSE BUT IN FLORIDA? [A8-4, add:]

Entrenched ideas yield grudgingly, and the question of tieing up to private property in an emergency leads to heated argument, so let us examine the cases, which are few. Note that seafarers were not under threat of being cast into the water; it was their property they sought to save. Note, too, that many marina and dockage agreements provide for removal of vessels when natural elements threaten unusual stress, often in exposed marine areas, for the facilities may not have been designed and built to withstand such stress. Now read and decide:

In Dutton v Strong, (1861) 66 US 1, 17 L Ed 29, Strong owned the Henry Ramsdell which sailed from Chicago to Racine in ballast on May 6, 1955 and arrived between midnight and 1:00 in safety. When it was a quarter mile from the harbor, the wind suddenly changed from south to northeast, blowing hard.

The ship headed for the only visible light on the supposition that it was on the northern pier in the harbor toward which it was bound. The anticipated pier had no light, but the light seen was on the bridge pier of defendants. The mistake was discovered upon the vessel's approach, but instead of changing course, they took in sail and dropped anchor to prevent beaching. This checked headway, and the vessel sagged against the pier without injury. They put lines on the pier to work the vessel away from another bridge pier to the south and to keep it from pounding. Successively, they put on more lines and hawsers. By 4:00 AM the bow still was 40 feet from the pier; by 10:00 AM it was at the pier. The wind and sea increased, so they fastened a chain to the opposite side of the pier. By noon the vessel was pounding and it pulled the chain and pile 8 feet through the pier. By 2:00 PM that pile and chain gave way and lodged against other piles where it held unless the pile broke or that part of the pier that held it gave way.

Now one of defendants appeared and ordered the master to get the vessel away from the pier or it would be cast adrift. The master said he'd see what he could do, but he made no attempt to leave, so defendants' employee cut the hawser which caused the rest of the piles to give way with attached stanchions and bulwarks. To prevent further damage, the master ordered the vessel to be scuttled.

Plaintiff sued in trespass upon the case [modern negligence] contending that defendants had no right to cut the hawser and cast the vessel adrift to save their pier because the erection of the pier impliedly licensed plaintiffs and others navigating the waters to moor their vessels at the pier, and such license included the right to use the pier according to the exigencies of the case.

The court ruled for defendants. Piers or wharves may be private or public. If private, the owner may have the right to exclusive enjoyment and exclude all others from its use. Here the master attached the vessel to the pier without any authority from defendants, either express or implied. There was nothing to be transacted between them, and all pretense of a license fails. The master wrongfully tied up to the pier as a trespasser to avoid peril to the vessel, but that endangered the pier and exposed it to destruction. Defendants had the right to interpose and disengage the vessel from the pier as the only means to relieve their property from the impending danger. They never had consented to incur that danger, they were not accountable for the insufficiency of the pier to hold the vessel, it had not been erected or designed as a mooring for vessels in rough weather, and it was plaintiffs' fault that the vessel was placed in the predicament in which it found itself.

In <u>Ploof v Putnam</u>, (Vt 1908) 81 Vt 471, 71 A 188, plaintiff, with wife and two minor children, sailed a sloop on

Lake Champlain on November 13, 1904. Endangered by a sudden tempest, he moored the sloop to a dock on defendant's island in the Lake. Defendant's servant unmoored it, and it was driven onto the shore by the tempest and destroyed. Plaintiff and his family were injured when they were cast into the Lake and on the shore. Plaintiff sued for trespass by unmooring the sloop, and for breach of duty to permit the mooring during the tempest; defendant moved for a dismissal.

The court denied defendant's motion. The entry upon the land of another may be justified by necessity, and the complaint showed the necessity for mooring the sloop. It was not necessary, as defendant contended, that plaintiff allege there were no natural objects to which he could have moored with equal safety, for that was a matter for proof at the trial.

In Compton v Hawkins, (Ala 1890) 90 Ala 411, 8 So 75, plaintiff sued for damages for refusal by defendant, owner of a landing on Tombigbee River, to receive plaintiff's timber preparatory to being rafted by river to the market even though defendant had the means to receive and store it for which plaintiff offered to pay.

Plaintiff lost. The better opinion, said the court, is that the right to use the stream as a highway is distinct from the right to use the land to receive and discharge passengers. Those navigating the river have no right, as an incident to the right of navigation, to land on and use the bank for loading and unloading vessels without consent of the owner unless in the case of necessity. The riparian owner has the same dominion and power to control such landing places as any other private property and to possess the same to the exclusion of the public. Plaintiff did not allege sufficiently a right to deposit his timber at the landing or defendant's duty to allow it to be stored.

LAND TRESPASS [A8-4, add at bottom:]

Trespass to a dock is trespass to real property. What of trespass to wetlands? Wetlands, as explained by Daniel L. Molloy in The Public Trust Doctrine and Ownership of Florida's Navigable Lakes, 29 U. of Fla. L.R. (1977), are those that can be used for agriculture by drainage or by diking, or that remain in trusteeship for the state for navigable use by the public [see M9-13].

The question of private appropriation of such land as an interference with navigation arose in Skipper v Phipps, (DC Fla 1980) 483 F Supp 1213. Plaintiffs, while duck hunting, carried their boat over a strip of land. They were confronted and told they were trespassing by Taylor who was employed by Phipps Broadcasting to protect their property from vandalism and other damages. Plaintiffs alleged they were "arrested" five times by Taylor for trespassing. These consisted of Taylor stopping them and asking for identification or warning that they were trespassing. Signs were posted. A jury found them not guilty on five counts of criminal trespass.

Taylor had been a deputy sheriff and an employee of the Game and Fish Commission, and he now carried powers of a deputy sheriff under a commission from the sheriff, and he filed an affidavit with the State Attorney's Office for the five counts of criminal trespass, so plaintiffs brought the present civil rights action for deprivation of rights under color of law. They had dragged their boat across a 50-75 yard strip of land between Carr Lake and Mallard Pond, although an alternate route allowed access between Mallard Pond and Carr Lake by water. They alleged the land they crossed actually was public because it was below the ordinary high water mark of Lake Jackson, a navigable water owned and held in trust by the State, of which Carr Lake and Mallard Pond were a part.

The court awarded summary judgment for defendants. After reciting the necessary elements, the court held there was no arrest; there was nothing more than warning of trespass with legal consequences to ensue.

Florida holds title to State sovereignty lands for the benefit of its people. Plaintiffs contended these were State sovereignty lands. Even if true, plaintiffs would have to identify a federal right or privilege to use State sovereignty lands, for lands underlying navigable waters within a State belong to a State in its sovereignty capacity and may be used and disposed of as it may elect. Before a possible finding of illegal arrest, plaintiffs must show a federal right to use such lands and that they were State sovereignty lands. In fact, they did not challenge the validity of clear chain of title in Phipps. The alleged federal civil rights action will not be used to transform the alleged action into a complex suit to quiet title between the State and Phipps.

OIL POLLUTION   [A8-5, add:]

In U.S. v Ward, (1980) ___ US ___, 100 S Ct ___, 65 L Ed 2d 742, on March 23, 1975, oil escaped an oil retention pit at a drilling facility near Enid, Okla. and entered Boggie Creek, an Arkansas River tributary. On April 2nd, Ward notified Environmental Protection Agency of the discharge and submitted a fuller report later which was forwarded to the Coast Guard. After notice and opportunity for hearing, the Coast Guard assessed a $500 civil penalty, later reduced to $250 by the District Court, which Ward appealed for violation of the 5th Amendment prohibition of self-incrimination. The Court of Appeals held that 33 USC §1321(b)(6) was sufficiently punitive to violate 5th Amendment protections, and enjoined collection of the penalty.

The Supreme Court reversed. Ward was required to report the spill by the terms of the statute, and failure to do so carried a fine. The statute provided that information so received would not be used in a criminal prosecution except for perjury or giving a false statement. Money paid went into a fund to pay for decontamination of the spill and defray costs of administration of the Act. Congress termed the sanction here involved to be a civil penalty. The Congressional intent was to allow imposition of the penalties without regard to procedural restrictions in criminal cases even though spills were designated criminal by the 70 year old 33 USC §403 (Rivers and Harbors Act). The statutory scheme was not so punitive in purpose or effect as to convert the governmental action into a criminal or quasi-criminal proceeding to justify 5th Amendment protection.

Ch. B9 MARKING AND REMOVING THE WRECK

[Ch. M9-4, after Ingram v Ohio River, add:]

After a wreck is marked, navigators are bound to heed the mark for their safety. In Ingram Barge Co. v Valley Line Co., (DC Mo 1979) 470 F Supp 140, defendant split a tow of 8 coal barges to get them through a bad stretch of the Illinois River. A set grounded temporarily in this relay procedure, and defendant was notified two barges had sunk. The Coast Guard, upon request, was unable to mark the wreck, but defendant purchased from the Coast Guard a buoy, buoy anchor with cable, and buoy lights, and caused the lighted buoy to be emplaced. One of plaintiff's barges in a tow struck one of defendant's sunken barges, and plaintiff sued for damage caused by the collision.

Defendant won. The court found, after reviewing the details of the placement of the buoy, defendant's duty under 33 USC §409 to mark the wreck in a navigable channel, and the attendant regulations, that the buoy was positioned in the exercise of good judgment consistent with Wreck Act regulations. Although plaintiff's tug captain disputed the fact of the light atop the buoy before collision, he admitted his searchlight picked up a buoy off the shoreline that he thought was a stray which he maneuvered to avoid striking in order to pass it on the wrong side in violation of navigation regulations.

The sunken barges protruded into the channel but there was room to pass properly as attested by numerous tows that passed properly without problems in the four days during which the damaged barge was being removed from the sunken barges. Moreover, the captain could have radioed the Coast Guard or a vessel traveling in the area to ask information regarding the buoy; but he took no precautions and proceeded on the risky assumption that the buoy was a stray on the justification that the icy conditions in the river at the time caused many buoys to be off station and out of position. Such possibilities do not warrant an absolute disregard of buoys as aids to navigation. 33 CFR §62.25-55 which cautions mariners not to rely solely on buoys for navigational purposes because of their potential unreliability does not advocate that they be ignored; it points out that buoys cannot be the sole source of navigational aid because of their potential unreliability.

Plaintiff failed to establish, under the Pennsylvania Rule [A22-1] that its failure to follow the buoy's directions could not have been a cause of the accident, and plaintiff's statutory fault must be the sole cause of the accident.

COAST GUARD LIABILITY   [M9-7, add after Lane:]

Government's discretion to mark and remove wrecks arose again in Offshore Transportation Corp. v U.S., (DC La 1979) 465 F Supp 976. Plaintiff's 62 foot supply boat, Golden Tiger, left Intercoastal City, La. for an oil rig near Eugene Island in the Gulf. The course, passing through Southwest Pass into Vermillion Bay, ran just south of Shell Key in waters 6 to 8 feet deep with a shifting bottom that limited below-surface visibility to a foot or less. The area generally is avoided by commercial and pleasure craft because of sandbars, shoals and a coral reef, and it is remote from any navigational channel or fairway maintained by the Coast Guard.

At 3:00 PM at Shell Key on high tide, visibility was excellent and seas were relatively calm when, at 6 knots, Golden Tiger struck a stainless steel shaft 6 inches below the surface, and it had substantial hulldamage. In 1968 the Nimrod was reported sunk and was charted at that location, but it never had been marked physically by a buoy or other marker. The Coast Guard reported Golden Tiger sunk in Notice to Mariners and advised caution in the vicinity.

Two months later, plaintiff's Flying Tiger went to Shell Key with precision navigational equipment to locate the object that wrecked Golden Tiger, but it drifted aground on an iron pipe nearby for 12 hours, and it sustained serious hull damage. Probably, it was caused by an 1880 wreck that similarly was charted but not marked. Both obstructions were in navigable waters, and plaintiff sued the U.S. for damages to both vessels.

Plaintiff lost. 33 USC §414 and 14 USC §86 were intended to protect marine traffic from danger posed by wrecks, and the needs of navigation measure the responsibility of Corps of Engineers and the Coast Guard in their decisions whether or not to remove a wreck, or mark it, respectively. These agencies have not the resources to remove or mark every wreck in the Gulf, and plaintiff's experienced masters testified that these waters were avoided by mariners because of the shallow water and coral reef. The boat charterer urged the owner to take the most direct route to the rig. The Coast Guard had no notice of such intention. Both agencies consider the waters frequented by vessels when the threat to navigation is deemed to be the greatest in order to carry out the duties with which they are charged by the statutes. In exercising their discretion to mark or remove wrecks, the agencies relied on map surveys of the area without making traffic studies of Shell Key. It would be an unreasonable burden on government to impose a duty over an extended period to conduct periodic traffic surveys to discover changed conditions. Instead, government's duty to use reasonable care is fulfilled by reliance on user requests or reports of accidents to reevaluate its decision not to remove or to mark a particular wreck. There was no abuse of discretion and thus no breach of duty to plaintiff.

In Owens v U.S., (DC Fla 1979) 474 F Supp 806, Owens charted a course from Mobile Harbor to No. 1 sea buoy off Pensacola, then turned over the piloting to Peyton. Darkness set in and the weather turned bad by time they approached the sea buoy which Peyton did not see, so he continued east hoping to pick up a reference point on land. When he saw the light of the Naval Air Station, he turned northwesterly to find the Caucus Channel entrance from the Gulf. He saw WR 2 marking the sunken battleship Massachusetts [M19-2] which he assumed to be the channel marker, and he went around it on a course he thought would place him in the channel. He hit the battleship. Owens and his intervening insurer claimed that the Coast Guard was negligent in failing to mark properly the Massachusetts and nearby Caucus Channel.

They lost. They contended that Caucus Channel marker C3 should have been a lighted buoy so that Peyton would have seen it and found his way into the channel; the lights on the port side of the channel should have been green instead of white so that they would not be confused with shore lights; and WR2 was obscured partially by bird droppings, and it should have been closer to the Massachusetts.

Under the weather conditions, Peyton did not see No. 1 which was lighted and to which the course had been charted. There is no indication that a lighted C3 on the northwesterly course change would have been seen in that weather. If he did not see the red lights on the starboard side of the channel, nothing indicates he would have seen lights on the port side if they had been green.

When the boat reached the wreck buoy, Doman and Johnson tried to determine its identity in the short period of view as the boat cruised at 15 knots. Doman told Peyton he thought he saw an "O" which he thought must be on No. 10. Peyton did not believe this because he didn't think he was that close to shore, but he acted on the assumption it was No. 10 which brought him to the wreck. He did slow down in passing the buoy, but he should have gone back to check it. Johnson said he thought he saw "W" but Peyton testified he didn't hear that; if he had, he would have realized it marked the wreck and he would not have taken the collision course. If Peyton had gone back to check it in the exercise of ordinary seamanship, it was not so obscured that he would not have been able to identify it.

The distance of WR2 from the wreck made no difference. It was not intended to deal with misidentification. While a buoy in open water normally is placed further from a wreck than would be the case in closed channel waters, it also helped to mark a shoal in this instance. The nature and extent of the turn governed the likelihood of collision with the wreck.

There was no negligence on the part of government that was a contributing cause of the accident, and it is not an insurer of the safety of those upon the water.

[M9-9, add after Marine Leasing Services:]
Reasonable conduct between related parties in removing a wreck was examined in Tennessee Valley Sand & Gravel Co. v

M/V Delta, (CA Miss 1979) 598 F 2d 930. While being towed by Delta, plaintiff's barge sank in an inlet to the Tennessee River in 25 feet of water, and it was tied off. Plaintiff, without full investigation, decided to try to raise the barge, so it contracted with a marine salvor which salvaged the cargo and sent a diver to ascertain the condition of the barge. He found it had buckled severely from lying across an underwater creek. The salvage operator had been working the wreck for 10 days and, after hearing this information, plaintiff's representative sought no counsel from Corps of Engineers but instructed the salvor to continue the work. The barge was raised and sold for scrap. Plaintiff's suit for damages for the sinking included $20,000 for raising the barge. The trial judge found the sinking to be the fault of defendant but he disallowed the $20,000 because plaintiff's failure to contact Engineers before incurring that expense showed an indifference to its obligation to mitigate damages.

The Court of Appeals reversed and allowed the $20,000. There was no duty to mitigate damages, said the court, for there was no correlative right upon its violation. There is a method of apportioning damages between the parties where the injured party, after the casualty, has used the degree of care that society demands of the reasonable person. The victim's neglect results in denial to him of the losses shown to result from his failure to use reasonable efforts to avoid or prevent them. The wrongdoer has the burden to show that the victim failed to minimize his damage. Although the victim's unreasonable conduct will preclude his recovery of such damages, defendant must show that the conduct was unreasonable and that it aggravated the harm. Thus, if plaintiff acts unreasonably but it doesn't affect the scope of the harm, defendant remains fully liable for his negligence; and if plaintiff's reasonable efforts are unsuccessful, an actual increase in loss will not preclude recovery for all expenses incurred in the process. In determining reasonableness the court must consider that the necessity for the decision was imposed by the defendant, and that judgments in crises are subject to human error.

Plaintiff had a duty under 33 USC §409 [M9-1, 7] to start immediate and diligent removal of the wreck sunk in a navigable channel. The duty of an owner whose actions are responsible for the sinking is non-delegable and inescapable. If he fails to act, government may do so for navigational safety, and the owner will be liable for this cost and for any intervening damage caused by the wreck. If the owner is without fault, he still has the duty to remove the wreck upon which he has the choice to remove it and seek recovery of expenses from the responsible party, or he may abandon it to the United States for removal and recovery of expenses from the negligent party. If the innocent owner abandons, he is not liable for cost of removal or for damages to third parties as a result of the wreck.

Plaintiff's position with respect to fault was uncertain in the face of the foregoing ascertainable consequences. Defendant alleged that the accident resulted from unseaworthiness of the barge or negligence of plaintiff or of third parties. Even if a court might find plaintiff free from fault several years later, Engineers might disagree and subject plaintiff to further litigation. If plaintiff had inquired and Engineers did not require the barge to be moved, that would not protect plaintiff from a suit by a third party for striking the wreck, or from a change of mind by Engineers. At best, plaintiff could have had a personal opinion of government's employee without warranty upon which plaintiff could scarcely rely.

When plaintiff decided to raise the barge, any subsequent liability was conjectural, and defendant failed to show that any contingent liability was so negligible as to make unreasonable plaintiff's decision to raise the barge without prior investigation. Plaintiff knew the barge sank because of a leak while unattended, and it believed the barge was on the bottom virtually unharmed. It was unaware of the extensive damage that made the barge unsalvageable. Yet, even if it knew this, the removal expense incurred would be reasonable under the obligations imposed by 33 USC §409. Plaintiff's decision may have saved defendant added expense from salvage by government at a later time after changed conditions upon which defendant might make the same claim for failure to mitigate damages.

The dissenting judge said that the policy for mitigation of damages is for the benefit of the parties and for society at large in requiring the injured party to use opportunities to hold down losses. "The majority opinion, written from the viewpoint of hindsight, seems to me to reward a party that pushed ahead without availing himself of sources of information furnished to its agent (the salvage company) and ultimately to it. This is antithetical to the underlying policy."

This case considers post-casualty mitigation. Compare it with those of pre-casualty mitigation in Ch. B22, BARGE V REAL ESTATE.

Ch. B10 BOAT SALES

SALE ON APPROVAL   [M10-4, add after WHEN DOES TITLE PASS:]

    A contrast to Manuel v Shaheen [M10-2] is Exchange Bank & Trust Co. v Glenn's Marine, Inc., (Ark 1979) 579 SW 2d 358. Beason bought a boat, trailer and 55 hp motor from Glenn's. They agreed that if Beeson was satisfied after a weekend trial period, he could keep that motor or exchange it for a larger one at a higher price. Glenn's did not consider the sale to be consummated at the time Beason took the smaller motor and Glenn's would bear the loss if anything happened to the "rig", so it required Beason to insure it. Beason left a deposit to assure he would buy one or the other, and he exchanged the motor for the larger one in 48 hours.
    Beason financed the purchase by a $4088 promissory note and security interest on the rig, and the bank filed a financing statement on the collateral. However, the bank had no knowledge of the subsequent exchange of motors. When Beason defaulted on his note payment, the bank filed replevin against Glenn's to recover the smaller motor or its value.
    The bank lost. This transaction was not an absolute sale, Glenn's had title to the original motor, and the bank was not entitled to its possession; it was a sale on approval. UCC §2-326 provides that if the delivered goods may be returned by the buyer even though they conform to the contract, the sale is on approval if the goods are delivered primarily for use. §2-327 provides that in sales on approval, although the goods are identified to the contract, the risk of loss and the title do not pass to the buyer until acceptance; and use of the goods consistent with the purpose of trial is not acceptance, but failure seasonably to notify the seller of election to return the goods is an acceptance.
    Contrary to the bank's contention, this was not an absolute sale with right to rescind.

VALUE   [A10-3, add after Barrington v Kelley:]

    In Couch v Frichter's Sportsmen's Haven, Inc., (La App 1979) 365 So 2d 901, Couch bought a 26 foot sport fisherman boat from Frichter's. In its first months it had engine problems which were fixed by M&L Marine under a Ford Motors Warranty. Almost two years later the starboard engine steamed. M&L inspected and told Couch the engine block was manufactured for automotive rather than marine use which was not covered by the automotive warranty. Couch installed a new engine and sued Frichter's for a reduction of the purchase price, claiming also that the engines were not a matched pair.
    The court held that the marine nature of an engine intended to be one of a matched pair for a fishing boat is a

principal motive for its purchase, and Couch was entitled to a reduction in the price for the one manufactured for automotive use. Frichter's was liable for the sale to Couch regardless of lack of knowledge of the automotive engine (Frichter's seller was now out of business) because a represented quality of the goods (the matched pair), a principal motive of the sale, was lacking.

The measure of damages in the case was the difference between the sale price to Couch and the price the parties would have agreed on if they knew of the defect: the amount needed to give Couch an installed marine engine rather than an installed non-marine engine. Here Couch could recover the amount necessary to rebuild the automotive engine into a marine engine rather than a marinized or converted engine, plus expenses of installation.

PUNITIVE DAMAGES   [M10-13, add:]

Punitive or exemplary damages are awarded to a plaintiff by increasing compensatory damages as a punishment, deterence or warning to deter a defendant's wanton, reckless, malicious, or oppressive acts. Such awards are uncommon - it would be a sad reflection on the state of our society if they were; yet, the growth of consumerism promotes awareness of this relief. Simply put, the key is not the degree of outrage of the plaintiff, but that of the court.

Such a case was Neil Huffman VW Corp. v Ridolphi, (Ala 1979) 378 So 2d 700. Ridolphi, an insurance salesman, wanted to buy a 1974 Datsun 260Z from defendant, but noticing the car had been repainted, he asked if it had been wrecked. Hinson, the business manager, said the repainting could have resulted from a bad paint job at the factory. Neither Hinson nor Mattingly, Huffman's general sales manager, told Ridolphi that Huffman had painted the car when, in fact, they painted it twice in three motnhs. The previous owner painted it once before trading it to Huffman.

Ridolphi was concerned because a repainted car is a suspect for having been wrecked. When he asked about a repaired spot he saw in the rear when the car was on the rack for tire changes, he was told it was minor damage. It turned out to be major when he learned over CB radio that the car was riding sideways. There being independent suspension on each wheel, the impact of a serious accident could shift the alinement 3 or 4 inches. He paid $4850 for the car, but a few months later the highest trade value was $2000-2500, and nobody would buy it. And when he put the car through a coin car-wash it came out with no paint on the hood. After spending $750-800 in repairs and driving 33,000 miles, he sued Huffman for fraud and misrepresentation when Huffman refused an adjustment.

The court affirmed a $27,500 jury award of which some

$3150-3650 were actual damages. Said the court:

"The doctrine of caveat emptor, if not already grounded, is a weak bird. The law now is consumer oriented, and federal and state laws (Truth-in lending, UCC, for example) have been passed for the protection of the consumer. It now appears that the seller is the one to beware. This certainly appears to be true in the matter of the sale of used cars. It is a rare case when the seller and the buyer of a used car stand on equal footing. In most cases the buyer is at the mercy of the seller, and when he pays a substantial portion of his monthly pay check in car payments, he does not want to drive a car running sideways down the highway or have the thing come out nude when he drives it through a car-wash."

The jury saw through the evasive answers. Punitive damages in this kind of case was discretionary with the jury. The nature of the conduct on Huffman's part justified the award.

Ch. B11 WARRANTIES

EXPRESS WARRANTIES   [M11-3, add:]

The right to rely on representations in sales was closely scrutinized by Florida courts in several new cases. In Upledger v Vilamor, Inc., (Fla App 1979) 369 So 2d 427, after buying an apartment building, buyers sued seller for false representations on which they relied as to the amount of apartment rents and duration of leases. Buyers admitted they did not check the accuracy of these items, and the court entered summary judgment against them on the authority of Potaker v Hurtak, (Fla 1955) 82 So 2d 502; and Folz v Beard, (Fla App 1976) 332 So 2d 219. Examining these cases:

- In Potaker, plaintiff leased a restaurant facility in reliance on the false statement by the lessor that the previous lessee had made a profit when, in fact, it never had been profitable. The court ruled against plaintiff, for in measuring the right of reliance, every person must use reasonable diligence for his own protection. In the absence of accompanying actual deception, artifice, or misconduct, if the means of knowledge are at hand and are available to both parties equally, and the subject matter is open equally to their inspection, the plaintiff may not complain of deception by misrepresentation if he did not avail himself of those means and opportunities, (citing 23 Am Jur §155, Fraud and Deceit).

- In Folz, plaintiff lost a suit to rescind the purchase of an employment agency for fraudulent misrepresentations. Without a fiduciary relationship, or actionable fraud for inducing the representee to forebear investigation, or of circumstances making an investigation impossible, difficult or expensive, the representee has a duty to use reasonable diligence for his own protection. Thus, absent accompanying undiscoverable deception, artifice or misconduct, where the means of knowledge at hand are available to both parties equally for their inspection, if one of them does not use those means and opportunities, he may not complain of deception by the other's misrepresentations.

The court reversed the summary judgment against these plaintiffs, noting Board of Public Instruction v Everett W. Martin & Son, Inc., (Fla 1957) 97 So 2d 21; and Martin v Paskow, (Fla App 1976) 339 So 2d 266:

- In Board, a contractor misrepresented to the school what it paid in substituting jalousies put into the construction job. That court held it was not the duty of the Board's architect to investigate the cost of the substituted material, but they and the Board were justified in accepting the representation from the contractor that he paid a certain sum without their having to go to the material supplier to determine the price.

- In <u>Martin</u>, similarly, where the buyer rescinded purchase of an apartment building for fraudulent misrepresentation, the court said that where the record shows that positive representations were made to induce plaintiff to act to his detriment, defendant cannot complain if plaintiff acted in reliance.

Now the appellate court found these two lines of authority to be difficult to reconcile. In reversing the summary judgment against Upledger, the court noted that misrepresentations of opinion and law are not actionable; but the judicial trend is toward the doctrine that negligence in trusting in a misrepresentation will not excuse positive willful fraud or deprive the defrauded person of his remedy. This is true especially where there is a relation of natural trust and confidence; even though there is not strictly a fiduciary relationship, the failure of the defrauded party to exercise ordinary prudence or vigilance will not deprive him of redress.

If the representation is more in the nature of "puffing", or is incredible, or is obviously false, plaintiff should not be entitled to rely on it. But if a specific false statement is made knowingly, and it is relied upon reasonably, the representee, in accordance with the growing line of authority, is not precluded from recovery because he failed to make independent investigation of the truth of the statement. This position is justified either by the desire to upgrade business morality, or by the pragmatic view that, as between the two, a negligent party ought to prevail over a fraudulent party. Here, the seller had superior knowledge of the apartment rents and leases. The buyer had no reason to believe that the misrepresentations might be false. The buyers, as a matter of law, must not be denied recovery for their failure to investigate.

In <u>Nessim v De Loache</u>, (Fla App 1980) 384 So 2d 1341, Nessim sued De Loache, seller of the 63 foot yacht Mi-Mar, and Bertram & Co. as broker to rescind the contract of sale and for fraud and deceit. The complaint alleged that defendants represented the yacht to be in good condition, knowing it had a latent defect - it had grounded and submerged partially to the damage of its electrical system; plaintiff had been switched after having been introduced to a better vessel which was not for sale; defendants had superior knowledge but plaintiff knew nothing of yachts and yachting and relied on Bertram to supply an independent surveyor as called for in the contract of sale; the independent surveyor, unknown to plaintiff at the time, was a former employee of Bertram and made only a cursory examination which failed to reveal the latent defect.

Bertram had sold the yacht to Mi-Mar Charters of Miami, Inc. in 1972. De Loache was president and sole stockholder. The Nessim contract was signed December 28, 1977 by De Loache individually. Minor repairs recommended by the surveyor were made by Bertram before closing. Nessim's interim captain was aboard during repairs with opportunity to inspect before the

January 31, 1978 closing between Nessim and Mi-Mar Charters. The trial court granted summary judgment in favor of De Loache on his defenses that he was not individually liable for the acts of the corporate owner, and plaintiffs action was barred by the doctrine of caveat emptor.

The appellate court reversed and remanded for trial. Fraud ordinarily is not a proper subject for summary judgment. Being a subtle matter, it requires a full explanation of facts and circumstances to determine if they constitute fraud collectively, and such a determination usually requires a trial. The classic illustration of fraud is where one party having superior knowledge intentionally fails to disclose a material fact which is not discoverable by ordinary observation, especially where coupled by trick or artifice. De Loache's deposition had not been taken when summary judgment was granted. There were questions as to whether Bertram was acting in the course and scope of its employment; whether Nessim had a right to rely on Bertram's representations; and whether he had an opportunity to inspect and learn of the defect, latent or otherwise.

Although the corporation had been dissolved involuntarily by the Florida Secretary of State in December 1976 until reinstatement September 13, 1978 under the express reinstatement provisions of F.S. 607.271(5), that reinstatement will not affect liability of its executive in the interim of dissolution. De Loache could be held liable personally.

IMPLIED WARRANTY OF MERCHANTABILITY   [M11-5, add after Moron:]

In Daigle v Robinson Bros., Inc., (La App 1979) 368 So 2d 186, plaintiff bought a white Ford from Robinson October 11, 1974. It was dirty, having been on the car lot five months before sale. After cleaning and delivery, Daigle told the salesman of rust spots, and he said he would clean the car with chemical compound. She accepted the car but she brought it back on a number of occasions. An October 21st repair order indicated the "rust problem" would be taken care of later.

The car had been shipped from the assembly plant in Atlanta through Birmingham to Baton Rouge. It was subject, we are told, to industrial fallout in transit, probably steel filings in Birmingham. These settle on the paint, oxidize in a few hours of exposure to moisture, and appear as tiny rust spots which are easily removed by washing with an oxalic acid solution. If this is not done, the rust will destroy the paint and attack the metal of the car. Robinson's franchise required it to inspect on delivery and note defects. Ford assumed the $10 cost of cleaning the vehicle because of fallout, but Robinson made no claim in this instance. The paint condition worsened until the old paint had to be removed. The trial court allowed $950 to plaintiff against Robinson for repainting, but plaintiff asserted a redhibition claim against Ford.

The court defined a redhibition defect as one which supports avoidance of a sale for rendering the property absolutely useless or so inconvenient and imperfect that the buyer, if informed, would not have made the purchase. Here the defect at the time of delivery was so minor that the car was neither useless nor its use so imperfect or inconvenient that Daigle would have declined acceptance because of fallout. This defect which Robinson could have and should have discovered became a redhibitory defect because of Robinson's dereliction; but as there was none at the time of sale, there was no such claim against Ford.

THE MARINE SURVEYOR   [A11-2, add after 2nd paragraph:]

As an unripened proposition of law, the extended liability of special knowledge people bears watching. There are pressures. In the 1980 session of the Florida Legislature, Senate Bill 656 and House Bill 1355 provided, among other things, that an officer, agent or employee of an engineering corporation shall be personally liable and accountable <u>only to the person for whom professional services were rendered</u>. The underlined part was not enacted. What was enacted, Ch. 80-223, amended F.S. 471.023(3) dealing with the liability of a registered engineer practicing through a corporation or partnership, which is not germane to our interest.

It led to a scanning of F.S. Ch. 471 Engineering, and F.F. Ch. 472 Land Surveying. Both were enacted in 1979 after "sunset" legislative review of prior law to regulate those professions. Purpose is stated: In §471.001, physical and economic injury would result to the citizens of the state if incompetent engineers performed engineering services, thus regulation of the practice of engineering is necessary in the interest of public health and safety; in 472.001, it is necessary to regulate land surveyors because improper land surveying of land, water, and space presents a significant threat to the public.

§471.005(4)(a) defines engineering to include service requiring engineering education, training "in the application of special knowledge of the mathematical, physical, and engineering sciences to such services" in a wide variety of technical undertakings of a mechanical, electrical, hydraulic, pneumatic, or thermal nature, insofar as they involve safeguarding life, health, or property. Comparably, §472.005(4)(a) defines land surveying to include professional service involving "the application of special knowledge of the principles of mathematics, the related physical and applied sciences", and other elements necessary for the performance of land surveys.

Engineering and land surveying are remote to the personal life of the average citizen, but they have long been with us. They are associated integrally with where we live

B11-4

or work. Marine surveyors are late arrivals in performing similar functions for vessels. It will be for the legislative wisdom to determine when the practice of marine surveying has become that important and prevalent to the affected public to require its inclusion among the regulated professions. In Florida, the size of the boating industry indicates such action to be timely. It is a multi-million dollar industry which only qualified professionals should be allowed to serve for the protection of property interests, and more importantly, human life and safety as will be noted from the cases throughout this text on Small Boat Law.

SPECIAL KNOWLEDGE PEOPLE   [A11-8, add:]

In *Investors Tax Sheltered Real Estate, Ltd. v Leventhal*, (Fla App 1979) 370 So 2d 815, plaintiff entered into a sale-leaseback transaction on an apartment complex in Dallas. When the seller could not make the lease payments, plaintiff sued the accountants for auditing the seller negligently and rendering an unqualified opinion in the financial statements which were included in seller's annual report. The controversy centered on the adequacy of disclosure of the largest asset: notes receivable on mobile home park sales that were merely conditional contractual rights based on critical variables.

Plaintiff lost. The financial statement disclosed the nature of the asset in the explanatory notes. The accountants were not in privity with plaintiff. Before they would be liable to such a third party for loss arising out of reliance on the statements they prepared, there would have to be a showing of gross negligence by the accountants, or having knowledge that the third party intended to rely on the statements prepared by the accountants, that there was fraud in connection therewith.

By contrast, in *Navajo Circle, Inc. v Development Concepts Corp.*, (Fla App 1979) 373 So 2d 689, the association of Navajo Circle condominium and a unit owner sued the architect and contractor because the architect negligently supervised the construction and subsequent repairs to the roof of the building, and the contractor negligently built the roof; and there was subsequent damage to the roof, interior and exterior walls, and rentals were lost. The trial court dismissed for lack of privity between the parties.

The appellate court reversed. Privity is an essential element in a contract cause of action, but not in tort. The issue is whether defendants owed a legal duty to plaintiffs and whether the injury resulted from a violation of the duty, but the absence of contractual privity does not affect the tort claim. The duty may have sprung from a contractual promise made to another, but the duty in the negligence action is to use reasonable care in performing that promise, and that duty is independent of the contract. Whether defendants' duty

of reasonable care extends to a plaintiff not a party to the
contract depends on whether plaintiffs and defendants are in a
relationship in which the law imposes a duty on defendants to
avoid harm to plaintiffs. A supplier of a product is liable
for his negligence which reasonably may be expected to cause
injury to another's interests if the product is defective.
The duty of reasonable care to one who may be in contact foreseeably is not diminished simply because the injury resulted
from performance of a contractual duty owed to another person.
A supplier of a service has a legal duty to use reasonable care
to avoid unreasonable risks if it is foreseeable that plaintiff
will be injured.

WARRANTY EXCLUSIONS OR MODIFICATIONS   [M11-9, add:]

In Knipp v Weinbaum, (Fla App 1977) 351 So 2d 1081,
plaintiff bought a three wheeled motorcycle from defendant who
did business as Homestead Cycle Shop. It had been built at
home by a motorcycle enthusiast for his own use, and it was
traded to three private individuals before it reached defendant. The bill of sale to plaintiff stated prominently: Cycle
Sold AS IS - ONE CUSTOM TRIKE THREE WHEELER. Several hours
later plaintiff was injured seriously on a major highway when
a defective weld on the rear axle allegedly gave way causing
loss of control. Plaintiff sued for breach of express and
implied warranties, and negligence. Summary judgment was
granted against plaintiff, but three days later the Florida
Supreme Court decided West v Caterpillar Tractor [M21-6]
adopting the law of strict liability, and plaintiff sought to
amend his complaint to include a strict liability claim which
was denied.

The appellate court reversed and remanded for further
proceedings. Implied warranties, despite ostensible disclaimers, may be imposed on the sale of used goods in limited circumstances. When the UCC in §672.2-316(3) excluded all implied warranties by "as is", it was modified by "unless the
circumstances indicate otherwise". This precludes automatic
absolution by use of "as is". Also, such automatic absolution
would contravene the policy of §672.2-719(3) which declares
to be unconscionable a limitation of consequential damages for
personal injury in consumer goods cases. The seller may disclaim with "as is" when both parties understand absolution to
be the intended meaning of the phrase, for the seller may disclaim warranties as long as the buyer reasonably understands
this is being done. But to be effective, a disclaimer must be
part of the basis of the bargain between the parties. Here
there were conflicting statements on the intended meaning of
the disclaimer even as to whether "as is" applied only to
minor defects preventing qualification for a vehicle inspection sticker. A summary judgment is improper when there is a
disputed issue of fact.

Even though "as is" negates liability for warranty, the absence of warranties in the sale of a chattel does not necessarily preclude liability for negligence. "As is" may bear upon a duty, in matter of degree, that defendant owed to plaintiff. The reasonable understanding of the parties as to the extent of the disclaimer would be a jury question.

Although not deciding whether strict liability in tort is applicable to the purchase of used merchandise not originally manufactured for sale to the public, the trial court should have allowed the amendment of the complaint for such pleading, for the rules allow amendments at any time in the furtherance of justice.

LEMON SQUEEZE - THE PATIENCE RULE   [All-13, add:]

Vigilance is appropriate to the consideration of warranties. If the product is subject to correction, how far shall the consumer's patience extend? If patience is a virtue, too much of it will sacrifice rights. In K/F Development & Investment Corp. v Williamson Crane & Dozer Corp., (Fla App 1979) 367 So 2d 1078, K/F built two warehouses and sold them to plaintiff. K/F warranted orally at the sale closing that the warehouses had a "good ten-year roof", but one began to leak shortly after closing. K/F notified Zack, the roofing sub-contractor, who patched it. After a two year patching pattern, plaintiff was informed a new roof was necessary, and it sued for breach of express and implied warranty and for negligence. An issue at the trial was whether the roof was installed in accordance with building industry standards in the community, and plaintiff won a jury verdict.

The appellate court reversed. The alleged oral ten year warranty at closing was after the date of agreement for purchase and sale, so it could not have been an inducement to make the deal. The statute of limitations barred the claim for cost of replacement under theories of implied warranty or negligence, and this was not tolled by the intermittent repairs, for plaintiff knew or should have known of the alleged defect when the roof began to leak. The modern rule is that people should exercise their rights within the time limited by the statute which should not be extended by good faith attempts to remedy a defect.

In Kelly Tractor Co. v Gurgiolo, (Fla App 1979) 369 So 2d 992, plaintiff sued for breach of express warranty of future performance of two engines bought from defendant for a charter boat. There were significant mechanical difficulties after delivery in October 1968 which continued until suit on June 30, 1976. The court held suit was barred by the 4 year statute of limitations. Plaintiff had discovered or should have discovered breach of express warranties on future performance by June 30, 1972 long before the suit.

Ch. B12 FEDERAL BOAT SAFETY STANDARDS

A MATTER OF MOOD   [M12-2, add:]

As in NEW STANDARDS [A12-1], changes in label displays exceed the scope of this text and will not be pursued.

Of broader interest in the regulatory process is the Coast Guard's Consumer Affairs Program which went through a period of public comment. Program implementation was planned for December 1, 1980 as part of a Government-wide effort to improve consumer participation in Federal programs. It contemplates an outreach to organized groups of various categories and to the individual boating consumer. Thus, consumerism for products of the boating industry will join the other products that are under surveillance in our society.

[A12-3, add after Outboard Marine v Apeco:]

Manufacturers of component parts incorporated into marine equipment can be drawn into admiralty in products liability litigation as held in Sperry Rand Corp. v Radio Corp. of America, (CA La 1980) 618 F 2d 319. A vessel grounded and was involved in a collision in Houston Ship Channel allegedly because of a defect in the gyro-pilot steering system. The owner sued manufacturer Sperry Rand and its insurer. As the case progressed, defendants determined that the failure was caused by components manufactured by others, so they settled, took an assignment of claims, and brought a products liability action in admiralty court for their economic loss against RCA, Texas Instruments, and Electro-Switch Corp.

The district court dismissed for lack of admiralty jurisdiction because the small component parts were not specifically manufactured for incorporation in marine systems and they had little relationship to traditional maritime activity. These components were used in every conceivable aspect of electronic equipment.

The Court of Appeals reversed. The shipowner was engaged in a maritime activity, the injury was on a vessel in navigable waters, and the instrumentality causing the injury was a marine steering mechanism with defective components. If the vessel owner had sued the makers of the component parts, admiralty jurisdiction should not have been precluded. That relief in admiralty will extend to this plaintiff notwithstanding that the parts were not unique to this navigational equipment to protect the national interest in uniformity of laws and remedies for those facing the hazards of waterborne transportation.

Ch. B13 FLORIDA YACHT AND SHIP BROKER'S ACT

The repealer of the Act [A13-1] became effective on August 5, 1979, but not before the Act came under court test in <u>United Yacht Brokers, Inc. v Gillespie</u>, (Fla 1979) 377 So 2d 668. Johnson approached United to find a yacht suitable for his purchase, allegedly agreeing orally to pay a commission for United's efforts. Brown, a broker with United, showed Johnson several vessels including Sea Prince owned by Siewert and Anstett. Brown negotiated an agreement for Johnson to buy Sea Prince for $400,000 cash and a house valued at $260,000 conditioned on Siewert's inspection and approval of the house. Siewert rejected the house and a subsequent offer by Johnson. Allegedly, Siewert told Brown he wanted to meet with Johnson alone, and he met with Johnson on Sea Prince where, purportedly, he induced Johnson to deal directly with him and not through Brown. Thereafter, Johnson dealt solely with Siewert, he refused to enter into a later purchase agreement proposed by United, he bought the yacht from Siewert, and he refused to pay United a commission on the sale.

United sued Johnson's estate (he died) for breach of the brokerage agreement without alleging United's compliance with F.S. 537.05(2) which required a yacht broker to have written authorization from his principal before engaging in a transaction. Also, United charged Anstett and Siewert with wrongful interference with a contractual relationship. The complaint was dismissed as to all defendants for non-compliance with §537.05(2). On appeal, United attacked the constitutionality of the statute because no other class of licensed brokers regulated by the state were required to have written authorization before acting on behalf of a principal.

The Florida Supreme Court upheld the constitutionality of the statute which was rationally and reasonably related to a legitimate legislative purpose and was not imposed arbitarily or capriciously. Its purpose was to provide all parties to the transaction with a measure of protection in Florida's important yacht marketplace. It did not violate the equal protection and due process requirements of the 14th Amendment to the U.S. Constitution because the legislature may establish different classifications in regulating occupations to serve valid purposes under the state's police powers. Equal protection concerns legislative classifications; due process of law protects against legislative deprivation of life, liberty or property. The statute had a reasonable relation to a permissible legislative objective, and it was not discriminatory, arbitrary or oppressive. No fundamental rights were involved, and the statute applied with substantial fairness upon practically all persons similarly situated without oppression or arbitrary injury to the substantial rights of any person. Thus, the dismissal of the claim against Johnson's estate was affirmed.

However, the court reversed the summary judgment on the tortious interference claim because the unenforceable nature of the alleged contract between United and Johnson did not bar the suit against Anstett and Siewert. There was a possibility that the unenforceable promise might have been carried out if no third person interfered. "Although we do not condone United's failure to comply with Section 537.05(2), neither will we permit Anstett and Siewert to use it as a shield to limit their liability for tortious interference, a practice to which brokers of all types are peculiarly susceptible."

The dissenting opinion contended that the broker should not recover the equivalent of his commission from sellers who never employed him. Dugas v Dubois [M13-4], in addition to barring commissions on an oral contract, denied enforcement under theories of ratification, estoppel. or quantum meruit. The statute is both regulatory and penal, a violation being a misdemeanor, and there should be no recognition of a right to damages from a third party for tortious interference because that would frustrate the legislative purpose of penalizing the violation of the statute.

Once more, in Hatteras of Lauderdale, Inc. v Erisman, (Fla App 1980) 383 So 2d 985, plaintiff, having an oral yacht brokerage agreement with the seller, sued the buyer for the sale commission and alleged an intentional interference with the contractual relationship. The trial court dismissed for failure to comply with F.S. 537.05(2) which required the broker to have written authorization from his principal.

The appellate court reversed under authority of United Yacht Brokers v Gillespie. The intentional interference with the contractual relationship will support an action against the eventual purchaser of the yacht, but not against the seller who had the oral agreement.

The underlying importance of a written brokerage contract in all respects as well as in every instance is shown by Eckert v Soverel Marine Inc., (Fla App 1980) 380 So 2d 569. Plaintiff executed an offer to buy a yacht and placed it with the broker who represented a foreign seller and who was unable to provide adequate title documentation. Plaintiff had requested certain repairs. The broker agreed to return the deposit less $1000 for the cost of these repairs and $75 for cost of the new name on the transom. However, the broker refused to return additional funds withheld for commissions.

The court held the broker was not entitled to the commission. The offer to purchase specified that the seller, not plaintiff, was obligated for the commission. Plaintiff had no contractual obligation in that behalf.

Ch. B14   FLORIDA SALES TAX

TAX GUIDES   [M14-3, add after §12A-1.71]

Administration imprecision prejudiced the tax collector in Anderson v State Dept. of Revenue, (Fla App 1980) 380 So 2d 1083. Out Island Charters, Inc. of which Anderson was president sold, leased, repaired and chartered yachts. After boat sales, they agreed pursuant to Yacht Charter Management Agreements, for a percentage of gross bareboat fees, to act as the owners' agent to charter boats to third parties, and to maintain, repair, and dock the boats at the owners' expense. An owner could use his vessel at any time without costs if no charters were pending, but some owners deleted that provision before signing. In most cases, owners used their vessels occasionally to test equipment and to do routine maintenance and repairs accompanied by wives, mechanics or friends who helped with handling or routine maintenance. They were not purely personal pleasure trips.

No Florida sales tax was paid on the boat sales, equipment purchases, repair parts, dockage, or other expenses incident to the management and maintenance of the vessels, but tax was collected on vessel rentals. When the owners bought these vessels they did not register with the State as dealers in yacht chartering, nor did they provide Anderson with a certificate of resale. Anderson believed the transactions to be exempt from sales tax because the owners bought the vessels for rental, and he was unaware that dealer registration and submission of resale certificates were required to establish exemption.

After an audit, the owners were advised to pay the sales tax if they had used their boats for personal business; but if use had been for chartering exclusively, they should execute affidavits so stating and apply for certificates of registration as dealers and blanket certificates of resale. Most owners did so. In one transaction, Morgan bought a vessel for full payment, removed it to Tennessee the next day, but Anderson did not know if Morgan had furnished an exemption affidavit. [See M14-1]

Anderson bought a boat from Coastal Sailing Services of Tallahassee and paid sales tax. Later he thought he was exempt because he bought it solely for resale, so he asked about refund procedures. A state sales tax examiner advised by letter that a refund from Coastal could be had if the vessel was bought solely for rental purposes, and a request to Coastal should be accompanied by a certificate of sales tax exemption on a form enclosed. Anderson had been the purchaser, but the state letter referred to Out Island Charters as buyer with its identifying sales tax registration number. The examiner later testified that it was department policy to grant an exemption if the property was bought for rental purposes even if the buyer was not registered as a dealer at the time of sale. The state's Executive Director testified that registration at or a few days after time of sale was a prerequisite to exemption in such cases.

Anderson received the refund from Coastal in 1975 but the exemption form again was executed to Out Island Charters, and an examiner assessed this sale in a current proposed tax assessment because he found no documentary evidence that Anderson intended to use the boat for charters when he bought it, or that he was registered as a dealer then, or furnished a resale certificate to the seller when it was bought. No evidence was presented that Anderson used the boat for personal purposes, and he testified he bought it solely for rental but admitted he had no dealer's registration number at the time of purchase.

The State conceded that "equipment" bought solely for rental could be tax exempt under Rule 12A-1.71(2) which, though questionable as "equipment", had carried a boat exemption in practice; but the State contended that Anderson should have paid the tax because he was not registered as a dealer at that time. The question raised before the court was whether Anderson's registration some months after the sale related back to exempt this sale.

The court said: Yes. Although Anderson failed to file the required dealer's certificate before the sale, it would be grossly unfair not to allow him to show the true situation, for double taxation is to be avoided. The State's change of position in its policy provision handicapped Anderson and Out Island Charters in their attempts to satisfy the State as to taxable status and sales. They had a right to rely on the original interpretation letter.

[M14-3, 3rd line from bottom:]
The allusion to propriety for a delivery captain to have an ICC license should have been omitted as a practical matter. 49 USC §10544, addressing miscellaneous water carrier transportation exemptions, provides that, except to the extent that the ICC finds it necessary to carry out expressed transportation policy, the Commissioner does not have jurisdiction over transportation by water carrier when the transportation is provided by a vessel of not more than 100 tons carrying capacity or 100 indicated horsepower. 49 CFR §1072 defines "smallcraft" as a vessel of not more than 100 tons carrying capacity or not more than 100 indicated horsepower; "large craft" means a vessel of greater carrying capacity or power.

Thus, this matter is better left unpursued in this text.

[M14-4, add:]
Although Ch. 14 addressed sales tax in Florida, sales tax is universal among the States and common propositions will be of interest. "Sailaway" as a tax avoidance device will vary with geography. Thus, in <u>Matter of Seafarer Fiber Glass Yachts, Inc.</u>, (DC NY 1979), Seafarer made and sold customized

fiberglass yachts. To avoid New York sales tax, it arranged out-of-state delivery to customers frequently by one of two devices: By "sailaway" delivery in which its employee and the buyer sailed from Huntington Harbor into the Connecticut waters of Long Island Sound where delivery was made "officially"; or the buyer hired a trucker to "pick-up" the boat in Huntington and deliver it out of state. Seafarer, in a Chapter XI proceeding of the Bankruptcy Act, continued business under court supervision during which New York claimed sales taxes allegedly unpaid because of use of these devices. The Bankruptcy Judge disallowed the tax claim.

On appeal, the State argued that the fiction of delivery at the far side of a buoy in the middle of Long Island Sound was not an actual delivery. The District Judge held this delivery issue to be one of fact, and the Bankruptcy Judge's finding was to be upheld because it was not clearly erroneous. The State had produced no evidence on this issue.

As to truck delivery, the Bankrupcy Judge had held that pick-ups by truckers without ICC licenses were not taxable because the State conceded that pick-ups by ICC licensed truckers for out-of-state delivery were tax free sales, and the distinction between the two truckers appeared to be arbitrary and unreasonable. The District Judge reversed this decision as being contrary to law under which pick-ups by non-ICC licensed truckers, employees of the buyers, were subject to New York sales tax.

Ch. B15 BOAT CHARTERS AND LIVERIES

BAREBOAT CHARTER   [M15-2, add:]

Bareboat chartering of yachts as a means of enjoying ownership while deriving income is a flourishing business as the advertising section of any boating magazine will show; but legal hazards appear in Harris v Waikona Corp., (DC Hawaii 1980) 484 F Supp 372. In 1965 Dr. Adolph bought the 83 foot staysail schooner Astor built in 1926 in Scotland. When he brought it to California he was cited by the Coast Guard for failure to report arrival of a foreign vessel in a U.S. port (19 USC §1433), and not entering the vessel in Customs (19 USC §1435). In 1970 he was cited for transporting passengers between U.S. ports on a foreign vessel (46 USC §289). He wanted nothing more to do with the schooner after his son died in an accident involving it in 1973.

In 1974 Katz identified himself as the late son's friend who would be happy to live on the boat while seeing to minor repairs looking toward its sale. He suggested the possibility of charters, but Dr. Adolph was wary of new fines. The boat was drycocked, but for further repairs, Katz suggested a free berth at the University of Hawaii where repairs would be cheaper than in California and Astor could be sold more easily. He said he would take some friends to help defray expenses, and Adolph agreed. Actually, to circumvent 46 USC §289, Katz gathered passengers who paid to sail to Hawaii under a sham bareboat charter agreement and an agreement electing him captain and ship's husband (managing agent) for the voyage. The passengers came to Katz and paid separately; crew members did not pay, or paid a lesser amount. They signed a bareboat charter contract indicating it was with owner Adolph who was to receive $300. He did not sign it and he received nothing.

After the voyage a passenger wrote Adolph that Katz was a terrible seaman and irresponsible master who allowed Astor to deteriorate rapid. He offered to repair Astor at his own expense if Katz was removed. In December 1975 the Coast Guard notified Adolph that Astor again had violated 19 USC §§ 1433 and 1435, and 46 USC §289, that fines would be assessed, and that Astor might be seized. Adolph phoned Katz to leave Astor but Katz pleaded that he and his small dog had no place to go, so Adolph agreed he could remain aboard temporarily, but told him he could not sail Astor.

In January 1976 the Coast Guard seized Astor constructively so that it could not sail more than 50 miles from Hawaii. But later that month Katz entered into a "Charter Management Agreement" with Waikona Corp., which purported to be with the boat's owner, to arrange bareboat charters for Astor. Waikona was to advertise and make all arrangements for charters and receive payment for every day Astor was chartered.

Waikona's promotions reached Donald Harris in Colorado who wanted Astor for his group of 8 for 10 days, and he sent a deposit of $200, balance due $2800. But Adolph decided to get Katz off the yacht and work with the man who had written to him about Katz. Katz was evicted on April 15th of which he informed Waikona. Simultaneously, the Harris party of 11 visited Astor to see how things were going, and they learned that Astor was unavailable. Their vacation dream was smashed, the $2800 certified check held by Waikona made them short of funds, they refused substitution of two smaller boats because they did not want to split the party, and they sued Waikona for breach of contract. Waikona filed a third party complaint against Adolph for indemnification, and plaintiffs sued Adolph for breach of contract and intentional infliction of emotional distress.

The court found Waikona liable to plaintiffs, granted summary judgment to Adolph as to the claim of Waikona, found Adolph not liable to plaintiffs for their damages nor for any tort arising from his rightful repossession of Astor, and Adolph could recover his costs from Waikona (which the court was advised in 1977 had become insolvent).

Vessel charters are maritime in nature. Harris was the contracting party who corresponded and negotiated with Waikona, the deposit was his personal check; therefore, only he can recover on the charter contract. However, the other plaintiffs can recover against Waikona as third party beneficiaries of that contract. The anticipations and plans of the group as beneficiaries were disclosed to Waikona by Harris acting as a group spokesman. The performance owed by Waikona was for the benefit of the group, which Waikona understood. In making the contract Waikona unqualifiedly promised availability of Astor for the time specified and warranted ability to provide the yacht. They did not tell Harris they were only an agent for the owner. Waikona could have made sure the owner would not withhold Astor by contacting the owner before making the contract. Its breach was not excused. Astor was unique, and two smaller boats which would divide the party did not represent "cover" to mitigate damages. Plaintiffs did have some vacation out of the trip, but it was impaired by attendant shortage of funds and necessary crowding, and they can recover from Waikona for this mental stress.

As to plaintiffs' claims against Adolph, the Waikona-Katz "Charter Management Agreement" involved no charter of a vessel. It provided that the owner hire Waikona as agent to arrange boat charters. The charter contract was maritime but this "Agreement" was not; however, there appears to be no conflict between maritime law and general agency principles. In December Adolph forbade Katz even to sail the yacht, much less make charter arrangements, and any contract was against explicit orders. The November 24, 1974 "Agreement of Participation of Captain of Schooner Astor" between Katz and Adolph indicates that Katz would draw no salary until such time as

Astor receives revenue from charters. It permitted Katz to
live aboard and reserved decision to the owner as final and decisive in all matters of the agreement. The import is that any
decisions on charters were to be made by Adolph. If Katz had
charter authority, it would have been spelled out as was permission to live aboard, and even if there had been such authority, it would have been revoked in December 1975.

Katz had no apparent authority to act; that depended on
representations from Adolph to Waikona of which there were none.
The display of the Katz-Adolph agreement gave every indication
that Katz' decision-making power was substantially less than
that of the normal master and that chartering was outside the
scope of his authority. It showed authority only to sail Astor.
Waikona saw Coast Guard seizure papers for violation of 46 USC
§289 which named Katz as captain, and the bareboat charter
papers for the trip from California which prompted the seizure.
It should have alerted Waikona to contact the owner who was
within reach of a 40 cent phone call to Los Angeles. Adolph
did nothing intentionally or carelessly to lead Waikona to believe Katz had authority to put out Astor for charter. Adolph
never knew Waikona believed it had a valid contract until Adolph
evicted Katz. Waikona had no reason to rely, and there was no
estoppel. Adolph had no actual knowledge of the "Charter Management Agreement", none should be imputed to him, and there
was no ratification.

INSURANCE [M15-5, add:]

Mariner Charters failed to recover from its insurer
for theft of a chartered boat because it did not fall under an
"infidelity" exclusion; but with "theft" coverage, as in Imperial v Ellington [M25-19], there was a contrary result in
Collins v Royal Globe Ins. Co., (Fla App 1979) 368 So 2d 941.
Plaintiff voluntarily gave possession of his motor home to a
party who falsely said he wanted to rent it, and he disappeared
with it. The rent check was returned for insufficient funds.
Defendant, insurer against loss by theft, acknowledged that the
thief intended to steal the vehicle at the time he got possession, but it refused to pay the loss because the policy excluded loss due to conversion, embezzlement or secretion by one in
lawful possession which, said, defendant, means possession
voluntarily relinquished.

In ruling for plaintiff, the court held that the thief
intended the theft at the time he got possession. All his representations were false and were designed fraudulently to induce plaintiff to deliver possession. Thus, the thief never
acquired lawful possession. Whatever the mode of operation of
the thief, the owner intended to insure against loss by theft.
If certain classes of thieves or types of theft are not to be
covered, the insurer must exclude them in clear language. A
thief acquires no lawful possession, and if he was a thief from

the start, then his possession was unlawful from the start.

BOAT LIVERIES   [M15-6, add after Osterlind v Hill:]

In Christian Appalachian Project, Inc. v Berry, (Ky 1972) 487 SW 2d 951, 94 ALR 3rd 871, Donny Berry, with several friends, came to the lake owned and operated by C.A.P. for public recreational use. Two young men rented a canoe and paddled off. They were given life jackets and instructed by an attendant to wear them. Berry had rented a flat bottom boat which he changed for a canoe. Out of sight of the boat dock, it tipped and he drowned. His estate sued C.A.P. for his wrongful death. There was conflicting evidence at the trial whether the attendant had furnished a life jacket. Plaintiff won a $16,000 verdict.

On appeal, C.A.P. contended it had no duty to furnish a life preserver and, alternatively, Berry had as much responsibility to ask for one as C.A.P. had to make one available; and if he was as inexperienced as plaintiff sought to show, it was unreasonable for him to rent a canoe without a life preserver and paddle off on his own. Plaintiff argued that C.A.P. knew of a canoe's propensity to capsize, Berry knew nothing of canoes, C.A.P. had a duty to warn of this, and no lifeguard was present.

Judgment was reversed, case dismissed. In the operation of a recreational facility for adult boating on a lake, defendant had no duty to furnish a lifeguard. There was no reason for its employee to know of Berry's inexperience, so there was no duty to warn Berry as an adult that a canoe might capsize. Even if a duty to furnish a life preserver had been pleaded and proved properly in this case, Berry's conduct was so unreasonable under the circumstances as to bar recovery. There was no evidence that the canoe was unusual or unsound, there was no unusual water condition, and he was an inexperienced swimmer. His conduct clearly involved a risk out of all proportion to its value which is contributory negligence as a matter of law.

[Note: As an annotation to this case, 94 ALR 3rd 876 discussing livery liability for injury to patrons collects cases in which the livery was or was not liable.]

The Berry case had a canoe but no lifeguard. Baroco, below, had a beach and lifeguard, but no watercraft. Why consider it? Private waters such as in Kaiser Aetna [B2-4], whitewater river runs, etc., may have patrols in a livery sense with rescue responsibilities. Glenview Park, below, had a safety patrol but direct rescue effort was not in issue. Thus, until we have a case closer in point, Baroco will span the legal responsibilities to be projected.

In Baroco v Araserve, Inc., (CA Ala 1980) 621 F 2d 189, Araserve contracted with Alabama to operate a recreational facility at Gulf Shores. The contract specified it was for the benefit of the public; operation of a pavilion was required for the Gulf Shores beach area; Araserv was to provide two lifeguards for the pavilion area and furnish all necessary life saving equipment; and it was required to take all proper safeguards for prevention of injuries or damage to the public. Only one lifeguard was hired, he was not told of available life saving equipment, and none had been purchased by May 12, 1974 when he reported for work.

That day, Anthony Baroco took his wife and family to the beach and noticed two teenagers playing in the water, one of whom later asked his aid for the other in the water. The water was choppy, waves were high, and Baroco told the girl to call the lifeguard. Baroco considered the waters dangerous under the prevailing conditions, but he was an experienced Gulf swimmer. Nobody should have been swimming in the Gulf under those conditions which were too rough for a rescue squad even to attempt to use a boat, as later shown by competent testimony at the trial. The lifeguard swam 150 yards to the pair, but the teenager already appeared to be dead and Baroco, preventing rescue by his panic, drowned.

In the action for his wrongful death, the complaint charged tortious breach of contract and negligence upon which a jury awarded $500,000 against Araserv. It contended on appeal that a breach of contract claim cannot support a wrongful death action because punitive damages, involved in this award, are not recoverable in contract actions in Alabama.

The award was affirmed. The complaint did not allege that death was caused by breach of contract, but rather that death resulted from non-performance of a duty established by the contract which is actionable in Alabama as tortious breach of contract. Araserve owed a duty to beach patrons as third party beneficiaries of the contract to provide two lifeguards and life saving equipment. By testimony, failure to observe these duties proximately caused Baroco's death. The lifeguard testified that because he was able to reach Baroco, rescue could have been effected if he had the proper equipment. The jury could infer that if a second lifeguard had been hired, Baroco need not have risked his life to save the drowning girl.

Araserve contended also that Baroco was contributorily negligent by placing himself in an obvious position of peril. As Baroco considered himself an experienced swimmer who faced a life and death decision which had to be made without time for reasoned deliberation, contributory negligence was a jury question, and a reasonable jury could have reached the decision it did. The dangers inherent in a beach operation are great, and the commensurate standards for comporting with this risk are great. In inducing the State to grant the concession contract, Araserve represented that it gave its employees extensive training and relied on the most modern equipment in the industry. By testimony, two lifeguards with rescue equipment were required as a minimum to safeguard a Gulf beach the size of this one. Araserve represented to the State that a Red Cross life-saving certificate would be a pre-requisite for the lifeguards, but the man hired did not have one. Thus, Araserve violated its own standards of care, those of the contract, and of common law. In imposing punitive damages for wrongful death, the jury could have been motivated by a desire to prevent future deaths caused by commercial concerns which fail to recognize and uphold the duties and responsibilities provided for by the contract with the State in similar circumstances.

The dissenting opinion commented that no reasonably minded jury could possibly find that Baroco was not contributorily negligent when he entered the waters too rough for the rescue squad even to attempt to use a boat. [But see DANGER INVITES RESCUE [M4-10].

In Glenview Park District v Melhus, (CA Ill 1976) 540 F 2d 1321, Glenview advertised a 4 hour 15 mile canoe trip down the Fox River. After checking the Illinois Conservation Department booklet, the Fox had been selected because it was a calm, slow-moving river, wide, with very few obstructions, and it was shallow enough for wading under ordinary conditions. Supervisors made a reconnaisance run, and they took through a group of people two weeks before September 30th. They assumed conditions would remain constant and did not check various sources to learn river conditions; but the Fox on September 30th was at flood stage and waters had overflowed the banks at places so that trees on the banks were in the water which, therefore, was closer to overhanging branches.

In response to the advertising for the trip: $8.00 per person including bus transportation, use of canoe, paddles, life preservers, and supervision down the river, Mrs. Melhus asked the secretary at the Glenview office what canoeing skill was needed. She was told it was minimal and it would be perfectly safe for her children, 5 and 8. She paid the fees and registered. Her husband was a non-swimmer. He had been in a canoe several times as a youngster, and he did not think canoeing was very complex.

For the trip on September 30th the supervisors laid out 8 canoes and various life preservers which were required for children but were optional for adults. Supervisor Guy Bacci said he would be in the last canoe, his brother in the lead, and all should stay relatively in the center of the river. There was no canoeing instruction and no inquiry as to swimming ability or canoeing skill. The Melhus canoe zigzagged considerably in the early part of the trip. After 45 minutes the group approached an island. The Melhus canoe was in the center of the river when they saw trees about 50 feet ahead. Dr. Melhus took over the sole paddling and tried to steer left to avoid the trees. The canoe struck a lowhanging limb which spilled the family into the river, and Dr. Melhus drowned in 8-10 feet of water.

Glenview petitioned the admiralty court for exoneration from or limitation of liability [Ch. M23], and Mrs. Melhus sued Glenview for wrongful death of her husband. The trial court denied Glenview's petition but entered judgment on the merits against the widow's suit.

The Court of Appeals reversed the judgment against Mrs. Melhus' claim. The evidence did not support a finding that there was no Glenview negligence proximately causing the drowning. Glenview's duty to use due care was not destroyed by the corresponding duty of Dr. Melhus. Glenview had some duty of care as a private entrepreneur, but that duty varied with the circumstances of the case. The failure to check the water level and warn of overhanging branches were negligent omissions proximately causing the Melhus canoe to encounter them. His contributory negligence in reduction of recovery should be determined under admiralty principles.

The denial of Glenview's limitation petition was affirmed. Being guilty of actionable negligence as recited, it cannot qualify for the requested relief. Glenview argued that Melhus was a bareboat charterer but, said the court, this canoeing trip was no more such relationship than as there would be in the purchase of a ticket and participating in a ride in a boat of an amusement park Tunnel of Love.

Ch. 16 MARINA AND BOATYARD DISPUTES

YARD SECURITY - THEFT   [M16-13]

A boatyard had a security problem like the truckyard in Gioe v Ducate and Lee Corp., (La App 1980) 381 So 2d 530. Plaintiff sued defendant depositary for theft of an outboard motor. The yard's chain link fence, topped with barbed wire, had a 10-15 inch opening at the bottom for a 3-5 foot length.

Defendant was liable. It knew of the opening at the bottom and it had been victim of motor theft in the past. It did not exercise reasonable care over plaintiff's new outboard.

Apart from theft of a vehicle, what is the bailee's liability for valuable personal property in it? In Insurance Co. of North America v Solari Parking, Inc., (La 1979) 370 So 2d 503, the Langes were relocating and honeymooning from Seattle to Key West and passed through New Orleans. Their car was loaded with personal effects so, for greater security, they went to Solari's, an inside attended facility. They gave the car key to attendant White, received a claim check, and he gave them directions to the location of a local night club they asked about. Two hanging clothes bags, a picnic basket, two automobile tires, a pillow, an afghan, a black pouch, and a cosmetic bag were in the back seat area, and a bag was on the front seat. Suitcases and items of real value were locked in the trunk. There had been no conversation as to the contents of the trunk or the car.

They left, White started the engine to park the car, he left to attend to another customer, a thief stole the idling car, and when the Langes returned four hours later, he helped them fill out a claim form which listed the car and its contents. They were paid for loss of the car and partially by their insurer for the contents, but Solari and its insurer denied liability for the contents of the car. The trial court ruled for the Langes and INA against Solari and its insurer, USF&G. The appellate court, in 367 So 2d 12, reversed and dismissed because Solari's liability was conditioned on its consent to receive, preserve and restore the property; there was no opportunity to inspect the car; there was no showing of White's actual or constructive knowledge from which could be presumed a consent to accept the car's contents; and Solari thus was not liable.

The Supreme Court reversed the appellate court and held Solari liable. The Langes expected White to take control of their possessions when they gave him the car key which was accepted without reservation as to the car's contents. Solari must admit that cars containing a substantial number of items are common, especially in the French Quarter because of the large number of tourists, and that the contents will be stolen with the car if its employees negligently afford the opportunity. Thus, the loss of the car's contents was a part of the damages contemplated by the parties to the breached contract.

Although Solari could not have contracted away its liability which was an essential element of the contract, it could have limited its liability by specifying the nature and extent of the liability for what it received for deposit or bailment. It could have had the attendant inform customers that the garage was a parking facility only for vehicles and that it would not accept responsibility for items contained in the cars.

Solari's USF&G policy insured "loss to an automobile caused by theft of the entire automobile". This language suggests coverage more general than merely for the automobile and equipment such as a spare tire and jack. Such a narrow coverage, as contended by USF&G, should be stated clearly and expressly and not foster several possible interpretations. Policy language is read broadly to favor coverage, and ambiguities will be construed against the insurer.

A house as real estate is outside a bailment relationship for personal property, but custody imposes a duty to warn where there is knowledge of high risk of theft as in Orkin Exterminating Co., Inc. v Culpepper, (Fla App 1979) 367 So 2d 1026. Plaintiff submitted her house to defendant for tenting and fumigation under an agreement. Defendant's written instructions required her to unlock all exterior doors or make the keys available. While the house was tented it was broken into by persons unknown [an operation spreading in Miami with wider availability of Scuba gear], and $450 worth of property was stolen. Other homes tented by defendant had been broken into by unknown persons previously, but defendant had not warned plaintiff of this. Plaintiff charged defendant with negligence by failure to warn her and to provide additional security for her home.

Noting that the complaint was based on negligence rather than a bailor-bailee relationship, the court held that the criminal act of a third party was not an intervening or superseding cause to absolve defendant of liability in a negligence action. From prior burglaries, this breaking was foreseeable by defendant upon which a failure to warn and to provide adequate security would sustain a finding of negligence.

CASUALTIES IN CUSTODY   [M16-14, add after Buntin v Fletchas:]

In Compania de Navigacion v S/S American Oriole, (DC La 1976) 474 F Supp 22, American Oriole was berthed with Todd Shipyard Corp. in New Orleans for repairs after which it was laid up as a dead ship for an indeterminate period. On December 4, 1974 her master conferred with Todd's docking master on the arrangement, alignment and number of mooring lines to be used in the coming winter months. Todd continued with repairs, and for the owner's account, Vinson Guard Service was engaged for 24 hour security as gangway watchman to prevent trespassing and theft. Todd provided electricity, mooring line handlers as necessary, and daily fire watch service which included checking of mooring lines. On December 11th the owner's port engineer instructed the gangway watchman to use the red emergency telephone near the gangway to call Todd for assistance if there was any difficulty.

Oriole was moored near the downriver end of Todd's property two berths below M/S Galaxias. Between them was several hundred feet of damaged wharf and planking roped off by a guard rail.

On January 10, 1975 beginning at 7:30 AM the weather bureau issued severe weather statements pertaining to a tornado watch in south Louisiana including: "Some of the thunderstorms will be accompanied by wind gusts to near 70 M.P.H. and a possible tornado". Todd's general superintendant issued instructions to check Oriole's lines, but when this reached the leaderman, he thought the checking was for changes in the height of the river as he was unaware of the severe weather forecast. He and his crew left Oriole at 10:00 AM.

At noon the Vinson guard telephoned that the gangplank was being pulled from the dock, and he took shelter from the rain in a nearby shed. Five minutes later he called again and was told help was on the way. He was given three numbers to call, apparently to the office of the general superintendant. He made a third call and, as he looked out from the shed, he saw that the bow line had come free. As he made a fourth call he heard lines snapping as Oriole went adrift. Meanwhile, the general superintendant attempted several calls, reached the general foreman, they drove to Oriole's berth, found it had broken free, and called the Coast Guard and for tug assistance.

Oriole drifted downriver, struck Aino, Damita and Golden Chalice, then drifted across the river and struck Locarno moored to the Amstar wharf, which it damaged also, on the opposite bank. Then the tugs arrived and held Oriole against the bank in a holed and listing condition. It was returned to Todd and drydocked.

The breaking adrift apparently resulted in part from the collapse of a 42 foot section of the wooden wharf. Double bitts securing the bow lines were missing and fresh damage was apparent otherwise. The ship had strained on lines in the gusting wind. When the mooring bitts were pulled into the river the sping lines parted under the uneven strain and the stern lines pulled over and off the canted bollards which held them.

The court held Todd liable to the owners of Locarno and of the anchored Aino, Damita and Golden Chalice, to Amstar, and to American Foreign Steamship Corp., as owner of Oriole. Todd did not suffer a tornado. Weather instruments three miles NNW of Todd recorded winds 39-60 mph between 12:29 and 12:38 PM; others 8.4 miles SSE recorded winds 46-48 mph between 12:42 and 12:47 PM; Galaxias moored 200 feet above Oriole on the same dock had no difficulty. There was no evidence of wind damage at Todd's yard nor of unusual wind damage in the New Orleans area on January 10th.

As a wharfinger entrusted with sole and exclusive custody and control of the unmanned dead ship, Todd was a bailee for hire. <u>Buntin v Fletchas</u> [M16-13] Although not an insurer, it had a duty to use reasonable diligence to ascertain the condition of the berth and the security of the mooring. It breached that duty by failing to maintain the dock in proper condition and in failing to secure the ship adequately in the face of impending bad weather.

A vessel which drifts into collision is presumed to be at fault, and a breakaway, such as this, shows prima facie negligence. However, the evidence rebuts a presumption of Oriole's fault. Its care and custody was given to Todd a month before the breakaway, and the ship is not responsible for Todd's failure to take adequate mooring precautions in face of the known weather forecast. Thus, Todd solely was at fault. It failed to establish vis major or Act of God despite substantial wind gusts contemporaneous with the breakaway. The weather was not so catastrophic as to preclude precautionary measures in securing the ship.

Ch. B17 MARITIME LIENS

NECESSARIES [M17-8, add:]

When does a repair lien adhere to a vessel? In Pan American Bank of Miami v O/S Denise, (CA Fla 1980) 613 F 2d 599, the bank's loans to Marine Exploration Co. were secured by first preferred ship's fleet mortgages under which Marine was required to maintain certain financial strength which it violated. Marine also violated terms by virtue of Tracor Marine having placed a repair lien on its vessel Tammy W. The bank foreclosed in admiralty and Tracor intervened to assert the claim in rem against Tammy W. The bank got judgment against Marine in personam, against several Marine vessels in rem, and Tracor got a judgment in rem against Tammy W.

The appeal questioned whether the maritime lien attached to Tammy W when it left the Tracor yard after repairs, which was before suit was filed, or later after suit was filed.

The court held the lien attached when Tammy W left Tracor's custody with the repair bill unpaid. The mortgage expressly prohibited the imposition of a lien against the vessel other than to the mortgagee or for crew's wages or salvage. This was consistent with the Ship Mortgage Act which provides for enforcement in rem upon default of any terms or conditions of the mortgage. Any arrangement for payment to Tracor at a later date would be material to the time when Tracor's lien might be enforced, but not when it came into being.

TIMELINESS OF CLAIMS [M17-13, add after 2nd paragraph:]

In the order of priorities of claims, diligence in enforcement at law was held to be an intervening factor in Salina Mfg. Co. v Diner's Club, Inc., (Fla App 1980) 382 So 2d 1309.

Diner's issued execution to the sheriff in October 1972 on its $5100 judgment against Newton. Salina issued execution in September 1973 on its $2300 judgment against Newton. Diner's did nothing more, but Salina learned by its discovery proceedings that Newton bought a boat on October 1975 with his own funds but took title in the name of Newton and his wife by the entireties, so it was subject to the writs of execution. Salina filed supplementary proceedings in April 1978, and in December the court voided the transfer in the joint names and directed the sheriff to sell the boat to satisfy Salina.

When the sheriff advertised the sale, Diner's, after doing nothing for 6 years, petitioned the court for priority over the Salina execution which the court granted, allowing Diner's to bit its judgment amount at the sale but requiring others to make cash bids. Diner's bid in the boat at $4000, Salina appealed.

The appellate court reversed. As against third parties

(Diner's), Salina's supplementary proceedings, regarded as a substitute for a creditor's bill to reach Newton's equitable interest in the boat, created a lien in Salina against that equitable interest which adhered upon commencement of that proceeding and was perfected upon the issuance of that judgment. Salina, as the diligent creditor who discovered and brought in the equitable asset, is entitled to priority over all other creditors with inclusion of its costs and expenses of suit. Thus, Salina was entitled to recover from the $4000 in Diner's hands the amount of its $2300 judgment, interest, and costs expended in the supplementary proceedings.

[Note, however, the general principle that, between two or more judgment creditors, priority of payment from property subject to writs of execution (legal rather than equitable process) is determined by the order of receipt by the sheriff of writs of execution.]

RESCUE AND PURSUIT OF PROPERTY   [A17-4, add]

Of passing interest, Florida enacted F.S. 861.045 criminalizing a boat operator's flight or attempt to elude a law enforcement officer after direction to stop. [See B5-4]

MARSHAL'S COSTS   [A17-4, add:]

A state court equally was concerned over the extraordinary expense of securing a vessel in judicial custody and the assurance of due process for debtor in Vintero Sales Corp. v Marsh & McLennan, Inc., (Ala 1979) 367 So 2d 461. Vintero insured Bonair Star through Marsh & McLennan who attached the vessel in their suit in state court for unpaid premiums. The sheriff would not take actual custody and guard it, so M&M nominated Mobile Protective Service as bailee for that purpose, but no court approval was obtained. The cost for 24 hour guarding for 6 months was $19,152. Also, M&M took out Hull and Machinery (Port Risk) and Increased Value insurance of $5,600,000, naming itself as loss payee for which the 6 month premium was $52,052, also without court approval. Vintero objected to the taxing against it of the guard service and insurance expenses.

Noting that Alabama and Federal §54(d) Rules of Civil Procedure relating to costs were substantially identical, the court held that where costs are substantial and will increase significantly the ultimate expense of a lawsuit, court approval must be obtained before expenses are incurred if they are to be taxed as costs. This allows the court to assure that expenses other than those routinely incidental to litigation, and where there is no express statutory authorization, shall be only those reasonably and necessarily incurred. It enables the opponent, who alternately may bear the expense, to suggest less expensive alternatives.

M&M insured the vessel for its full value, when its

interest was for a smaller amount, to shield it from possible liability for damage or destruction. This expense rivaled the judgment itself, but Vintero never had an opportunity to suggest alternatives or to object to the type and amount of insurance.

The guard service was necessary, for the sheriff otherwise would not have attached the vessel. Here the failure to obtain prior approval was understandable, but it is essential that the court maintain control over custodial expenses.

Being a case of first impression, it is remanded to the lower court for a hearing on the reasonableness of the insurance premiums and guard expenses, and the determination of which party shall bear the entire burden of these costs or of a prorata portion.

The court examined due process in the vessel arrest in Karl Senner, Inc. v M/V Arcadian Valor, (DC La 1980) 485 F Supp 287. Senner directed the U.S. Marshal, under Admiralty Supplementary Rule C, to arrest Valor for enforcement of a maritime lien for services rendered. The owner, Arcadian Offshore, was joined in the action in personam. Defendants challenged the constitutionality of Rule C for deprivation of property without due process of law for lack of notice and right to be heard.

The court granted the motion to dismiss the in rem proceeding against the vessel, but emphasized the feature of in personam jurisdiction over the owner as distinguished from the traditional view most recently stated in Hjalmar Bjorges Rederi v Tug Condor, (DC Cal 1979) 1979 AMC 1696, in which the Fuentes [M6-3] conditions of due process were found to be satisfied because:

1) The arrest procedure was an integral and necessary feature throughout the history of maritime law;

2) Arrest was necessary to get jurisdiction and provide a forum for maritime claims because of the mobile and international character of shipping;

3) Prompt action peculiar to admiralty was needed;

4) Governmental interest in admiralty procedures far exceeds that involved in garnishment proceedings.

But Condor did not explain the justification for these conclusions, and this court now held that the seizure under Rule C failed to comport with basic concepts of due process where the court has personal jurisdiction of the vessel owners and seizure of the vessel in rem is done without prior notice or judicial intervention. To do otherwise would amount to a finding that due process stops at the water's edge.

Rule C is overbroad for indiscriminate application for seizure of all vessels without regard for factual distinctions. With personal jurisdiction, there is no basis to ignore fundamental due process. This arrest was to secure payment rather than to acquire jurisdiction.

The Supplementary Rules permit seizure of a vessel

merely under a warrant of arrest issued by a clerk upon the filing of a complaint containing merely conclusory allegations without notice to the owner or opportunity to be heard. No pre-seizure or judicial review is contemplated and no bond is required of complainant for protection of the owner.

Calero-Toledo [M15-8] indicated that acquisition of jurisdiction is not an end in itself unless done in aid of an important governmental or public interest; but when private interests are involved, as here, the situation is not unusual.

Due process was upheld in arrest of vessels in foreclosure of preferred ship mortgages where the owner had notice in Merchants Nat. Bank of Mobile v Dredge Gillespie, etc., (DC La 1980) 488 F Supp 1302. Several owning vessels involved in a gravel dredging operation pledged them under preferred ship mortgages for over $2,000,000. The mortgages were in default and the owners were unsuccessful in efforts to sell them to satisfy the mortgages and realize something on the balance. The Arlington was seized by the U.S. Marshal on May 25, 1979, the others July 19, 1979 in mortgage foreclosures in rem and in personam in admiralty. They were moored together on the Mississippi when several broke loose on April 10, 1980 and floated downriver and under the Vicksburg Bridge. Some were in a sunken or dilapidated condition, they were without routine maintenance and were subject to deterioration of hulls and engines, and they incurred $17,000 costs monthly during seizure. On August 27, 1979 the bank had requested interlocutory sale as to which hearing was held in December, but the owner of Gillespie moved to vacate the seizure for denial of due process by Admiralty Rule C authorizing seizure on filing a complaint.

The motion to vacate the seizure was denied. Due process is weighed in the individual case giving consideration to the functions involved and the considerations affected. These defendants were afforded due process protection, Fuentes [M6-7]. The foreclosures were filed for failure to make payments on principal indebtedness for a year. Local Rule 21 provided that defendants, upon showing an improper practice in manifest want of equity, could require the bank to show cause instanter why the attachment should not be vacated. After seizure July 19th, defendants requested and were granted a continuance to September 30th to retain local counsel to answer or otherwise plead. On August 27th the bank moved for interlocutory sale, defendants filed answer and counterclaim September 17th questioning constitutionality of involuntary prejudgement seizure under Rule C as to which the bank was given to October 27th to respond. Extensive discovery proceedings followed and a two day evidentiary hearing was held.

These defendants had ample notice of plaintiff's claims for the alleged mortgage payment defaults, but they made no request for judicial post-seizure consideration under Rule 21.

8 months elapsed since seizure, but the owners never posted bond, entered into any stipulation, or otherwise attempted to secure release of the vessels. They were not denied due process under the facts.

THE PREFERRED SHIP MORTGAGE   [M17-18, add:]

What goes wrong often illustrates better the elements of an idea than what goes right. Such was Matter of Meredosia Harbor & Fleeting Service, Inc., (CA Ill 1976) 545 F 2d 583. In 1970 Rasco formed Meredosia Harbor & Fleeting Service, Inc., also its wholly owned subsidiary River Road Marine Repair, Inc., to build and repair boats. They engaged in building a river tow boat and a harbor tow boat. To obtain funds, Rasco opened checking accounts in the corporate names and in his own name with Meredosia Bank and Rushville Bank, as also with another Illinois bank and an Oklahoma bank. He began kiting checks among these banks which was discovered by Meredosia Bank in early September 1970.

Neither of Rasco's corporations ever had any paid in capital, neither issued any stock, and both were insolvent in early September 1970. Meredosia Bank was aware of the check kiting in July and Rushville realized in early September that Rasco was insolvent and overdrawn.

On October 1, 1970 River Road mortgaged the two unfinished boats to these two banks to secure pre-existing debts of $300,000 and $170,000 for cash advanced. The affidavit of Rasco attached to the mortgage stated, as president of River Road, that the mortgage was made in good faith without any design to hinder, delay or defraud any existing or future creditors. On November 16, 1970 both corporations filed plans of arrangement but were declared bankrupt on January 4, 1971, and the bankruptcy referee, without objection, ordered sale of the two uncompleted vessels. One brought $21,000, the other with other property brought $25,000.

The two banks claimed the vessels or the sale proceeds. In denying their claims, the referee found that the mortgage was given for an antecedent debt of $300,000 caused by the check-kiting, the bankrupts were hopelessly insolvent at the time, the mortgage was void as a preference; also the mortgage was invalid for lack of a proper supporting affidavit and because both vessels were incomplete at the time. The claims of both banks were allowed only as general unsecured claims.

The district judge affirmed and held there was no valid preferred ship mortgage because Rasco's affidavit was not made in good faith; also, the banks had only a voidable preference because they had reasonable cause to believe River Road was insolvent at the time of mortgaging.

The Court of Appeals affirmed. The property passed into the custody of the bankruptcy court on the date of bankruptcy adjudication. Having first obtained custody, it had jurisdiction to determine all lien claims against the vessels and the validity of the maritime mortgage even though not a court of admiralty. The affidavit, for validity, had to comply with statutory requirements. Here the "good faith" affidavit required by 46 USC §922, necessary for preferred status under §953, was made in bad faith. As to the argument by the banks that recourse thus should be sought against Rasco rather than to impair the status of the mortgage, the statute requires good faith in the mortgage transaction and in the mortgagees, which will be defeated by bad faith. There was connivance between the bank officers and Rasco to create a status preferred above other creditors which was a voidable act under the Bankruptcy Act. The court noted in passing that the documentation of the uncompleted vessels was fraudulent.

Ch. B18 SALVAGE

THE FAIR WEATHER TOW   [M18-5, add after SALVAGE AWARD ELEMENTS]

In W.P.L. Services, Inc. v Bisso Towboat Co., Inc., (CA La 1979) 598 F 2d 417, the Alma S grounded at its mooring during the night. The Jerri Watson undertook to assist, and suddenly Alma broke free and drifted behind Jerri. The sudden movement and the abrupt change in the aspect of the two vessels resulted in Alma pulling-over Jerri which flooded and sank. Jerri's owner sued Alma's owner and contended that salvage law applied.

The claim was dismissed. A salvage claim involves a marine peril, a voluntary service to assist, and success in whole or in part in saving the vessel or in contributing to that success. Here there was no marine peril. Alma had run aground previously under similar circumstances and it could have broken free without assistance. Such groundings were considered insignificant events, and the assistance by Jerri was routine courtesy by one vessel to another. Alma, while moving backwards, could not have anticipated that Jerri would not have taken the normally expected precaution of casting off the towline or turning to eliminate the possibility of sinking.

CONSERVATION v SALVAGE   [M18-18, add after DERELICTS:]

As in U.S. v Mitchell [A19-5], an administrative hazard arose to confront a salvor in U.S. v Alexander, (CA Fla 1979) 602 F 2d 1228. On May 18, 1977 a shrimper stranded on a coral reef at Looe Key about 30 miles off Key West. Nobody came forward to claim the abandoned vessel. While the Coast Guard removed 300 bales of marijuana on the 19th, defendant, a commercial salvor with 30 years experience in the Keys, approached with his salvage barge and radioed the Coast Guard that he would salvage the vessel.

After several days during which the wreck shifted from atop a reef into a groove between two reefs, he removed the electronic equipment and propeller. Later he removed the generator and diesel engine.

Allegedly, he damaged the coral reef on two occasions: About May 24th, in an effort to get at the engine, he cut a boom with an acetylene torch as it lay across the engine after which it fell and broke nearby coral. Then, on removing the engine about May 30th, he caused a long scrape in the coral ridge. He was charged with criminal violation of 43 CFR § 6224.1-1 on both counts for that, without first having obtained a permit, he damaged a viable coral community on the Outer Continental Shelf, this being a regulation promulgated under 43 USC §1334(a) of the Outer Continental Shelf Lands Act. He admitted cutting the pipe and removing the engine, but denied

causing any damage to the coral. He sought to show at the
trial that his salvage operation was an emergency action taken
to preserve property inasmuch as the permit requirement under
43 CFR §6224.4 does not apply to emergency activities taken to
save human lives or property jeopardized at sea, and the valuable engine would have been destroyed within 3 or 4 weeks which
would have occurred long before a permit could have been obtained. The trial judge refused to allow this defense to be
raised, and the jury convicted on both counts.

The Court of Appeals reversed. The enabling portion of
the Act provides that the Secretary of Interior shall administer provisions relating to the leasing of OCS lands and prescribe attendant rules and regulations for prevention of
waste and conservation of its natural resources; and such
rules and regulations shall apply to all operations conducted
under a lease issued. It deals with oil and gas transactions
and operations on submerged lands. This language, in context,
relates only to OCS mineral leases. Thus, the Secretary could
regulate damage to coral by OCS lessees or others engaged in
operations substantially related to mineral activities; but
the section does not give the Secretary authority to promulgate conservationist measures regulating other activities such
as these salvage operations that have nothing to do with mineral leases. This was not an independent source of regulatory
authority. By making these regulations applicable expressly
to leasing operations, Congress intended to exclude their application to other unrelated operations. Where Congress has
acted in other instances to preserve the marine environment,
it has enacted specific conservation statutes, typically
under Title 16, the conservation title of the U.S. Code.

Furthermore, the permit scheme is inconsistent with
43 USC §1332(b) which provides that the Act shall be construed
in such manner that the character as high seas of the waters
above the Continental Shelf and the right to navigation and
fishing shall not be affected. A prudent party who operated
in the high seas over a coral reef could not know in advance
if he might damage coral, so he would have to obtain a protective permit in advance - a 60 day procedure - which would
affect the right to navigation and fishing. This, therefore,
is beyond the scope of the Act, and the Secretary exceeded
his authority in attempting to regulate the activities of
this marine salvor. Preservation of the marine environment,
when coupled with due consideration for other legitimate competing interest, is a proper concern of Government, but it is
for Congress to make that determination by means of explicit
statutory authority.

FLORIDA SALVAGE JURISDICTION   [A18-1, add:]

O'Neill v Schoenbrod, (Fla App 1979) 374 So 2d 70, continued its appellate course after dismissal of the salvage claim because exclusive jurisdiction resided in a court of admiralty. [Note: The first appeal as reported in A18-1 actually was based on salvage under the saving to suitors clause, not unjust enrichment.] Now plaintiff filed a complaint for the salvage service based on unjust enrichment.

The appellate court dismissed this complaint for being nothing more than a disguised salvage claim over which the court had declined jurisdiction. Technical differences between the two kinds of claims were of gossamer strength. It was completely inadvisable to authorize the bringing of a kind of limited salvage claim under the heading of unjust enrichment, for it would invite confusion and unnecessary state-federal jurisdictional conflict.

DOUBLE STANDARD

As a fabricated proposition, a commercial boat and crew rendering a salvage service to a pleasure boat may be considered for a traditional liberal salvage award, but the converse apparently is not true. This is not to say that the pleasure boat and its complement never will be considered, or the award will be none; the liberality probably will be lacking. Such a sweeping statement does not appear in a reported decision; it evolves from an examination of derivative thinking appearing in salvage law. Let's trace it.

In the first O'Neill appeal [A18-1] wherein the court held that salvage was peculiarly within the jurisdiction of admiralty court because, among other things, of the peculiar system of awarding compensation, it did not elucidate, but it refused to be drawn into this area of law. Norris' Law of Salvage states, at page 18, that salvage cases were not tried in American common law courts before the establishment of the United States; thus, the saving to suitors clause [M2-3 ADMIRALTY - THE LAW] did not give common law courts a jurisdiction over this class of cases it never had possessed.

The Right of a Volunteer Agent against his Principal in Roman Law and in Anglo-American Law by R.J. Heilman, 4 Tenn. L.R. 34, examines certain classes of voluntary actions and the expectation of compensation. The right arises from negotiorum gestis (uncommissioned agency) which occurs when one person acts for another without previous authority. For our interest, it quotes, at page 83, from the English case of Falcke v Scottish Imperial Ins. Co., (1886) L.R. 34 Ch. D 234, at 248:

"The general principle is, beyond all question, that work and labour done or money expended by one man to preserve or benefit the property of another do not according to English law create any lien upon the property saved or benefitted, nor, even if standing alone, create any obligation to repay the expenditure. Liabilities are not to be forced upon people behind their backs any more than you can confer a benefit upon a man against his will."

"There is an exception to this proposition in the maritime law. * * * With regard to salvage, general average, and contribution, the maritime law differs from the common law. That has been so from the time of the Roman law downwards. The maritime law, for the purposes of public policy and for the advantage of trade, imposes in these cases, a liability upon the thing saved, a liability which is a special consequence arising out of the character of mercantile enterprises, the nature of sea perils, and the fact that the thing saved was saved under great stress and exceptional circumstances. No similar doctrine applies to things lost upon land, nor to anything except ships or goods in peril at sea."

The law of unjust enrichment is part of the law of restitution. In Restatement of the Law of Restitution, §117 Preservation of Another's Things on Credit, states at page 491: "A statement of the rules of admiralty relating to salvage is not within the scope of the Restatement on this Subject." So much for the O'Neill court's refusal to combine the law of unjust enrichment into the law of salvage in any guise.

What of the peculiar system of awarding compensation in salvage cases? Norris discusses the type of persons who may be entitled to a salvage award. He indicates kinds of landsmen (page 91) and others who are salvors, noting that neither sex nor age has a bearing, and women and a boy have been held to be salvors. As to principles considered in making awards, he states at page 375:

"There is no set rule or fixed formula by which a salvage award can be determined. Most courts find little difficulty in ascertaining whether or not the service rendered was that of salvage, but the determination of the amount of a just and proper award is quite often a very troublesome matter."

His discussion of ingredients comprising the salvage award (page 376) leads directly to The Blackwall [M18-4] at which point we need go no further than review our own chapter on salvage to understand the second refusal of the O'Neill court to become involved in this peculiar system of awarding compensation.

Now the double standard concept emerges. Turning to the Small Boat Law Laboratory [M1-1]: On a Sunday afternoon, one of our students crossed the Gulf Stream from the Bahamas in a sailboat. About 10 miles off Miami he came upon a 65 foot party fishing boat dead in the water with engine trouble. The radio was out. Wind was high, water was rough. There was no way the sailboat could tow the party boat, so the student radioed Coast Guard Miami which dispatched a commercial towboat while the sailboat stood by for several hours. Would this support a salvage claim? Yes. Any personal injuries or damage to the sailboat's hull or gear? "No, we just stood off, waited, and got bounced around in the rough water while the sails got torn up." Cost of sail repairs? "Nothing.

Any ragman, to keep from going broke, must learn to make sail repairs. We did it ourselves. We used a little gas, but it was negligible."

These facts will support a salvage claim, but a substantial award would not be a good prospect. A judge does not keep a bag of awards from which he plucks plums. The claimant must present demands for evaluation, yet the most important loss to the student was the intrusion into his recreational activity, and this item is problematical as we have seen in Seemann v Berger [A10-2].

In contrast, consider this story: The father of a legal secretary owned a 40 foot cruiser. It had seen better days, but he cherished it until, one bright Sunday afternoon on Biscayne Bay, it began to fill with water, and he radioed the Coast Guard. Instead of the Coast Guard, an open boat drew alongside almost immediately. It carried some men in wetsuits with an assortment of strange-looking gear, and they asked if he needed help. They went overside and stopped the leak in a matter of minutes. He was outraged when the mail brought their bill for $50. She inquired upon the outrage; Answer: Don't argue, pay the bill, get a general release.

These men were licensed Florida wreckers [see In Re Andrews, M19-3]. They made their livlihood among other things, by swift radio response to emergencies such as this for which they maintained a substantial investment in their vessel and its specialized equipment. Their experience was inevitable, their skill was demonstrated, the result was beneficial, the sustained expense for their ongoing operation was obvious. Biscayne Bay is a large body of water with most of it on top, but three or four feet of it inside the hull of a 40 foot cruiser, debilitated though it may have been, had to cause substantial financial loss. Routine though this incident may have been to them, a $50 payment appeared to be a good alternative to admiralty court litigation.

Beneficial to our inquiry are some 1000 cases tabulated in Norris in 159 pages under 12 salvage service categories. They date from 1790 to 1972. While not exhaustive, the list is representative, and only four cases reflect salvage service by those not involved with a commercial activity:

In the towing category, in an 1883 case the Yacht Mary salved the SS Carrie which leaked and was abandoned in the James River. Time spent was 2 or 3 hours, value of property saved was $2400, the award was $600.

In a 1926 case, a boathouse and three yachts were swept by flood in Union River in Maine. Yachts Kalmia, Duchess and Normanda were valued at $25,000, $20,000, and $15,000 respectively. They were retrieved by individial salvors over a span of 23 days for which there was an award of $3600.

In a 1919 case in the stranding group, five miles off Long Key, Florida, the motorboat Cossier carried out two anchors of the bark Boildieu, spent four hours, then left. There was no award because there was no contribution to the floating of the bark.

In a 1908 case in the miscellaneous group, two small boats spent a day assisting the barge New Haven off Cowls Point, Conn. The court made no award because no benefit was conferred in securing the vessel.

A 5th case, <u>Dominguez v Schooner Brindicate</u>, is given at our M18-9.

In <u>Cram v Steam Tug Whiz and Barge Joe</u>, (DC La 1927), 1927 AMC 573, a case not included in the list, on March 13, 1924 Whiz and Joe operated as an auto ferry across Atchafalaya River. 7 automobiles were aboard Joe when a squall struck suddenly against which Whiz had insufficient power to withstand and make headway. Drifting toward the railroad bridge, the captain blew for help and the motorboat L.J. responded. Its small additional power was sufficient to hold against the wind until a larger vessel helped tow the ferry to safety. The court found that Cram in the L.J. undoubtedly prevented a collision with the railroad bridge. Values involved were Whiz $1250, Joe $800, and L.J. $800. The court awarded Cram $300 for a salvage service of a moderate order. The suit in rem was restricted to property actually seized; therefore, no award could be made for salvaging the cargo of automobiles.

These investigations show slight expectation of liberal salvage awards to pleasure boatmen without undue bias. Some recreational boatmen, by long and sustained devotion to their pastime, learn care and skills far exceeding some of their commercial brethren, but certain physical differences usually will affect the operations - size and weight of the salvaging vessel, mechanical power, and diversity and sophistication of gear and equipment available in the emergency. Likely, there is a difference in manpower available to meet certain situations. It would be redundant to reiterate each applicable factor in the Salvage chapter of Small Boat Law, but it is submitted that this exposition supplies a plausible explanation of the reason for the Double Standard. Above all, only an exceptional case will justify the high cost of litigation for a speculative and illiberal award.

Does the Double Standard obviate the justification for our study of salvage law? Hardly. To the extent that any vessel may be subject to a salvage award, an understanding of this law is necessary.

<u>FINDER'S RIGHTS</u>   [M18-24, add]

In <u>Weber Marine, Inc. v One Large Cast Steel Stockless Anchor</u>, (DC La 1979) 478 F Supp 973, Weber found a 30,000 pound anchor in the Mississippi River and tried to locate the owner by notifying Corps of Engineers, Coast Guard and various marine associations, without result. It then filed this proceeding for any interested party to answer, and that it be declared the owner or be given a salvage award. After advertising in the newspaper, a default was entered.

Weber contended it became owner by abandonment, but the court held that the mere fact of discovery and inability to locate the owner were insufficient to constitute abandonment. These facts entitled plaintiff only to a salvage award and a lien on the property for that amount, and a marshal's sale to provide funds for compensation. If undistributed funds remained after sale, the balance would be deposited in the registry of the court for a year and a day. If no owner appeared within that period, the deposit would be paid to Weber.

A normal find with strict regulatory effect appeared in Peterson v Diaz, (Fla App 1980) 379 F 2d 990. On November 11, 1977 Peterson, Favor and Young found a camera case in a restaurant where they were employed in a hotel in Miami. It contained $17,215 in U.S. and Canadian currency, and hashish oil, and it was turned over to the Dade County Public Safety Department. On May 30, 1978 Young filed an action for return to her of the money. On January 11, 1979 Diaz, a Chilean resident, intervened in the case to claim rightful ownership of the currency for return to him.

He had reported the loss to the hotel prior to its finding, and he made no further inquiry or claim until December 10, 1978 some 13 months after the property was found. The court entered a summary judgment for Diaz because his claim made on the day following the loss of the currency satisfied the requirement of F.S. 715.01 as to calling for or claiming the property within 6 months after its finding.

The appellate court reversed. Claiming the property before it is found does not meet the statute which requires the rightful owner to call for or claim the property within 6 months _after_ its finding. The statute is a limitation on the common law, not an enlargement of it.

Ch. B19 FLORIDA SUNKEN TREASURE

[A19-3, after 4th paragraph, add:
     Florida v Treasure Salvors, Inc., (CA Fla 1980) 621 F 2d 1340 was a further appeal on the find of Atocha, and again the court reviewed its history. After a hurricane broke up the Spanish treasure fleet, 8 ships foundering, a Spanish salvage fleet tried to salvage Atocha at a 55 foot depth with its masts above water. A second hurricane scattered the salvage fleet, broke up Atocha, and scattered its remains over the sea floor. Hostile activities ended a 20 year search for more than 3 centuries when research by Salvors led it to the location 40 miles west of Key West. Believing it to be in Florida waters, Salvors executed a series of salvage contracts [M19-2] with the State which received 25% of the finds until the decision of U.S. v Florida [M2-12, (1976)] which determined that Florida never had an interest in lands here involved, and Salvors sued in rem for possession or confirmation of title to Atocha. After the U.S. intervened with Florida's assistance, the court ruled for Salvors and directed the U.S. Marshal to take custody of all property, which Florida resisted.
     On this appeal, Florida contended that this court lacked jurisdiction under the 11th Amendment which provided that federal court jurisdiction did not extend to suits against a State by citizens of another State or foreign State; and if Florida owned the artifacts, then the court's attempt to adjudicate ownership was a suit against the State. However, said the court, on Salvor's challenge of Florida's title, there was no presumptive title in Florida, and the court had to consider jurisdiction which was intertwined with the merits of the case; thus, the court determined it had jurisdiction.
     The Court of Appeals affirmed the trial court's conclusion that Florida had no interest in this treasure. The salvage contracts assumed situs on State lands, but after the Supreme Court decision which adjudicated otherwise, the contracts were void for mutual mistake without which the contracts never would have been made. Also applicable is the common law doctrine of failure of consideration. The promise to pay a 25% share of the finds in return for the right to conduct salvage operations on lands in which the State had no interest was a promise without legal support, and Salvors, upon discovery of this state of affairs, was free to rescind the agreement and recover what it had paid.

Ch. B20 SEAWORTHINESS

IMPROPER MAINTENANCE   [M20-14, add:]

Another condition which renders a vessel unfit for the intended use is improper maintenance. In Cargill, Inc. v Taylor Towing Service Inc., (DC Mo 1979) 483 F Supp 1094, plaintiff engaged defendant's tug to move grain barges. The tug needed repairs and operated on one 225 hp engine, the twin being out of service. The tug lost control of the tow a few hundred yards up the Mississippi, wind and current shoved the head of the tow toward the river bank, the tug's rudder had insufficient effect to maneuver with only one propeller, the barge and tug were pushed back downriver, and they struck and destroyed plaintiff's river dock facility.

The court held the tug to be unseaworthy at the time which proximately caused the damage to the loading facility for which defendant was liable. Defendant, for its privity and knowledge, was not qualified to limit liability.

IMPROPER NAVIGATIONAL PRACTICE

In Complaint of Thebes Shipping Inc., (DC NY 1980) 486 F Supp 436, after Argo Merchant ran aground 25 miles off Nantucket Island December 15, 1976 and broke in two, spilling its fuel oil cargo into the ocean, numerous claims were filed against the owner which sought exoneration from or limitation of liability. The court found the vessel was 21 miles off course at the time of grounding.

The court then found the vessel to be unseaworthy for the improper navigational practice of failing to maintain the gyro compass. The owner had ample notice but took no corrective action. The radio direction finder dated from 1953 when the vessel was built. Its components were water-intruded, corroded, and the cables would have been replaced. Short circuits were potential at any time. This unseaworthiness was a contributing cause of the grounding. A calibration curve was required to be made at least every 12 months, but its latest was of May 8, 1975. Not only was it out of date, but evidence showed it to be a total fabrication which was gross misconduct in the management of the ship.

Aboard, the pilot chart for November depicted currents in the area which were different from those of the pilot chart for December. The outdated pilot chart was a factor causing the ship to steer off its proper course. The lack of a current pilot chart was an unseaworthy condition which contributed to the grounding, and the owner failed to show reasonable efforts to provide an up-to-date chart.

The causes of the grounding were general mismanagement and neglect by the owner combined with navigational errors by the officers during the voyage. The casualty occurred with privity and knowledge of the owner. Limitation of liability was denied.

UNSAFE WORK PROCEDURES

A variety of deficient work procedures were encompassed in Vargas v McNamara, (CA Mass 1979) 608 F 2d 15. Plaintiffs were seamen employed by defendant in contemplation of a fishing trip. Defendant brought his vessel to Cape Cod Marine Service where repair work was to be done. He instructed plaintiffs to clean the engine room and he provided equipment consisting of hose and spray gun, and an unlabeled 5 gallon bucket of Verisol cleaning agent and steam cleaner which he got from Cape Cod Marine. It was not known if Cape Cod provided information on the cleaning component or precautions to be taken.

In accordance with defendant's instructions, plaintiffs sprayed an area of the engine room with Verisol, scraped the grime, then applied the steam cleaner, working without respirators or other equipment to offset toxic fumes. When the engine room filled with steam, they coughed and had difficulty breathing. They took frequent fresh air breaks but their symptoms worsened, and they became disabled from working for a period of time. They sued McNamara and Cape Cod for negligence. Their expert testified that Verisol is a toxic industrial solvent which is particularly hazardous in spray form because droplets are absorbed into the respiratory system if no respirator is worn.

The trial court granted defendants a directed verdict for lack of plaintiffs' prima facie case. There was no evidence that defendants knew or should have known the toxic qualities of Verisol or the circumstances governing its use, and there was no evidence Cape Cod furnished incorrect information or failed to pass along what it had. The court then raised the question of unseaworthiness but refused to allow amendment of the complaint to include that because the evidence failed to show it.

The Court of Appeals vacated McNamara's judgment and remanded for consideration of an unseaworthiness count. There was sufficient evidence to find unseaworthiness such as may arise from an unsafe method of work from failure to provide adequate or necessary safety equipment. Propriety of use of a toxic solvent in spray form in a poorly ventilated room is questionable, and a fact-finder might conclude at the very least that protective masks should have been provided. McNamara's knowledge would be irrelevant, for liability under unseaworthiness principles is not dependent upon fault. Trawler Racer [M20-13].

THE JONES ACT [M20-16, add after Hopson v Texaco:]

In Brown v Stanwick International, Inc., (Fla App 1979) 367 So 2d 241, Brown was injured riding a motorcycle in Iran when he swerved to avoid a truck. He sued his employer for maintenance and cure, Jones Act negligence, unseaworthiness, and breach of contract of employment for watch and standby duties on the Imperial Iranian Ship Chah Bahar stationed at Bandar Abbas; also, he was to train Iranian personnel and perform other assignments for Stanwick. Stanwick was to provide living accommodations aboard.

The ship's boiler room was inoperative and it received power from an electrical shore tie. He started work on the boilers to make them operational, but this never was completed. The ship was used extensively to repair other Iranian ships and it trained Iranian personnel in that regard. It was uninhabitable because of vermin, and the employees were moved to a team house 10 kilometers away from which they commuted to the ship. Brown was instructed to repair the boiler at the team house, and he was seriously injured on the way.

Brown claimed seaman status engaged in the service of his vessel at the time of accident based on failure to maintain habitable or "seaworthy" living quarters aboard the ship. The trial court granted summary judgment against him.

The appellate reversed in part, and remanded. There was a jury question whether he was a seaman at the time of accident. He had a more or less permanent connection with the vessel, his duties contributed to the vessel's mission, and they were those traditionally performed by seamen. It was a jury question if the vessel, on lease from the United States, was in navigation. Many cases hold that unseaworthiness and Jones Act benefits apply to special purpose structures without motive power and do not perform the conventional functions as a means of transportation by water but which perform a water-based function as being "in navigation". As a functioning repair ship and naval training facility riding in navigable waters, a jury could find that this ship met such a test. He was injured in the service of his ship while going to repair the crew's living quarters. If a jury should find him a seaman, he would be entitled to maintenance and cure.

However, although Brown might have the seaman's right to sue under the Jones Act and for unseaworthiness, he cannot recover under Jones Act liability as that requires a showing of negligence by the employer; unseaworthiness requires a showing of breach of warranty of the vessel's seaworthiness; and both require a causal link between the deficient condition and the casualty. The only relationship between the accident and a lack of shipboard living quarters is a "but for" condition of the vessel which is too remote from the trip to fix the boiler at the team house to be legally significant for the imposition of liability. Similarly, damages for breach of employment contract to provide living quarters aboard did not result in damages to Brown which would result naturally from the breach. The maintenance and cure count is reversed.

Ch. B21   PERSONAL INJURIES

STRICT LIABILITY IN TORT   [M21-7, add after West v Caterpillar:]

Obviousness of risk in product use was in issue in Hethcoat v Chevron Oil Co., (Fla App 1978) 364 So 2d 1243. Hy-Way manufactured a machine to heat asphalt by coils which circulated hot oil within the storage tank. A small integral furnace supplied the heat. The innerliner of the furnace deteriorated with the intended use during which combustible residue built up on the exposes surfaces. The innerliner had to be burned out with an acetylene flame for the designed replacement. The welder's oxygen rich flame caused an explosion of the volatiles present in the enclosed space, and it killed him.

His estate sued the manufacturer, the owner, and the manufacturer of the heat transfer oil because the design was defective. Also, there was no warning on the machine, nor in the manufacturer's literature, of the danger of applying a cutting torch without first purging the system by steam; thus, a manufacturer who markets a machine which inevitably requires maintenance involving a grave risk, but who does not warn of risks that cannot be eliminated, should be liable even to those whose vocational experience should be warning enough.

The court held there was no showing of a design defect. The fact of an injury while using or being near a machine does not impose liability, for virtually every machine is capable of being the instrument of hurt. The machine did not harm. The explosion resulted from exposing acetylene and oxygen to petroleum vapors. As to giving warning, there is no duty on a manufacturer for risks which should be known to an experienced user. To require a posted warning for every part subject to repair at grave risk would be impossible. West v Caterpillar Tractor Co. [M21-6] and Blackburn v Dorta [A21-1] never were intended to impose an impossible and unreasonable burden upon a manufacturer.

In Auburn Machine Works Co.,Inc. v Jones, (Fla 1979) 366 So 2d 1167, Jones was instructed by his supervisor of a crew laying underground telephone cable to enter the trench behind the trench digging machine to place the cable flat on the trench bottom. He lost his balance when the trench caved in, his foot tangled in the exposed machine chain, and his leg had to be amputated below the knee. The trencher had no shield and it was obviously dangerous.

His suit charged negligence, breach of warranty, strict liability for defective manufacture and design, failure to provide shields on exposed dangerous parts of the machine, lack of operator's field of view of dangerous moving parts, inadequate operation instructions, implied warranty of fitness for intended purpose and of safe design, unmerchantability for lack of safety devices, and strict liability in tort. The trial judge granted summary judgment in favor of Auburn, but the appellate court reversed and refused to apply the "patent danger" or "open and obvious hazard" doctrine which would shield the manufacturer from liability.

The Supreme Court affirmed the appellate court. "We reject the doctrine and hold that the obviousness of the hazard is not an exception to liability on the part of the manufacturer but rather is a defense by which the manufacturer may show that plaintiff did not exercise a reasonable degree of care as required by the circumstances." Comparative negligence will apply when the defense is raised. The modern trend in the nation is to abandon the strict patent danger doctrine as an exception to liability and to find that the obviousness of the defect is only a factor to be considered as a mitigating defense in determining whether a defect is unreasonably dangerous, and whether plaintiff used that degree of reasonable care required by the circumstances. The patent danger doctrine encourages manufacturers to be outrageous in their design, to eliminate safety devices, and to make hazards obvious. It protects manufacturers who sell negligently designed machines which pose formidable dangers to their users. It puts the entire accidental loss on the injured plaintiff notwithstanding the manufacturer's partial fault. "Accordingly, we reject the patent danger doctrine and conclude that it does not create an absolute exception to liability on the part of the manufacturer."

CRASHWORTHINESS   [A21-3, add:]

In our search for a boat case, Nicolodi v Harley-Davidson Motor Co., (Fla App 1979) #78-1089 draws us closer. Plaintiff was a passenger on a motorcycle manufactured by defendant which collided with a truck; she lost a leg. Her suit was based on the crashworthiness doctrine as applied to automobiles in Ford Motor Co. v Evancho, (Fla 1976) 327 So 2d 201, as being applicable also to motorcycles under counts for negligence, breach of implied warranty, and strict liability. There was no safety device to protect a passenger's legs in a collision. The trial court dismissed the complaint because a motorcycle is not within the conceptual ambit of crashworthiness.

The appellate court reversed. Defendant argued that the crashworthiness doctrine cannot be applied to a motorcycle because it is inherently unsafe for crashes. The court held crashworthiness to be an aspect of negligence principles. It extends to manufacturers of motorcycles as well as automobiles because foreseeability of involvement in an accident is its basis. For transportation purposes, a motorcycle is as much a motor vehicle as an automobile, and the scope of reasonably foreseeable use is the same (emphasis supplied). Crashworthiness applies to the motorcycle even without a secondary collision.

The negligence count charged defendant with a breach of duty of reasonable care to equip the motorcycle with a safety device to protect the legs from injury in an accident as reasonably might be foreseen; the implied warranty count raised reasonable fitness for ordinary use as a motorcycle in transporting a passenger with reasonable safety, and the failure to have a safety device for leg protection in a collision; the strict liability count charged marketing with a defect unreasonably dangerous to a passenger for lack of a protective safety device for protection of a passenger's legs in a collision. For all three counts, plaintiff is entitled to present to a jury the question whether defendant failed to use reasonable care, or breached its implied warranty of merchantability and manufactured an unreasonably dangerous product.

In *Cryts v Ford Motor Co.*, (Mo App 1978) 571 SW 2d 683, Cryts drove south in a 1957 Ford Thunderbird on a two lane access road adjacent to an Interstate. Unterdorfer drove north and, as they approached, he edged into the opposing lane, swerved back, disconcerted Cryts, and they crashed into each other. Cryts pitched forward and to the right, then back into the left armrest, and his broken back resulted in permanent paraplegia.

In his suit against Ford for defective design and Unterdorfer for negligence, his expert, Diboll, testified to two basic methods of energy absorption: (1) padded material to distribute the force of impact over an area rather than concentrate it at one point; (2) removal of protrusions to avoid concentration of high stress energy at a narrow point. He found the armrest was made of hard plastic covered by .11 of an inch padding, and its pointed shape concentrated energy absorbed by the body. Ford's expert testified that the armrest was to provide a handle to close the door, to be an armrest, and to prevent contact with door hardware in a collision. Furthermore, the design suggested by Diboll would not provide these functions, nor conform with federal regulations in effect at the time of trial (there were none in 1957, the accident occurred June 3, 1967).

Ford was held liable. In a product liability "second collision" as here, the manufacturer's liability is extended where construction or design of the product caused separate or enhanced injuries after an initial accident brought about by an independent cause. Plaintiff need prove only that the design was so defective as to make the product unreasonably dangerous for its anticipated use. Negligence, knowledge or fault of the manufacturer are irrelevant. The focus is on the dangerous condition of the product designed in a particular way. In a negligence case the concern is with the reasonableness of the manufacturer's action in designing the article. Thus, even though the designer's actions were reasonable in the light of what was known at the time the product was planned and sold, the product may be dangerous to a degree imposing strict liability.

Plaintiff had to prove the product was defective in condition or design when it left the manufacturer, that he was using the product in its intended manner, and that it was dangerous beyond the contemplation of a user having ordinary knowledge common to the community as to its characteristics. Testimony of plaintiff's expert reasonably justified a verdict that the armrest was defective and that it was unreasonably dangerous for its anticipated use.

Collision was a foreseeable incident of use of a motor vehicle. The question at hand was the defective condition of the product, not the manufacturer's knowledge, negligence or fault. The principles of energy absorption adduced by Diboll have been known for 300 years, and they could have been applied to the 1957 design even though there may not have been a governmental regulatory standard. A governmental standard will not mitigate strict liability unless it required the defective condition to exist. The 10 year age of the car is not relevant to shield the manufacturer from liability if the evidence showed the design to be unreasonably dangerous.

In Harris v Bardwell, (La App 1979) 373 So 2d 777, five weeks after plaintiff bought a boat, he cruised it with his daughter and a friend at 15-18 mph on Lake Bistineau. An insect hit his face, his flinch caused the boat to turn abruptly, the screws securing the pedestal of his seat pulled loose from the boat, he was thown in the water, and the propeller of the circling boat twice cut into his flesh and bone. When the boat struck a tree, the passengers got control of the boat and rescued him. He sued the seller and manufacturer.

The seat pedestal had six 1-1/2 inch sheet metal screws holding it to the 1/2 inch plywood floorboard covered with fiberglass. Below the floor was a 2 x 6 inch keelboard. Proper installation required that two of the six screws go into the keel while the other four simply went through the plywood; but none of these went into the keel. This was a high performance bass boat with 50 hp motor. Plaintiff's expert testified that the pedestal would come loose in an 18 foot diameter turn at 15 mph, or a 26 foot turn at 18 mph; and in either case, it was reasonably foreseeable that the occupant of the seat would be forcibly propelled from the seat if the screws pulled out. Under Louisiana law, a defective installation triggered liability.

The court upheld a $175,000 jury verdict against the manufacturer, but the seller was not liable. A seller who knows of defects or who, with reasonable inspection, can find obvious or apparent defects in the products he sells stands in a position similar to that of the manufacturer; but he does not have to make minute inspection or disassemble the product to look for latent defects. Unlike the manufacturer, he is not presumed to know the latent defects in the product he sells. None of the six screws that went into the floor (or keel) was detectable by naked eye inspection. In over 20 years sales experience, the seller never before experienced a pedestal failure. The defective installation was latent as undetectable by simple inspection. The verdict in favor of the seller was correct.

[M21-7, add after Frumer and Friedman:]

Any gasoline container case will be of interest in boating considerations. In Hurd v Munford, Inc., (Fla App 1979) 378 So 2d 86, Hurd, a minor, bought gas at defendant's Majik Market by pumping it into his own plastic milk carton. He put it in the family utility room without replacing the top of the carton. Four hours later he went there to get some clothing. Perhaps he did or did not knock over the carton, but the gasoline poured over his clothing, spread to the hot water heater, the pilot light ignited it, and he was burned severely.

He sued the market for breach of implied warranty, strict liability for a dangerous defective product, and negligence. The trial court directed verdicts against him on the first two counts, and the jury found in favor of defendants as to negligence. The trial judge opined that the sale involved only gasoline and did not include the carton supplied by Hurd so that there were no factual questions for the jury on that matter.

The appellate court affirmed. These facts were stated in an opinion by one judge who affirmed on the negligence count but dissented on the dismissal of the breach of implied warranty and strict liability counts: F.S. 526.141 requires self-service gasoline stations to have an attendant on duty when open and to prevent dispensing of gasoline in non-approved containers. The UCC implied warranty of merchantability requires goods to be adequately contained, packaged and labeled as the agreement may require. Thus, said the judge, by operation of law the retailer must be deemed to have supplied both the gasoline and container without which Hurd could not have bought the gas.

§402A, Restatement (Second) of Torts [M21-4] and West v Caterpillar Tractor Co. [M21-6] impose liability on one who sells a product in a defective condition unreasonably dangerous to the user. Where the container is dangerous, the seller is deemed to have sold the gas and container, so the product was sold in a defective condition. While Hurd may have been negligent in the use of the container, that would not bar a jury from deliberating on the question of strict liability and implied warranty.

Defendant's violation of the dispensing control of the statute was negligence, and the jury passed on this. Hurd contended that this violation imposed liability regardless of whether it proximately caused the injury. The statute, however, was intended to protect against a particular type of injury, not to protect against the inability of a class of persons (minors) to protect themselves.

EXTENDED MARKETING

The novel question of a manufacturer's liability for a casualty during a demonstration arose in Nat'l Bank of Mobile v Cessna Aircraft, (Ala 1978) 365 So 2d 966. The U.S. District Court for Alabama requested the Alabama Supreme Court to answer the question: Did the Alabama Extended Manufacturer's Liability Doctrine apply to injury or death from use of a defective product (aircraft) which was placed in commerce by demonstration although no sale of the product had been made?

Alabama had adopted the Doctrine which imputes negligence as a matter of law to a manufacturer, supplier, or seller who markets a product not reasonably safe when applied to its intended use in the usual or customary manner. Restatement of Torts 2nd, §402A on which the doctrine is based limits its principles to sales situations, but its policy supports the extension of liability to other situations such as marketing the product. This includes supplying market information, and the tendency of strict liability cases is to extend the liability in non-sale situations: demonstration of a fork-lift truck, lease of a truck, free sample to a prospective customer, free lacquer reducer furnished after sale.

The Alabama Supreme Court held, therefore, that when a product is placed in the "stream of commerce", whether by demonstration, lease, free sample, or sale, the Doctrine should attach. Profit is the motivation of each, whether or not a "sale" takes place. For consumer protection it is the manufacturer who is in the better position to know and correct defects in his product in accordance with the concept of strict liability.

DEATH ACTIONS [M21-9, add:]

In Sanders v Richmond, (Mo App 1979) 579 SW 2d 401, Sanders owned a 16 foot john-boat powered by a stern-mounted 20 hp motor. It did not have the running lights required by law, and between 10 and 11 PM he and his brother-in-law, Dillon, left the Missouri bank of the Mississippi River near Lake Shore to check trot lines at Two Branch Island. Sanders, wearing a camouflage jacket, operated the outboard motor from a swivel-type chair on the thwart just forward of the stern. On his head he carried a lighted reflector lamp like a miner's light. Dillon, wearing a reddish-orange life jacket, sat on a thwart ahead of Sanders and faced aft. It was necessary to cross the main channel of the Mississippi to reach Two Branch

Island in the middle of the river. Weather was clear, waters were calm

As the boat headed for the island at 12-15 mph, Dillon looked at Sanders' clubhouse astern which was near the dock they had left when he heard a thump and lost consciousness. He never heard the sound of another engine nor saw an approaching light. When he regained consciousness he saw Sanders in the stern, unconscious.

Richmond and a lady friend ran unriver from a restaurant at 18-20 mph in a 19 foot Sidewinder runabout powered by a 455 hp jet engine. His running lights were on as he ran on plane in the main channel. He sat and steered at the starboard side looking ahead. His guest sat on the port side, faced him, and looked out across the water. Just before the collision, Richmond saw a shadow to his left, but no lights. Damage photographs showed that the bow of the runabout at the waterline struck the starboard of the john-boat just ahead of Sanders' thwart.

Sanders' widow sued for his wrongful death and appealed a verdict and judgment against her. The appellate court reversed. The situs of the collision on the Mississippi was a navigable stream governed by navigation rules for Western Rivers. The Federal Boat Safety Act of 1971 preempted state law except where state boating safety programs are directed at implementing and supplementing the Act. Plaintiff brought her claim in state court as provided by the Missouri Wrongful Death Statute. This, however, did not deprive her of the benefits of admiralty law and expose her to a defense of contributory negligence under Missouri substantive law. Under Moragne [M21-7], the state court is required to apply federal maritime law in a cause for wrongful death on navigable waters in the state in whose court the remedy is pursued. Jurisdiction required that there be a maritime tort cognizable in admiralty which bore a significant relationship to traditional maritime activity. St. Hilaire Moye [M21-23] held that the operation of a pleasure craft meets this jurisdictional requirement.

GUESTS [M21-10, add:]

Armour v Gradler, (DC Pa 1978) 448 F Supp 741, is a classic of its kind, for it fulfills the search for the characteristic small boat "guest" liability case, touching upon every applicable element of law examined in the text and its cases. Thus, the case and text references will be given to integrate the doctrines considered. The painstaking skill of the court and counsel will emerge in this carefully litigated case.

At 8:00 PM September 9, 1972, Gradler and Armour left Presque Isle Marina in Erie on Gradler's boat Kamai, a 1967 30 foot Revelcraft Express Cruiser which was equipped with ship to shore radio. Gradler was the operator, Armour the guest. They were to fish and return by midnight. Small craft warnings were displayed at the Coast Guard Station which they had to pass in going to Lake Erie, and others in the marina who had larger boats cautioned Gradler about this, although the weather was clear at the time with 3 to 4 foot seas. But Gradler enjoyed rough water boating and he frequently exposed Kamai to rough seas.

At 1:35 AM Mrs. Gradler called the Coast Guard. Kamai did not answer its radio. A Coast Guard search expanded until the patrol found Kamai at 7:25 AM, submerged with cabin top visible just above the water. Nobody was aboard. At 12:45 PM the two dead bodies were found a considerable distance from Kamai, floating within 100 feet of each other in almost vertical position in life vests. They had suffered from exposure prior to death from asphyxiation.

Coast Guard examination showed that Kamai's half-inch plywood hull was split and set in on the bottom under the floorboards of the main cabin with screw fasteners torn out a considerable distance from the break which was 8 feet aft of the bow and 18 inches to the starboard side of the keel. Kamai was found in open water with no indication as to what obstacle, if any, it had encountered.

Mrs. Armour sued Mrs. Gradler in state court individually as co-owner of Kamai, as personal representative of her husband's estate, for personal injuries and death of Armour pursuant to the Pennsylvania Wrongful Death Act, for common law negligence, for violation of the Pennsylvania Motor Boat Law (55 P.S. §483), the Federal Boat Safety Act (46 USC §1451), the Jones Act (46 USC §688), later abandoned, and the general maritime law.

The case was removed to admiralty court where, after a non-jury trial, judgment was awarded to plaintiff. Armour's injuries and death took place on a vessel upon navigable waters which subject them to the jurisdiction and measuring standards of maritime law without regard to whether they be judged in state or federal court, Kermarec [M21-9], Branch v Schumann [M21-14], even though a non-commercial pleasure craft, St. Hilaire Moye [M21-23]. Admiralty jurisdiction having attached, maritime rather than common law standards of negligence will apply. [M21-2].

Plaintiff asserted liability for Gradler's breach of warranty of seaworthiness [M20-1,2]. The duty of seaworthiness is owed to a seaman which Armour was not. By the Kermarec case, however, a duty of care is owed to others aboard with the owner's consent. The intent to go fishing does not entitle Armour to the benefit of the seaworthiness doctrine until his seaman's status is established [see Read's Petition, M20-3]. There was no evidence that the craft required two people for safe operation. Although Armour was a boat owner and was familiar with elements of boat handling such as mooring, anchoring and casting-off, he did not come aboard for the

B21-8

purpose of aiding in navigation or performing crewman's duties.

As to negligence of Gradler under maritime law, he created an unreasonable risk. This included venturing onto the Lake when weather and sea conditions were such that going out with knowledge of the unseaworthy condition of his boat endangered the lives of those aboard. He knew of hull structure deficiencies that made the boat dangerous in rough water. When the boat was discovered, the floor boards were in place and undisturbed, and the Coast Guard removed them to expose the site of the leak. The hull had longitudinal girders running along each side of the keel 18 inches from it. They were connected to the keel by transverse strong backs which were 18 inches apart but not in contact with the plywood sheathing. Thus, there were unsupported plywood sheathing expanses of approximately 15 inches by 8 or 10 feet long.

Dr. Yagle, professor of naval architecture at the University of Michigan, testified as plaintiff's expert witness that large pressure load in the absence of framing allowed the hull to be displaced freely. This panting or flexing gradually delaminated the plywood causing its deterioration at an accelerated rate making it difficult and unsafe to maintain. Usual design has a skeleton which supports the sheathing and integrates it into the frame as a unit. But Kamai did not meet this standard because the unsupported panel, lacking contact with the framing, yielded to panting from water pressure at rest in still water and underway at high speeds with rough seas and continuous flexing of the wood. As the condition develops, the boat will not perform as a reasonably prudent boat operator would expect. He concluded that the damage in the area discussed was caused by an outside object striking the weakened hull sheathing causing a puncture. A strong hull would have more resistance and cause an object, such as a log, to roll under without penetration.

This opinion was supported by comments Gradler had made about the condition of the boat. He was an experienced carpenter and a building contractor by trade, and he was aware of Kamai's hull deficiencies. In September 1971 it partially sank at the dock which he reported to his insurer as having been caused by coming down on a log on the port side in rough waters. During the year following he examined the hull several times with Clarence Fleckinger, also an experienced boater and carpenter. They discussed the need for framing to prevent flexing in rough water, and Gradler expressed concern to Fleckinger about the bottom opening in rough seas. At various times he had discussed the unseaworthiness with Mrs. Fleckinger and its susceptibility to damage, especially in rough water. He knew debris frequently was encountered in Lake Erie, especially in a rough sea, to which Mrs. Gradler also testified.

Defendant's expert, Alanson Mang, a ship's carpenter, disagreed with respect to the excessive flexing. He found no unseaworthy condition due to the longitudinal construction, nor on visual examination of the boat on the eve of trial (the boat was salvaged, reconditioned, and sold twice, without incident. Thus, no sample piece was available for testing four years after the accident.). Although the hull would have been stronger if transverse members had been fastened to the skin, the lack of support did not create an unseaworthy condition. The hull at the time of his examination was sturdy and sound.

The court found Kamai to be unseaworthy at the time of departure from the marina. Gradler breached the duty of reasonable care he owed to Armour when he went onto the Lake under the conditions described with awareness of the frailty of his vessel. This was maritime negligence in violation of Federal Boat Safety Act §12(d) [MII-5] and proximately caused Armour's death.

As to the defense of limitation of liability, the court agreed that the Limitation Act [M23-1] should not be applicable in pleasure boat cases such as this, noting dicta in Richards v Blake [M21-26], but the courts have applied the Act. However, defendant is not entitled to consideration of such relief in this case because Gradler had knowledge [M23-1] of the dangerous condition and deficiencies in Kamai's hull which led to the casualty and drowning. He was not free of privity and knowledge of the occasion for the injury. But Mrs. Gradler was free of any liability for Armour's death. There was no showing of fault on her part and the negligence of her husband could not be imputed to her, so there was no need to consider the applicability of the Act to her.

The court went on to itemize damage elements against the estate which are illustrative, but beyond our interest.

A design defect case that looked extensively into proof is Wolff v Whittaker Marine & Mfg. Co., Inc., (DC Mo 1979) 484 F Supp 1021. Whittaker manufactured the 39 foot fiberglass houseboat Patty Kay in 1969 with twin 225 hp engines and a 6.5 automatic start generator. Port and starboard fuel tanks were located forward in the bilge with the water tank and generator.

On June 27, 1969 Deutsch leased Patty Kay from L&L Leasing Co. which bought it that day from Lake Center, Inc. which bought it on the 23rd from Whittaker. Deutsch had possession from June 27, 1969 to May 7, 1972 when it exploded at Lake Center Marina on the Mississippi. Deutsch and his son Charles boarded the boat which had not been moved since the end of the 1971 Fall boating season. They ran the engine and fuel compartment blowers for 10 minutes, started the engines, ran to the fuel dock 100 yards away, and shut down. Deutsch left the boat. Marina employee Kevin Bell handed the fuel hose to Charles who filled the tanks until the vent holes overflowed, then hosed down the spillage from the dock's water supply. He did not recall if he closed the doors and windows before fueling. Deutsch returned with Merle Bell to look into a balky engine problem. Between 30 and 60 minutes after fueling, Merle Bell switched on a cabin light, Deutsch actuated an electric stove burner, and the boat exploded and burned. The three managed to escape with serious burns from which Deutsch died May 22nd. His executor sued Whittaker for wrongful death on a theory of strict liability in tort.

Plaintiff alleged three defects: (1) A stress riser in the copper tubing at the end of the fuel line between the port tank and the main fuel line which caused a crack after three years of normal usage. (2) The connection nut on that line was tightened insufficiently at manufacture so that it loosened gradually until it leaked. (3) Siting the generator in the fuel compartment was inherently dangerous design because explosive vapors were likely to gather there. Defendant showed the boat had been in Deutsch's possession three years during which repairs had been made which altered its condition after leaving defendant.

The court entered judgment for defendant for failure of plaintiff's proof. A product malfunction is some proof of a defect, the existence of which plaintiff could show by circumstantial evidence without establishing any specific defect. But plaintiff's circumstantial evidence required negation of causes other than a product defect plus a showing that a product defect was introduced into the product by defendant. The standard of proof is not that beyond a reasonable doubt, but by a preponderence of evidence.

Thus, the crack in the fuel line, after expert testimony, could have been caused by the explosion, and it could have pre-existed the explosion. There was no evidence that the flare at the end of the tubing was made improperly, or that the fracture resulted from a manufacturing defect.

The connection nut which was found after the explosion to be only finger-tight was not likely to have been in that condition at manufacture three years earlier in view of expert testimony that a connection starting as finger-tight would have become even looser after three years to the point where it leaked. Also, the threads on the nut were more worn than those on the nut at the other end of the line which would indicate it was taken off and on several times. It is more probable that the nut was re-tightened insufficiently at some time after manufacture than at manufacture.

There was no evidence of unreasonably dangerous design. The testimony showed Patty Kay met standards of the American Boat & Yacht Council, National Fire Protection Association, and state of the art in the pleasure craft industry in allowing the placement of electrical equipment where flammable vapors are present. The generator complied with ABYC recommendations that it be placed as high above the bilges as possible.

The ventilation system was more than adequate. Vapor tight compartments and spark proof generators exist only on Navy vessels. The fuel lines were adequately designed to withstand vibration. There was no evidence that placement of the electric range in relation to the gas tanks was unreasonably dangerous or that the electrical system was defective. On the other hand, plaintiff did not negate negligent fueling procedure or tampering with the fuel lines and the finger-tight nut. This is failure of proof.

OVERHEAD POWER LINES   [A21-18, add after McKowen v Gulf States]

Foreseeability continues to control in Williams v City of Alexandria, (La App 1979) 376 So 2d 367. Williams was employed by Carbo Foundry. Lary Carbo told him to drive a crane to the front of the Foundry building so steel beams could be loaded on a flat-bed truck. Lovato, general foreman and crane operator, helped guide the beams as they were lifted by Williams over a tall "hurricane" fence under the City's electrical transmission lines. Williams held one end of a steel bar, the boom touched the overhead wires or was so close that current arced, and plaintiff's right arm and left leg had to be amputated as a result of the shock.

The Foundry, the only industrial facility in a residential area, covered two blocks divided by Ashley Street. The lines ran parallel to Ashley nearest Carbo's and were built in 1958 to connect power to Carbo. Three lines at the Olive Street intersection where the accident took place were 42 feet 5 inches from ground level. Plaintiff appealed a dismissal, for the trial judge concluded the sole cause of the accident was Lovato's raising the boom knowing the lines were there, and contacting them.

The appellate court affirmed. Negligence is conduct creating an unreasonable risk of foreseeable harm to others. It becomes a cause of harm if it was a substantial factor in bringing about that harm, and it is determined by the existence of the hazard and the violation of duty to protect others from the risk. The utility agency of such a dangerous facility has a high degree of care. It is liable to those who foreseeably might contact the wire which creates the hazardous condition, McKowen v Gulf States Utilities [A21-7], and a utility is negligent if it does not take practical steps to reduce the hazard by providing clearance reasonably required for reasonable foreseeable use of the surface below, or provide effective guards to isolate lines from accidental contact by persons using the surface below. The utility must use utmost care to reduce hazards to life as far as practical, and in places where contact by persons reasonably may be anticipated. But the utility need not guard against hazards which could not be anticipated reasonably. The mere fact of existence of transmission lines is adequate notice of that fact and the utility is not required to post notice that the line is energized in the absence of some peculiar and unusual circumstance.

Plaintiff charged the City with negligence for failure to insulate the lines in an industrial area at a height at which industrial equipment users foreseeably might contact the lines. The City was not negligent in construction and erection of the lines and it was not reasonable at the time of erection for the City to foresee a risk of contact with the wires at the location and height. The foundry did not use any equipment capable of reaching the lines at the time of their erection and it did not produce anything which would require equipment that possibly could contact the wires. The crane involved was acquired a year before the accident. It was used on job sites away from the foundry, it had been used on Ashley Street on several occasions, and on Ashley behind the machine shop to load and unload structural steel; the occasion of this accident was the first time it had been used at the location.

Plaintiff's experts agreed reluctantly that the classifications in the National Electrical Safety Code, most recently applicable, required vertical clearance of 20 feet from the ground to the lowest point of the wires. The highest vertical clearance required by the Code over land is 28 feet, and the highest under any circumstances is 40 feet for crossing water areas in excess of 200 acres where sailboating could be expected. Thus, the lines were 20 feet higher than Code requirements for the location. The City could not have foreseen a risk of harm by the wires at the location, and it owed no duty to plaintiff to prevent the risk he encountered which would have been foreseeable in these circumstances. The sole proximate cause of the accident was the negligence of the crane operator in moving the crane too close to the wires of which he was aware and tried to avoid. Also negligent was plaintiff's employer who instructed the truck loading to take place at the situs. They should have foreseen that the lifting operation in close proximity to the overhead wires would risk contact. The record amply supported the jury verdict.

Design defect was added in McPhail v Municipality of Culebra, (CA P.R. 1979) 598 F 2d 603. McPhail sailed a 16 foot Hobie Cat to a dock located in a small inlet to offer a sailing lesson to the owner of the dock. When he left the dock he was blown further inshore while trying to tack out of the inlet. About 50 feet from the inshore end of the inlet the 27 foot aluminum mast touched a high tension wire that hung 20 feet over the water and he was killed. His mother sued the authority responsible for the power lines (Culebra) and the manufacturer and seller of the boat.

The mast was mounted on a metal frame positioned on two fiberglass pontoons. The operator sat on the metal frame and steered by holding a metal tiller arm that descended into the water. The fiberglass pontoons were effective insulators, so current from the mast, to reach ground, passed through the helmsman who was between the frame and the tiller arm. The owner's manual warned to avoid power lines when launching.

Plaintiff's expert testified that a $10 wire to ground the frame to the tiller arm would conduct most of the current entering the mast and would have saved McPhail's life. Defendant's expert contradicted this. The jury found Culebra not liable for the condition and position of the power lines, but found for plaintiff against the seller and manufacturer. However, the trial judge upset this and entered judgment for defendants notwithstanding the verdict.

The Court of Appeals affirmed. Under Restatement (2nd) of Torts §388, a supplier must know that a chattel is unreasonably dangerous in order to incur liability and fail to use reasonable care in warning of that danger. This is a standard akin to common law negligence. There was no duty to warn of the danger of sailing into power lines; but the warning of the obvious in the owner's manual was the exercise of reasonable care, for the danger was patent and obvious.

Plaintiff relied on §388 at trial. The facts could make out a case of defective design under Puerto Rico law based on foreseeable misuse of the product, or accident and failure to provide readily available and economically feasible safety measures. Puerto Rico adopted the California definition of strict liability in tort. After the instant trial the Puerto Rico Supreme Court made clear that defect of design is included in "defect", and imposition of liability does not require that the product be unreasonably dangerous as in Restatement (2nd) of Torts §402A. Thus, even if McPhail were negligent in sailing near power lines and that negligence contributed to the injury, there could be some recovery. But this was not the theory of liability presented at the trial. Plaintiff may not present one theory at trial (§388) and argue another (§402A) on appeal.

On denial of a petition for rehearing the court said that sailing into power lines was not an intended purpose of the product. The charge to the jury did not allow for liability for failure to provide safety measures for unintended misuse.

SKI CASES [M21-30, add after McDonald v Hanneson:]

In Strickland v Roberts, (Fla App 1980) 382 So 2d 1338, Roberts was director at a camp at which Strickland, an experienced slalom skier, was in charge of water-ski activity. He asked Roberts to pull him around the lake. On the first loop, Strickland swung out and turned his ski to spray youngsters sun bathing on the dock. On the second loop, he struck the last piling of the dock and was injured. His suit charged that failure to have an observer in the boat per F.S. 371.54 (1) was negligence per se, and it was a violation of §371.54 (4) to operate the boat close enough to the dock for Strickland to swing out on the ski rope and hit it.

The trial court found that Strickland was a skilled skier who, independently, could control his position and direction of the boat which merely provided the pull through the water, that the boat was going in a straight line to the dock at the time of collision, that Strickland propelled himself into the piling solely as a result of his failure to maintain proper watch for the dock or by error of judgment while spraying the dock after he directed his ski out of the boat's wake, and that there was no causal relationship between defendant's actions and plaintiff's injuries which were self-inflicted. Defendant got summary judgment.

The appellate court affirmed. Plaintiff's reliance on the statute is unavailing. At the time of the accident, Roberts was observing Strickland, and there was no evidence that he manuevered Strickland to collide with the piling. Plaintiff skied as close as possible to the dock to spray it as he had done many times in the past; and this action by plaintiff was an aberrant form of skiing which normally would not be considered a contact sport. The risk of hitting the dock inheres in a sport of narrowly missing it. Contact sport is an exception to the merger of contributory negligence and assumption of risk set out in Blackburn v Dorta [A21-1]. This, too, was a basis for summary judgment.

A different aspect of management of a ski boat arose in Stansbury v Hover, (La App 1979) 366 So 2d 918. Jeff Hover, David Stansbury, Eddie Wasson and Paul Delaune, all about 15 years old, went on a boating outing on Lake Palourde. Jeff drove, Eddie skied, and David sat as the front of the bass boat as lookout. Eddie finished skiing, Jeff turned off the engine to pick him up, and David helped Eddie put the skis in the boat. Eddie climbed into the front. David moved to the rear and asked Jeff if the ski rope should be pulled into the boat. Jeff agreed and said they were going to pick up Paul on the beach.

Jeff and Eddie watched David as he pulled the ski bridle into the boat, and he sat down. Jeff and Eddie discussed Eddie's skiing as Jeff started the engine and accelerated. David was winding the rope around his arm and the "V" between his thumb and forefinger when Jeff accelerated. The nylon rope sank into the water although the handle was supported by a large float. The rope in the water pulled David's arm, the acceleration of the boat tended to jerk the boat out from under David, and he thought he would be pulled out of the boat and over the propeller, so he jumped over the side of the boat. When Eddie saw David go out, he screamed immediately for Jeff to stop. Jeff throttled to neutral instantly, but the rope slack ran out and David's arm was jerked. Nerve and tissue damage required amputation between shoulder and elbow.

The trial court found that Jeff was grossly negligent in accelerating without alerting his passengers, that he was negligent in moving without ascertaining that the ski rope was completely inside the boat after directing the inexperienced David to bring it in, that he was negligent in accelerating when he knew David was not looking at him but was looking astern while pulling the rope into the boat, and Jeff negligently failed to keep a proper lookout. The judge found Jeff's father guilty of independent negligence for failure to instruct Jeff in the dangers of sudden acceleration and need for proper lookout.

The appellate court affirmed judgment for plaintiff. Jeff owed a duty of ordinary and reasonable care to avoid unreasonable risk of harm to his passengers. After instructing David he should not have moved the boat until the rope was inside and David was seated, for David could have become entangled in the rope and fall or be pulled overboard. Jeff never looked back to see that the rope was in the boat. Although the rope may not have pulled David from the boat, he could have believed it would in his lack of experience. David's risk came within the scope of Jeff's duty of care. David, in his inexperience, was not contributorily negligent.

LAUNCHING RAMPS   [M21-30, add:]

Between the law of land and water, launching ramp cases were bound to arise. Ramps are slippery and dangerous. What are the duties of care? In Metropolitan Dade County v Yelvington, (Fla App 1980) #79-1588, Mrs. Yelvington slipped on an algae-coated boat launching ramp, a recreational facility operated and maintained by the County. There was evidence also of recently washed up seaweed of which the County may not have had notice, but there was evidence upon which the jury could have concluded she slipped on a 2 or 3 month buildup of algae. She won a jury verdict but with a finding she was 60% negligent. Both appealed.

The judgment was affirmed. There was ample evidence to support the verdict of her 60% negligence, but that was not a bar to her recovery under the rule of comparative negligence. A possessor of land may be liable for a condition on the land despite the obviousness of the hazard where it should anticipate the harm which may be caused, Restatement (2nd) of Torts, §343A. The slippery algae condition was not, as a matter of law, so open and obvious as to relieve the County of liability completely, nor can it be said, as a matter of law, that the County was not chargeable with any knowledge of the danger.

In Abdin v Fischer, (Fla 1979) 374 So 2d 1379, while preparing to launch his boat, Abdin slipped and fell on algae on the concrete boat ramp. He sued the lessee of the ramp, Sea Fresh Frozen Products, Inc. and its president, Fischer, for his injuries. The ramp, leased from Canaveral Port Authority, had a sign immediately adjacent: "Free boat ramp - courtesy of Fischer's Harbor Seafood, Bait, Ice, Fresh Seafoods". This retail business operation, along with a parking lot, restroom, and fish cleaning tables, was located near the boat ramp, and the wholesale fish house was nearby.

Defendants answered with the shield of liability for persons making available to the public, without charge, certain areas for recreational purposes as provided in F.S. 375.251. Its purpose was to encourage availability to the public of recreational areas in return for which the owner or lessee would be relieved of specified duties of care except for gross or wilful acts.

Plaintiff challenged the constitutionality of the Act because it would bar a common law action against owners and lessees for defective or dangerous conditions on the land. Defendants countered that plaintiff, absent a statute, would be a trespasser to whom they would be liable only for gross negligence, so that the only change in plaintiff's status made by the statute is that now he may enter the land lawfully if he chooses.

The court held that the legislative alteration of standards of care need only be reasonable, and this was a reasonable exercise of legislative power which did not violate the Florida Constitution's provision that the courts shall be open to every person for the redress of any injury.

However, a summary judgment in favor of defendants was not warranted. A jury reasonably could infer that commercial activity was taking place on the property which defendants alleged to be a "park area". The court, therefore, reversed and remanded for further proceedings on that question.

SUBMERGED OBSTRUCTIONS   [A21-11, add:]

In _Driskell v Alabama Power Co._, (Ala 1979) 374 So 2d 265, plaintiff operated a motorboat on defendant's Weiss Lake when it ran into a submerged tree trunk. He was thown into the water and injured. His suit charged negligence and wanton conduct in causing or allowing the submerged tree trunk to exist hidden from view, and in failing to mark it and warn plaintiff of the danger.

Plaintiff lost. The court had held before that submerged conditions hidden by water which add to the danger of a trespasser entering a pool, by definition, are not to be regarded as a pitfall or trap. _Wright v Alabama Power Co._ [A21-11] involved an invitee who hit a submerged fence. The present accident took place in a slough created in the early 1960's when the lake was backed up. A row of trees 10-20 feet high lined the entrance to the slough. By about 1975 they had rotted and fallen into the water, but their stumps remained. Stumps appeared when defendant reduced water level in the Fall; they disappeared a few inches below when the water level was raised in the Spring and in the Summer months when water sports were popular.

As in _Wright_, defendant raised and lowered the water level only for its own purposes. In _Wright_, that conduct was held not a positive act to create a new hidden danger, trap or pitfall. Again as in _Wright_, defendant had no duty to warn plaintiff, an ordinary licensee, of a possible danger concerning a condition brought about by its ordinary use of the land - raising and lowering the level of the lake.

Ch. B22   COLLISION

LOOKOUTS [M22-6, add:]

Operation in the confined waters of a busy harbor calls for an operator's close attention, but the question of a lookout during mooring arose in Marcona Corp. v O/S Shifty III, (CA Fla 1980) 615 F 2d 206. M/V Marcona was in the final process of mooring at a cement terminal in Tampa Harbor with two tugs then operating at right angles to Marcona. Shifty, towing a barge, met turbulent water generated by the tugs which caused Shifty and its barge to collide with Marcona. The trial court found the proximate cause of the collision to be the negligence of Shifty for failure to appreciate possible danger from the quickwater, or to maintain a proper lookout, or to communicate by whistle signal or radio.

On appeal, Shifty's owner contended that Marcona committed statutory violations as applicable to vessels underway, thereby invoking The Pennsylvania Rule [A22-2], and Marcona and its assisting tugs failed to post a lookout and to signal.

The Court of Appeals affirmed Shifty's negligence as the sole proximate cause of the collision. That included the conclusion that Marcona and its tugs were not negligent, so they could not have violated statutory requirements for a lookout or signals to invoke application of The Pennsylvania Rule. There is no absolute duty to maintain a lookout or signal other vessels during the final stages of mooring. The necessity of such precautions are to be determined from all the circumstances on the basis of common prudence.

BARGE v REAL ESTATE   [M22-7, add after THE RULE OF DAMAGES]

The complex case of S.C. Loveland v East West Towing, Inc., (CA Fla 1979) 608 F 2d 160, is of interest to those who may need to defend their real estate from onslaught by a derelict vessel.

East West's tug Miss Carolyn was to tow Loveland's 115 foot barge from New Orleans to Jacksonville. When it reached Panama City, the home office sold Carolyn to E&I Inc. which wanted early possession to send it to Grand Cayman, so E&I's Capt. Landreth flew to Panama City to board Carolyn. East West dispatched its tug Gary Stephens to cross the Gulf to tow at Tampa where E&I was to take title to Carolyn, and Gary was to assume tow of the barge. But Gary, through error, trailed Carolyn through the Intracoastal Waterway and never caught Carolyn in time.

Beyond Panama City, Carolyn's Capt. Verdin was out of his licensed waters and in over his head, so he relied on

Landreth for advice. At the mouth of Tampa Bay they discussed where to anchor the barge. They selected the spoil bank just east of Sunshine Skyway Bridge south of the channel at 10:00 AM August 18th and Carolyn proceeded to Nilo Docks <u>30 miles and 3 hours away</u> (emphasis supplied) of which Verdin notified East West that afternoon.

Meanwhile, Loveland asked East West the location of his barge. They did not know, and he learned for the first time time of the projected substitution of tugs. This upset him because it was his practice always to examine tugs and gear in advance for performance capability. He telephoned Intracoastal Waterway bridge tenders south of Tampa Bay (Apalachee Bay to Tampa Bay is an outside passage) and the Coast Guard to locate the tow, without result.

Although the barge was not required to have an anchor, it had a 500 pound Danforth which was suitable for the barge without superstructure - it had 2-1/2 feet of freeboard. However, it carried two large reactors which, for wind resistance, constituted a superstructure needing a heavier anchor. Thus, the barge dragged anchor in a thunderstorm the afternoon of the 19th and moved from the south to the north side of the channel. Bridge employees watched the barge with binoculars and they could identify it as it moved closer to the bridge. In a rain squall on the 20th, the barge hit the bridge with damage to both, $2700 and $123,000 respectively.

Three suits resulted: Loveland sued Carolyn, East West and E&I; they cross-claimed; Florida intervened. The trial judge apportioned comparative fault 50% against Carolyn in rem, 25% against East West for its own fault and that of Gary for failure to pick up the barge promptly, and 25% against the Florida Department of Transportation.

The State had called the Coast Guard on the 19th when the barge was noticed to be dragging anchor. On the 20th the bridge tender called the bridge foreman between 3:00 and 3:30 PM, and the Coast Guard was called between 4:00 and 4:30 PM. The bridge tender repeated between 5:00 and 6:00 PM, and again the bridge foreman called the Coast Guard. Shortly thereafter, the toll taker called during a rain squall to say the barge was up against the bridge. Then the Coast Guard arrived and took 15 minutes to draw the barge away from the bridge while calling Mr. Loveland to say they found his barge against the bridge. He called a Tampa tug, and in 30 minutes the Onslow was underway to take the barge from the cutter.

The court said the State was negligent because it did no more for its self-protection than call the Coast Guard. It could have checked to determine barge ownership and called Loveland who would have taken steps for a tow; or it could have called a local tug which would have had a lien on the barge so that there would have been no expense or damage to the State. Such failure to act was unjustified since previously at least one Liberty ship and a barge had drifted into the bridge. Severe thunderstorms on August afternoons in the Tampa Bay area were not unusual and the possibility of eventual collision with the bridge was foreseeable.

The Court of Appeals affirmed. East West was negligent for leaving the barge unattended in an exposed area near the bridge, anchoring the barge improperly in a spoil bank, failing to notify the barge owner of changed circumstances, and failing to obtain a relief tug.

Florida contended that if it had any duty to act, its duty was to the people of Florida and not to the barge owner; it acted reasonably and discharged any duty to act by calling the Coast Guard, the agency with the duty of removing hazards to navigation. But it made no effort to summon any of the many tugs in the area to come to the assistance of the apparently abandoned barge. The quick response of the tug hired by Loveland indicated that this course of action would have prevented the collision. While this might have involved some expense to the State, more importantly, it would have prevented damage to the State. The State's negligence was in its failure to take responsible precautions for the safety and protection of its own property. "We find the state's argument that it did all it reasonably could be expected to do by repeatedly notifying the Coast Guard, the agency responsible for floating dangers to navigation, forceful. This argument, however, was addressed to the finder of fact and we cannot say that the district judge lacked sufficient evidence to find the state negligent." Proximate cause is a finding of fact binding on the appellate court unless clearly erroneous.

A plaintiff is not entitled to recover damages he could have avoided by use of reasonable effort or expenditure after commission of a tort. The possibility of collision was foreseeable to the agents of the State, and this had happened before. The reasonableness of plaintiff's acts or omissions depends on the extent of the threatened injury as compared with the expense of remedying the situation and the practical certainty of success in the preventive effort.

"We do not base our resolution on what may well be an issue of first impression in admiralty law on the absence of cases finding negligence in fact patterns identical to those in the instant case. Rather, because no statute, regulation, or maritime custom controls, we again turn to common law, specifically the law of nuisance as related to contributory negligence and the rules of damages involving avoidable consequences." The court drew analogy under the law of nuisance to a landowner failing to use self-help to avoid foreseeable consequences and reduce damages by burying a dead animal lying on adjoining land.

The decision is wrong. Compare <u>Loveland</u> with <u>Petition of Alva S.S. Co., Ltd.</u>, (CA NY 1980) 616 F 2d 605. On June 16, 1966 petitioner's Alva Cape, carrying 133,000 gallons of naptha, collided with an empty tanker off the New Jersey coast causing an explosion and fire. It was extinguished by an epic fleet of sea-borne firefighting equipment after loss of 28 lives and personal injury to many others. For continuing threat of explosion and fire from flammable liquids and gases still aboard, it was taken to the Federal Explosion Harbor off Brooklyn. Alva's New York agent, Navcot, hired Merritt-Chapman & Scott to salvage the vessel, after gas-freeing the hold, by repairing if feasible, or scrapping. MCS unloaded naptha down to 2000-3000 gallons for which the ship's onboard pumps then became needed. But the New York Fire Department saw naptha leaking into the harbor and decided the best way to counter the combustion hazard was to inert the cargo with a gas such as nitrogen or carbon dioxide, and they issued such an order.

MCS and Navcot thought the order foolish and said so, but agreed to follow it. They thought a better procedure to be the flushing of the cargo with warm water. They decided to pump a token amount of CO_2 into the hold for which MCS ordered ten 50 gallon canisters from Walter Kidde & Co., much less than the 200 tons specified by the Fire Department. Kidde's salesman, Becker, inquired MCS's use of the CO_2. MCS's Varnum described the token plan. Becker said this would be extremely dangerous because an electric spark might trigger an explosion unless the fill apparatus was grounded properly by a wire to the hull. Varnum told him to mind his business.

Nullification of the sparking danger was the basis of the entire operation. Avoidance in this instance would be to ground the canister to the ship by a copper wire to prevent accumulation of an electrical charge around the point of contact. Lee, a marine chemist for a firm hired by MCS, warned Varnum of this, but Varnum said it was too late to change plans. MCS's salvage master, Zickl, had no personal knowledge of the dangers involved in the inerting procedure, and Varnum did not tell him of the warnings by Lee and Becker.

On the 28th when the first canister was discharged into the hold, Rush of the Fire Department realized that MCS and Navcot did not intend to perform inertion in the manner ordered so he left on a Department launch to phone his superiors. <u>His training as a fireman and his experience using CO_2 in ordinary land-based fires did not lead him to believe the operation in progress was dangerous</u>; (emphasis supplied) but within seconds after the beginning of discharge of the second canister, an accumulated electrical charge at the head of the nozzle sparked naptha gas in the hold. The explosion killed 4 salvage workers and injured several more. The next day the Fire Department ordered the ship to be removed from the Harbor within 24 hours. Navcot asked for more time to withdraw rented salvage equipment, but its efforts toward that end, under purported Coast Guard permission, were ended by threat of arrest, so Navcot had the vessel towed to sea to be sunk by hired gunfire.
In apportioning liability for explosion during "inerting", the

trial court found Navcot 20% liable, MCS 70% liable, the City 10% liable. On appeal <u>the City's liability was reversed</u>. Alva urged that it should not be liable because, even though it knew the inerting operation commenced by MCS to be futile, it did not know it was dangerous. But Alva had the Fire Department order requiring presence of a marine chemist during inerting who would have been aware of the danger of static electricity explosion as warned by Lee. The order had force of law, and Alva's failure to comply was negligence per se. Moreover, Alva was liable vicariously for MCS's negligence. An employer ordinarily is not liable for its independent contractor's negligence, but an exception is where the independent contractor performs a duty imposed by statute. The Fire Department order imposed a non-delegable duty for performance of the salvage if done at all. Failure to provide an overseeing chemist and refusal to do more than token inerting were acts of negligence by MCS which were imputed to Alva. Salvage of 30,000 gallons of naptha from the hull damaged by the prior explosion so that its closures could not be made secure was an inherently dangerous activity. The negligence of the contractor may be imputed to the employer in such an activity.

MCS contended that if Alva had a non-delegable duty, Alva should be fully liable. However, an independent contractor is liable for its own negligence even though the owner was liable under the non-delegable duty rule. Allocation of greater liability to MCS was justified because it had actual knowledge of the explosion danger from two independent sources on which it neglected to act or to warn Alva.

In marine negligence cases the court has the power to review the ultimate question of liability, and there was no basis to find the City liable. The finding of the City's 10% liability is reversed to be apportioned 77.78% against MCS and 22.22% against Alva. Rush merely knew that the inerting procedure as it was being carried out was useless. His decision to seek higher advice rather than to halt operations on his own was not lack of due care. Also, <u>the City had no duty to supply a fireman who would have had knowledge of the danger of the procedure being followed by MCS</u> (emphasis supplied). The record does not show that the order to use inerting gases rather than warm water treatment was without reasonable basis or due care.

CRITICISM

Imposition of liability against the Sunshine Skyway Bridge is disturbing. As a fixed structure, the ruling will apply to threatened damage to a dock or seawall - real estate [see <u>The Rock Island Bridge</u>, M17-2], the harried owner or dockmaster of which will be chargeable with knowledge of vessel registration systems and maritime law which was exhibited only by Mr. Loveland and the admiralty court. Small Boat Law classroom experience has shown that students sophisticated in maritime affairs, both lay and professional, require analysis and explanation of such legal elements which proved to be beyond a bridge tender or bridge foreman.

The trial judge in Loveland said there would have been no expense or damage if the State summoned a local tug; the Court of Appeals expanded that to some expense. Following the example set by the court, we can offer a variety of fanciful scenarios:

- The final solution for Alva Cape was to blow it up; why not also the barge? That would be fast, certain, cheap, and within reach of the Florida DOT which, in dealing with roads and bridges, is familiar with dynamite. Such could be ferried to the barge by Florida Marine Patrol boats which are much faster than tugs. The barge's 2-1/2 feet of freeboard would pose no problem. Shocking? Not at all. Remember we are talking about burying a dead animal.

- Hiring a tug is not as simple as hailing a taxicab, and for purposes of this criticism a salvage operator was consulted. Astonished by the decision, he expressed no doubt as to ignorance of bridge personnel of the above elements. On the pointed inquiry of hiring practice, he said this: The towboat rate at the time of the bridge collision was $1.00 per horsepower per day. But an operator would not respond automatically to any call; such response would be given where there was credit through a course of dealing or identification in the industry such as Loveland's; it would not be given to bridge personnel or a government agency without first assuring payment. Government in particular in not credit-worthy in such circumstances. This, therefore, involved much more than swinging a shovel which was a reality not faced by the Loveland court.

- Imagine a bridge tender or foreman, facing firing, being asked: What was your authority to obligate the State for tug hire? You knew the Coast Guard had been summoned; why didn't you wait for them? Why did you think the Coast Guard would not respond in time? Why did you think a private tug would arrive sooner? The imaginary dialogue leads to the larger issue of the State's capability to act which will be considered below.

- Parenthetically, the DOT is a complex system governed by the Florida Transportation Code consisting of 6 Parts, F.S. Ch 334 through 339. §339.281 imposes misdemeanor penalties upon an owner, agent, or master of a vessel who fails to report as soon as possible to the Marine Patrol, Sheriff, Highway Patrol, or Game and Fresh Water Fish Commission any damage caused to a bridge by a vessel. There is provision for rulemaking power; but nothing on the books reaches the subject of emergency action or tug-hire on threat of collision notwithstanding the experiences of the Sunshine Skyway Bridge's collisions or threats thereof. Thus, the bureaucratic firedrill we might project in the Loveland emergency teases the imagination.

- By similar instructional license, we can have the <u>Alva</u> court rewrite <u>Loveland</u> in the pattern of position of fireman Rush and New York City thusly: "The State had no duty to supply a bridge tender or bridge foreman who would have had knowledge of the Coast Guard system of vessel documentation and knowledge of the uncommon and unfamiliar of maritime liens and salvage rights and remedies in admiralty." With equal or greater effect we might extend this revisionary device to the owner or manager of a private seawall, dock or marina, the people foremost in our concern in this argument.

On the question of capability, the <u>Loveland</u> Court of Appeals cited <u>U.S. v Barge CBC 603</u>, (DC Ga 1964) 233 F Supp 85, in which a barge laden with 100 tons of rock became grounded in the Chattahoochee River 7 miles north of Bradley's Landing at Fort Benning for two months. Waters rose after Hurricane Flossy, the barge broke the manila line securing it to a tree trunk, and the barge drifted downstream. Soldiers, trying to clear floating debris from the Army's pontoon bridge, saw the approaching barge. They were ordered off the bridge which the barge struck. They tried to remove the barge by cables attached to winch-equipped trucks which lacked sufficient traction in the rain-soaked earth. The bridge gave way. The court found that the barge charterer failed to offer evidence that equipment was available to the Army to secure the barge in time, but the Army showed that removal in time was not feasible due to an obstruction and to insufficient traction for its equipment - lack of capability.

If the <u>Loveland</u> court had considered the central question of DOT's capability to decide and act, it would not have applied the simplistic analogy of burying a dead animal. However, this ill-advised ruling appears to bind private dock and seawall owners in the 5th Circuit.

For passing interest, compare these cases with the post-casualty mitigation in <u>Tennessee Valley Sand & Gravel Co. v M/V Delta</u> [B9-3].

Ch. B24   LIABILITY OF GOVERNMENT

LIABILITY FOR INSPECTION   [M24-3, add at bottom:]

In a wide sense, inspection results in particular information to be communicated. However, let us set apart government's inspection function as a separate category applicable to new activities subject to the familiar rule that where government has the discretion to act, it may decide without liability; but having acted, it may be liable for the manner of that performance as examined in Gercey v U.S., (CA RI 1976) 540 F 2d 536. Comet, a 30 year old 49 foot wooden motor vessel with 39 passenger capacity, failed a Coast Guard inspection in 1971 because its hull was rotten. Its certificate to carry 6 or more passengers for hire was revoked; but that revocation did not preclude its lawful operation otherwise than for that purpose. Comet was sold in the Fall to Jackson who continued to carry large groups of fee paying passengers in 1972 and 1973 to and from the port of Galilee past a Coast Guard Station. On May 19, 1973 he took a large group of fee paying passengers on a fishing trip off the east coast of Rhode Island in normal weather and sea, but Comet split and sank 5 miles off Point Judith, and Jackson and 16 passengers perished.

Gercey's parents sued for his wrongful death on that trip due to the Coast Guard's negligence because they failed to take positive, feasible steps to protect the passengers from the danger of voyaging on Comet. The sole action by the Coast Guard had been to remove Comet's certificate which, presumably, had been displayed in a conspicuous place most likely to be observed by the passengers.

Plaintiffs contended that the Coast Guard had either a statutory or common law duty to protect the passengers by: (1) informing the public of the condition of the vessel by a public notice or sign placed on the vessel; (2) checking periodically to determine if it was being used contrary to the safety regulation; (3) informing any new purchaser of the condition of the vessel; (4) notifying all Coast Guard units which vessels are decertified.

The court held the U.S. was not liable. Congress mandated only that the Coast Guard make periodic inspections and revoke certificates of non-complying vessels, but it did not impose on the Coast Guard a duty to devise, fund, staff and implement the kind of follow-up system which plaintiffs urge as ordinary prudence. The Coast Guard had discretionary authority, but it did not so act.

Such a decision is one of policy for promotion of the public interest. The Coast Guard has limited resources and a myriad of regulatory responsibilities. Plaintiffs' program would require a major commitment of resources balanced against effectiveness of current enforcement measures, degree of increased protection by plaintiffs' program, and whether the degree of increased protection would warrant the increased commitment of Coast Guard resources and their possible diversion from other regulatory activities.

The federal court does not have the power to impose liability on the Coast Guard for failure to make and implement such a program as a basic policy decision involving commitment of its limited resources. The Suits in Admiralty Act, which waived sovereign immunity of the U.S. for certain maritime claims, has no express exception for harm caused by the exercise of discretionary functions.

[A24-2, add after NATURE v COAST GUARD:]
In Bearce v U.S., (CA Ill 1980) 614 F 2d 556, Chicago harbor has an exterior breakwater running parallel to the shore. 97 feet from its north end the Coast Guard maintained a 4 second flashing green light as an aid to navigation. Shore Arm Extension breakwater runs perpendicular to the shore. Its eastern end terminates 400 feet from the exterior breakwater; it had no light. The main harbor entrance used by commercial vessels was located elsewhere.

Bearce, an experienced power boat operator familiar with the harbor, operated a new fiberglass speedboat with 233 hp engine the night of May 10, 1975. He had passed through the gap earlier that day, and at 10 PM he followed another boat out the gap at about 30 mph. Just before he cleared the breakwater he swerved left, collided with the Shore Arm Extension 20 feet from its eastern end, and was killed instantly. His passenger was badly injured.

His estate charged government with negligence for failure to place a light on the eastern end of Shore Arm Extension. In 1966 the Illinois Boating Council held public hearings, attended by the Coast Guard, on navigational aid needs of the gap. The Coast Guard noted that the exterior breakwater light should be changed from white to green, and a flashing red light should be placed on the end of Shore Arm Extension. It changed the white light to green to distinguish it from the lights of the city, but it never acted on the red light.

The court held the U.S. was not liable. The decision on whether to place a light at the eastern end of Shore Arm Extension fell within the discretionary authority of the Coast Guard to establish aids to navigation. 14 USC §81 provides that the Coast Guard may establish, maintain and operate aids to navigation. Although the U.S. may be liable for the negligent operation of aids, that can arise only after the Coast Guard exercises its discretion to act at all. The liability arises from breach of the non-discretionary duty to operate the aids with due care. Here the light was operating as planned and there was no operational error.

The Coast Guard decided similarly to provide only a single light for Milwaukee and Buffalo harbor secondary entrances. At the time of trial the Coast Guard had a priority list of aids to navigation approved for construction of $300 million which had not yet been funded by Congress. The Coast Guard cannot implement every recommendation. Thus, construction of navigational aids requires policy judgments concerning the public interest as a discretionary function which courts should not review in the context of a tort claim.

In Inter-Cities Navigation Corp. v U.S., (CA Fla 1979) 608 F 2d 1079, plaintiff's tug pushed a notched barge up the St. Johns River. Together, they were 647 feet long, 85 feet wide, with 32 feet draft. Five minutes before the accident the captain gave over the helm to mate Rakyta. When the bow of the unit reached buoy 69, Rakyta put the rudder left for a turn. It did not respond, so he reversed his port engine to twist from the approaching Shell Pier and accelerate the turn. They hit the pier.

Plaintiff sued the U.S. because the Coast Guard failed to maintain 69 on its charted position on which plaintiff's vessel relied, and this caused the collision. The trial court found the buoy to be 400-600 feet off station which the Coast Guard could and should have corrected. This helped cause the collision; but on the presumption that a moving vessel is at fault in colliding with a stationary object, which plaintiff did not overcome, the U.S. was only one-third liable for the $484,000 damage to the pier.

The Court of Appeals held the U.S. not liable. Rakyta did not rely on the charted position of the buoy in making his turn. The wrongful act or omission must have a reasonable connection in fact with the collision in order to find contributory fault in the actor or omitter, but a failure to act, even if unreasonable, cannot contribute to a collision if the act would have had no effect, example: lack of a lookout in a collision with a pier when the pier was in plain sight. Thus, for an improperly placed buoy to contribute to a collision, its position must reasonably affect the intended navigation. Rakyta testified he steered by the actual offstation position of the buoy, not by some invisible grid in his mind, and he was going to make his turn at the buoy. The evidence shows that a prudent navigator would start his turn well before the buoy, even when it was on station. There was no evidence a chart was aboard the vessel or ever had been. There was no substantial evidence he knew or relied on the buoy's charted position.

The tow was loaded more heavily at 32 feet draft than on previous voyages up the river at 20-22 feet. While not overloaded technically, the tug handled sluggishly which was a factual and legal cause of the collision. Failure to keep the buoy on position is not to be condoned, but its dislocation was not a cause of the collision.

Ch. B25 INSURANCE

THE INSURANCE CONTRACT   [M25-2, add]

As will have been noted, ambiguities can be as varied in an insurance contract as there are contractual provisions. Thus, in Zautner v Liberty Mutual Ins. Co., (Fla App 1980) 382 So 2d 106, plaintiff's floater policy insured his outboard motor and 22 foot boat designated in "Class of Property" as "outboard boats and motors". The "Newly Acquired Outboard Motors or Boats" clause required notification within 30 days of acquisition of "any outboard motor or boat". Plaintiff acquired a 25 foot inboard powered by two inboard engines which was damaged the next day when the steering failed while underway. The insurer won a summary judgment because the clause extended only to newly acquired outboard boats.

The appellate court reversed. Whether "outboards" related to "motors" only, or to "boats" as well, it was for the insurer to clarify the meaning, and the ambiguity would be construed against it. If only newly acquired "outboard boats" were to be covered, the insurer should have said "outboard motors or outboard boats", or "outboard boats and motors" as used earlier in the policy text. The use of the different term "Newly Acquired Outboard Motors or Boats" was some indication of a more expansive insuring agreement, possibly to mean coverage of all newly acquired boats or newly acquired motors. Plaintiff got summary judgment on his cross motion.

In Ross v Royal Globe Ins. Co., (CA Ark 1980) 612 F 2d 379, Ross bought a one year homeowners policy on May 9, 1972 from Royal Indemnity Ins. Co. On May 28th he bought a 14 foot boat with 35 hp outboard. On May 9, 1973 Royal Globe issued a one year policy, and on May 9, 1974 it issued a three year policy. On June 15, 1975 daughter Tresa was injured in a boat accident, their boat being operated by her boyfriend at the time. Tresa sued Royal Globe alleging coverage by the policy's omnibus provisions of the accident and operation.

The last policy excluded coverage of watercraft with more than a 25 hp outboard if owned by the insured at the inception of the policy and not endorsed thereon unless the insured gave the company written notice within 45 days after acquisition of his intention to insure the boat and motor, ownership of which was acquired before the policy term. Tresa contended that the exclusion applied only to watercraft acquired before the inception of the policy. The trial judge said the exclusion as drafted was nonsensical, a mistake, and he granted summary judgment to Royal Globe.

The Court of Appeals reversed and remanded for further proceedings. Globe argued that the exclusion applied to an instance where one applied for a policy, then acquired a boat, then was issued a policy so that the individual would have 45 days after purchase of the boat to notify Globe of an intention to insure, otherwise the exclusion would become operable; also, the exclusion would not apply if the insured bought a boat after the inception of the policy. Said the court, in examining at least three possible constructions of the exclusion, it was not for the trial judge to decide to "reform" the exclusion so as to deny coverage, but he should have applied the established rule that ambiguity in an insurance exclusion is to be construed strictly against the insurer with all reasonable doubts as to interpretation to be resolved in favor of the insured.

The three policies had not been placed in the record to determine whether they were renewals, as contended by Tresa, or different policies as contended by Globe, for under Arkansas law, where a renewal is made pursuant to a specific renewal provision in the policy, the renewal is treated as an extension of the first policy. There remains for determination the same exclusion clause in the 1972-1973 policy and whether it had a renewal clause, and whether Royal Indemnity and Royal Globe are to be considered the same firm for purposes of determining if the 1974-1977 policy is an extension of the 1972-1973 policy. Thus, the case was not in proper status for a summary judgment.

EVIDENTIARY STANDOFF   [M25-12, add after Mathis:]

A contrast to Mathis for implied warranty of seaworthiness is D.J. McDuffie, Inc. v Old Reliable Ins. Co., (CA La 1979) 608 F 2d 145. McDuffie's submersible drilling barge capsized, and defendant refused to pay on the marine hull policy which covered damage caused by latent defects in machinery or hull; also negligence of the master and crew, providing the loss or damage did not result from want of due diligence of the owner. The trial court ruled for defendant, finding an extensively deteriorated condition which breached the implied warranty of seaworthiness which attached at the outset of the policy.

Judgment was affirmed. There had been no dry-docking or inspection for 6 years before the capsize. The vessel was exposed to the normal abuses attendant upon an inland barge's operation during that period of regular use. McDuffie's expert witness testified to a recommendation one month before the policy was to take effect that the barge be drydocked for critical repairs. It lacked necessary deck plating, manhole systems, compartmental separation, and bottom plating to give the vessel watertight integrity. Constant pumping for recurrent listing to port or starboard became standing operating procedure. It was not reasonably suited for its intended use as an inland drilling barge. The breach of implied warranty of seaworthiness voided the insurance contract.

EFFICIENT NEGLIGENCE

In Goodman v Fireman's Fund Ins. Co., (CA Md 1979) 600 F 2d 1040, plaintiff used professional help in 1975 for winter layup of his 55 foot twin diesel Chris-Craft yacht, but he undertook to do this himself in 1976 when he failed to drain the sea water cooling system and close the sea valves. During winter cold the plastic filter jackets in the system froze and broke which allowed sea water to flow into the system and the broken jackets until the boat filled and sank to the stretched limits of its mooring lines.

Plaintiff sued his insurer for rejecting the loss. The hull insurance policy covered all risks of physical loss or damage from any external cause; also, if the loss or damage did not result from lack of due diligence by the assured, owners or managers of the yacht, it covered specified losses under the Inchmaree clause [M25-7] including latent defects and negligence of masters including the owner when he acted in that capacity. Policy exclusions were loss or damage by ice and/or freezing. It warranted that the vessel would be laid up and out of commission from October 1 until May 1 [see Yacht Rambler, M16-14; Yacht Almar, M16-17].

The trial court ruled against plaintiff because the loss was not covered by the policy: (1) to the extent that the freezing of water in the cooling system came within the policy exclusion; (2) the loss was not covered by the "all risks" clause of the policy [M25-2]; (3) the Inchmaree clause insuring against negligence of masters was inapplicable.

The Court of Appeals, disagreeing with most of these reasons, affirmed. "All risks" policies cover all fortuitous losses [M25-2]. A loss is not fortuitous if it results from an inherent defect, from ordinary wear and tear, or from intentional misconduct of the insured; but loss due to negligence of the insured or his agents has been held generally to be fortuitous and covered by all-risks, unless expressly excluded.

"External cause" in the all-risks clause did not limit the scope of the risks because the cause of loss necessarily was external if it did not result from inherent defect, ordinary wear, or intentional misconduct. The Inchmaree clause did not limit liability; its purpose in marine insurance policies is to broaden, not to restrict, coverage. However, it did not extend coverage to plaintiff under the facts in this case.

Although the trial court reasoned that the freezing water in the cooling system caused the sinking so that the loss came within the express policy exclusion, it was plaintiff's negligence that caused the freezing which, coupled with failure to close the sea valves, caused the sinking. When two or more causes combine to cause a loss, one of which is insured against and the other not, the loss is not insured unless the cause which is covered is the predominant efficient cause of the loss. Plaintiff's negligence was the predominent efficient cause of the sinking. While the freezing was an intervening cause of the series of events, it was not unforeseeable.

The trial court found it to be customary in the Chesapeake Bay region at least to close the sea valves as part of the winterizing program. Local custom governs interpretation of the layup warranty in a marine insurance policy. The breach of this express warranty released the insurer from any liability due to the breach.

THEFT COVERAGE   [A25-4, add after Sills v Boston]

In St. Paul Fire & Marine Ins. Co. v Veal, (Ala 1979) 377 So 2d 962, Veal took his 1971 GMC Diesel Tractor to a local mechanic for engine repairs, and he contracted to trade the entire engine, frame, transmission and $5,000 for a completed Cummings running gear installation. Eight months later he learned the replacement assembly was stolen property. His insurance covered loss by theft or larceny, so he sued his insurer for loss of the original running gear as having been stolen. The trial judge concluded that since the Cummings gear was stolen property, there had been a failure of consideration in Veal's contract so that he remained the owner of the GMC gear, and the court awarded him $12,000.

The Supreme Court reversed. Veal was induced to surrender possession and title to the GMC gear by the false pretense that he was obtaining good title to the Cummings replacement. The intended transfer, although induced by fraud or fraudulent pretenses of the taker, did not constitute theft or larceny within the ordinary meaning of the terms as used in the policy.

INTENTIONAL MISCONDUCT   [M25-20, add after THEFT COVERAGE:]

Boats frequently are co-wned by partners. Material, therefore is one's intentional misconduct as in Auto-Owners Ins. Co. v Eddinger, (Fla App 1979) 366 So 2d 123. A married couple insured their jointly owned home (each owned an entire interest in it). After divorce, they held the home as tenants in common (each owned an undivided half interest - partners). The original policy was renewed to insure their continuing interests as co-owners. When fire destroyed it, the ex-husband, Chafin, sued the insurer which denied liability on the ground that he had committed fraud and that he was responsible for the fire. Eddinger, the ex-wife, intervened and crossclaimed against the insurer. It was conceded she was innocent of any fraud, but the insurer contended Chafin's fraudulent act voided the policy which so provided in case of fraud by the insured; the company intended to insure Chafin and any named insured jointly, and the insurance was not severable so as to provide separate insurance of the interests of joint owners and coinsureds. It appealed a summary judgment for her.

The appellate court construed the policy in favor of Eddinger since there was no indication whether the policy coverage was joint or several. Although Florida had no case law, other jurisdictions held that the fraud of a coinsured does not void the coverage of an innocent coinsured, the significant element being the responsibility or liability for the wrongful act which is severable and separable rather than joint, and it is not to be attributed or imputed to the co-owner who is not implicated therein.

That policy of law was extended to a marina's tenants in American Eastern Development Corp. v Everglades Marina Inc., (CA Fla 1979) 608 F 2d 123. American and O'Donnell kept their boats in rack storage in the marina's building in Ft. Lauderdale from which they were removed and launched regularly by forklift to obviate salt water storage and keep the hulls barnacle-free. They were damaged in a fire set by the president and sole stockholder of the marina who had business difficulties. The marina's insurance covered loss or damage to vessels stored in the marina with no specific policy exclusions. The trial court upheld the boatowners' claims, and the marina's insurer appealed.

The decision was affirmed. This is an admiralty, not a land-based tort, case. The boats were not withdrawn from navigation [see The Bankrupt Queen, M17-2], but such storage is an alternative to tying up to docks or moorings to avoid exposure to deteriorating effects of water and weather.

The rack storage contracts were governed by Florida law. The Florida Supreme Court certified to this court, Everglades Marina, Inc. v American Eastern Development Corp., (Fla 1979) 374 So 2d 517, that the insurer is not liable to indemnify the insured for losses directly incurred by the fraud or misconduct of an insured, which precluded recovery under a policy when the insured has committed a criminal act with known or necessary consequences; but that public policy prohibition does not extend to third party beneficiaries of the insurance. Eddinger. There was no express exclusionary clause in the policy, and the court will not insert one. The boat owners neither knew nor participated in the criminal act. Their position is conformable with basic law principles for protection of innocent third parties.

That, said the Court of Appeals, is the law of this case.

PREMISES COVERAGE   [M25-22, add after HOMEOWNER'S POLICY:]

In Parliament Ins. Co. v Bryant, (Fla App 1980) 380 So 2d 1088, Bryant was injured in a boat accident during alleged demonstration ride when the boat was operated by an employee of Ultra Marine Corp. in an effort to sell her the boat. Ultra's insurer, Parliament, contended that there was no coverage for this casualty under the Owner's, Landlord's, and Tenant's Policy: it insured against bodily injury or property damage caused by an occurrence and arising out of the ownership, maintenance, or use of the insured premises, and all operations necessary or incidental to the business of selling boats. The policy excluded bodily injury or property damage arising out of the ownership, maintenance, operation, use, loading or unloading of any watercraft if the bodily injury or property damage occurs away from the insured premises.

The court held the boatride, which of necessity occurred away from the insured's premises, was not a covered activity. The rule that inconsistencies in insurance contracts are to be construed in favor of the insured applies only when a genuine inconsistency, uncertainty or ambiguity in meaning remains after resort to the ordinary rules of construction, but it does not allow courts to rewrite insurance contracts. The language clearly excluded coverage of activities away from the insured's premises. This was a premises liability policy, not a general liability policy. It recited a premium base of 5000 square feet of land upon which Ultra conducted its business. There was no ambiguity.

APPENDIX BI

FLORIDA MOTORBOAT LAW
Chapter 371

Amendments to the statute in the main text [MI] and 1978 Supplement [AI] are:

371.021 Definitions. [MI-2]
(1) [MI-2] Substitute:'"Vessel"is synonymous with boat as referenced in s. 1(b), Art. VII of the State Constitution and means a motor or artificially propelled vehicle registered as provided herein as property and includes every description of watercraft, barges, and air boats, other than a seaplane on the water, used or capable of being used as a means of transportation on water. However, live-aboard vessels are expressly excluded from the term "boat" for purposes of s. 1(b), Art. VII of the State Constitution and for purposes of license fees imposed by this part, if assessed as tangible personal property."
(16) [MI-4] Renumber: "(16)" to "(17)".
(17) [MI-4] Renumber: "(17)" to "(16)".
(18) [MI-4] Add: "Live-aboard vessel means:
(a) Any vessel used principally as a residence; or
(b) Any vessel represented as a place of business, a professional or other commercial enterprise, or legal residence, and providing or serving on a long-term basis the essential services or functions typically associated with a structure or other improvement to real property, and, if used as a means of transportation, said use is clearly a secondary or subsidiary use; or
(c) Any vessel used by any club or any other association of whatever nature when clearly demonstrated to serve a purpose other than a means of transportation.
Commercial fishing boats are expressly excluded from the term "live-aboard vessel"'

371.041 Operation of unnumbered motorboats prohibited. [MI-5]
On 2nd line after "numbered" and 6th line after "registered", insert: "within 10 days after purchase by the owner".

371.051 Application, certificate, etc. [MI-5]
(1)(b)(2) [MI-6] On 12th and 14th lines, change "50 cents" to "$1". On 15th line change "forty" to "20" days.
(1)(b)(5) [MI-6] Substitute: "Each certificate of registration issued shall state among other items the numbers awarded to the boat, the hull identification number, or hull serial number, the name and address of the owner, and a description of the boat, except that certificates of registration for boats constructed or assembled by the owner registered for the first time shall state all the foregoing information except

hull identification number or hull serial number. The numbers shall be placed on each side of the forward half of the vessel in such position as to provide clear legibility for identification. The numbers awarded to the boat shall read from left to right and shall be in block characters of good proportion not less than 3 inches in height. The numbers shall be of solid color which will contrast with the color of the background and so maintained as to be clearly visible and legible; i.e., dark numbers on a light background or light numbers on a dark background. The certificate of registration shall be pocket-size and shall be available for inspection on the boat for which issued whenever such boat is in operation."

371.053 Crimes relating to registration decals [MI-8] Add:
(1) It is unlawful for any person to make, alter, forge, countefeit, or reproduce a Florida registration decal unless authorized by the department.
(2) It is unlawful for any person knowingly to have in his possession a forged, counterfeit, or imitation Florida registration decal, or reproduction of a decal, unless possession by such person has been duly authorized by the department.
(3) It is unlawful for any person to barter, trade, sell, supply, or aid in supplying, or give away a Florida registration decal, or conspire to barter, trade, sell, supply, agree to supply, or aid in supplying, or give away a registration decal, unless duly authorized to issue the decal by the department, as provided in this part, or in rules of the department.
(4) Any person who violates any of the provisions of this subsection is guilty of a felony of the third degree, punishable as provided in s. 775.082, s. 775.083, or s. 775.084

371.141 Collisions, accidents, and casualties. [MI-12]
On 3rd line, change "marine resources" to "law enforcement"; on 6th line, after "division", add "of law enforcement".

371.63 Legislative declaration. [MI-27]
Substitute: "All boats registered as provided herein, except live-aboard vessels assessed as tangible personal property, are hereby declared to be motor vehicles and shall be taxed and certified as motor vehicles; however, nothing in this section shall be construed to prohibit any municipality that expends money for the patrol, regulation, and maintenance of any lakes, rivers, or waters in such municipality from regulating such boats resident in such municipalities and charging a license fee therefor. All moneys received from such fee shall be expended for the patrol, regulation, and maintenance of the lakes, rivers, and waters of such municipality."

371.64 Exemption from personal property tax. [MI-27]
On the 5th line after "fee." insert: "However, live-aboard vessels are subject to the tax on tangible personal

property and shall be annually exempt from the license fee under this part if assessed as tangible personal property for the current year."

371.65 Classification and license. [MI-28]
    (1) Class A-1. Change text to: "Less than 12 feet in length, and all canoes to which propulsion motors have been attached, regardless of length".
    (2) Renumber sections: "(3)" to "(2)"; "(4)" to "(3)"; "(5)" to "(4)"; "(6)" to "(5)"; "(7)" to "(6)"; "(8)" to "(7)".
    (3) Distribution of fees.- [MI-29]
    On 4th line, change "fix" to "ascertain"; on 6th line after "receive", delete "according to" and insert ","; on 9th line change "§371.65" to "subsection".
    (4) Fractional registration fee.- [MI-29]
    At end, change "December 1" to "December 31".
    (6) Exemption.- [MI-29] Substitute:
    "Vessels and motorboats owned and operated by Sea Explorer or Sea Scout units of the Boy Scouts of America, the Girl Scouts of America, the Associated Marine Institutes, Inc., and its affiliates, live-aboard vessels assessed as tangible personal property, and any boat used exclusively for commercial fishing and not propelled or powered by machinery of any horsepower are exempt from the provisions of subsection (1). Such vessels or motorboats shall be issued certificates of registration and numbers upon application and payment of the service fee provided in subsection (2). However, for live-aboard vessels proof of assessment by the county property appraiser as tangible personal property must be shown upon application in order to qualify for said exemption. Vessels assessed as live-aboard vessels on the 1980 assessment rolls shall be eligible for exemption from the registration fees imposed by this section beginning June 1, 1980. Similarly, any live-aboard vessel deleted from an assessment roll shall be subject to said regulation fees commencing in the year of deletion."
    (8) Mail service charge. [MI-30] Add new provision:
    A mail service charge shall be collected for each registration or reregistration mailed by the department or any tax collector. All registrations or reregistrations shall be mailed by first class mail unless otherwise requested by the purchaser. The amount of said mail service charge shall be the actual postage required rounded to the nearest 5 cents, plus 25 cents handling charge. Said mail service charge shall be in addition to the service charge provided in subsection (2), and shall be used and accounted for in accordance with law. [Eff. June 1, 1981]

371.66 Jurisdiction.- [MI-30] Add:
    "All applicable safety regulations and requirements under this part shall apply to live-aboard vessels. Live-aboard vessels shall be exempt from only the license fee

provisions of this part if assessed as tangible personal property."

371.68 Penalties. [AI-1]
(2) After "10 days" insert: ", and except as otherwise provided in this part,".

371.75 Application for certificate of title. [MI-32] Substitute:
(1) The owner of a motorboat required to pay the boat registration certificate license fee under this chapter, except federally documented vessels, shall apply to the department for a certificate of title.
(2) The application shall include the true name of the owner, the residence or business address of the owner, and the description of the boat, including the hull identification number or hull serial number, except applications for certificate of title for boats constructed or assembled by the owner which shall state all the foregoing information except hull identification number or hull serial number. The application shall be signed by the owner and shall be accompanied by the prescribed fee.
(3) The owner of a vessel exempt from the registration certificate license fee may apply to the department for a certificate of title by filing an application accompanied by the prescribed fee.

371.76 Certificate of title required. [MI-33]
(3) Delete "part II of chapter 371" and substitute "this part".
(4) Change "two dollars" to "$3"; change "fifty cents (50¢)" to "$1.50". [Eff. June 1, 1980]
Add: (5) The department shall provide a labeled place on the title where the seller's price can be indicated when a boat is sold. However, the department shall not be expected to provide a labeled place for the seller's price until such time as new boat title forms are awarded. It is the intent of the Legislature that, except as provided in this subsection, all certificates of title issued after the effective date of this act shall contain a labeled place for the seller's price to be indicated, and no notary public shall notarize a title transfer until the seller properly indicates the sales price, if a labeled place is provided on the title. It is the further intent of the Legislature that no title shall be accepted for transfer by any county tax collector or other agent of the state unless the sales price is entered in the appropriately labeled place on the title by the seller, if a labeled place is provided on the title.

371.763 Crimes relating to certificate of title. [MI-33] Add:
(1) It is unlawful for any person to procure or attempt to procure a certificate of title to a vessel, or pass or

attempt to pass a certificate of title or any assignment thereof to a vessel, knowing or having reason to believe that such vessel has been stolen. Any person violating any provision of this subsection is guilty of a felony of the third degree, punishable as provided in s. 775.082, s. 775.083 or s. 775.084.

(2) It is unlawful for any person, knowingly and with intent to defraud, to have in his possession, sell, offer to sell, countefeit, or supply a blank, forged, fictitious, counterfeit, stolen, or fraudulently or unlawfully obtained certificate of title, registration, bill of sale or any other indicia of ownership of a vessel, or conspire to do any of the foregoing. Any person violating any provision of this subsection is guilty of a felony of the third degree, punishable as provided in s. 775.082, s. 775.083, or s. 775.084.

371.77 [New title] Hull identification number or hull serial number required. [MI-33] Substitute:

(1) No person shall operate on the waters of this state a vessel the construction of which began after October 31, 1972, for which the department has issued a certificate of title or which is required by law to be registered, unless the vessel displays the assigned hull identification number issued by the United States Coast Guard. The hull identification number must be carved, burned, stamped, embossed or otherwise permanently affixed to the outboard side of the transom or, if there is no transom, to the outermost starboard side at the end of the hull that bears the rudder or other steering mechanism, above the waterline of the boat in such a way that alteration, removal or replacement would be obvious and evident. The characters of the hull identification number must be no less than one-fourth inch in height.

(2) No person shall operate on the waters of this state a vessel the construction of which was completed before November 1, 1972, for which the department has issued a certificate of title or which is required by law to be registered unless the vessel displays a hull serial number. The hull serial number shall be clearly imprinted in the transom or on the hull by stamping, impressing or marking with pressure. In lieu of imprinting, the hull serial number may be displayed on a plate in a permanent manner. If the hull serial number is displayed in a location other than the transom, the department must be notified by the manufacturer as to such location. Vessels for which the manufacturer has provided no hull serial number or vessels constructed or assembled by the owner shall be assigned a hull serial number by the department.

(3) No person, firm, association, or corporation shall destroy, remove, alter, cover, or deface the hull identification number or hull serial number, or plate bearing such number, of any vessel.

(4) It is unlawful for any person to knowingly buy,

sell, offer for sale, receive, dispose of, conceal, or have in his possession any vessel or part thereof on which the assigned identification number has been altered, removed, destroyed, covered, or defaced, or maintain such vessel in any manner which conceals or misrepresents the true identity of the vessel. Any person violating any provision of this subsection is guilty of a felony of the third degree, punishable as provided in s 775.082, s. 775.083, or s. 775.084.

(5) Failure to have the hull identification number clearly displayed in compliance with this section shall be probable cause for any Division of Law Enforcement officer or other authorized law enforcement officer to make further inspection of the vessel in question to ascertain the true identity thereof.

371.78 Refusal to issue or cancellation of certificate of number or title. [MI-34]
(2) At end delete: "after a hearing upon ten days' notice".

371.791 Manufacturer's certificate of origin to be furnished. [MI-34] Substitute:
(1) Any person selling a new vessel in this state shall furnish a manufacturer's certificate of origin to the purchaser thereof.
(2) It is unlawful for a vessel manufacturer, manufacturer's representative, or dealer to issue a manufacturer's certificate of origin describing a vessel, knowing that such description is false or that the vessel described does not exist or for any person to obtain or attempt to obtain such manufacturer's certificate of origin knowing the description is false or having reason to believe the vessel does not exist. Any person violating any provision of this subsection is guilty of a felony of the third degree, punishable as provided in s. 775.082, s. 775.083, or 775.084.

371.81 Notice of lien on motorboats; recording. [MI-36]
Substitute:
(6) The department shall be entitled to a fee of $1 for the recording of each notice of lien. No fee shall be charged for recording the satisfaction of lien. All of the fees collected shall be paid into the Motorboat Revolving Trust Fund.

371.82 Penalty. [MI-36]
Except as otherwise provided in this part, any person convicted of violating any of the provisions of this part is guilty of a misdemeanor of the second degree, punishable as provided in s. 775.082, s. 775.083, or s. 775.084.